FDI IN CHINA:
CONTRIBUTIONS TO GROWTH, RESTRUCTURING AND COMPETITIVENESS

IN: CHINA IN THE 21ST CENTURY

Xiaowen Tian (Series Editor)

GOVERNMENT AND MARKET IN CHINA: A LOCAL PERSPECTIVE
Jian Zhang
ISBN 1-59033-883-9.

THE EXTENT OF MARKETIZATION OF ECONOMIC SYSTEMS IN CHINA
Chen Zongsheng, Wu Zhe, Xie Siquan, et al
ISBN 1-56072-778-0.

BUSINESS COMMUNICATION IN CHINA
Zhu Yunxia
ISBN 1-56072-655-5.

CHINA'S RELATIONS WITH JAPAN IN AN ERA OF ECONOMIC LIBERALISATION
Dong Dong Zhang
ISBN 1-56072-625-3.

DYNAMICS OF DEVELOPMENT IN AN OPENING ECONOMY: CHINA SINCE 1978
Xiaowen Tian (Australia National University)
ISBN 1-56072-551-6.

FDI IN CHINA: CONTRIBUTIONS TO GROWTH, RESTRUCTURING AND COMPETITIVENESS

JIANG XIAOJUAN

Nova Science Publishers, Inc.
New York

Library of Congress Cataloging-in-Publication Data

Jiang, Xiaojuan, 1957-
FDI in China: contributions to growth, restructuring and competitiveness in China in the 21st century / Jiang Xiaojuan.
p. cm.
Includes bibliographical references and index.
ISBN: 1-59033-894-4.
1. Investments, Foreign—China. 2. China—Economic conditions—2000-. 3. China—Foreign economic relations. I. Title.

HG5782 .J5 2003
332.67'3'0951—dc22 2003022247

400 Oser Ave, Suite 1600
Hauppauge, New York 11788-3619
Tele. 631-231-7269 Fax 631-231-8175
e-mail: Novascience@earthlink.net
Web Site: http://www.novapublishers.com

Printed in the United States of America

CONTENTS

PREFACE

By the early 21st century, the FDI sector had carved out a major niche in the Chinese economy and exerted a remarkable impact on the nation's economic growth, industrial restructuring and its degree of integration with the global economy. The major role of the FDI sector manifests itself in many aspects, such as serving as a source of funds, improving investment efficiency, boosting output, introducing advanced technology and research capacities, ameliorating the industrial structure, expanding exports, upgrading the export commodity mix, and promoting economic restructuring. All these are described and analyzed in great detail in this book.

The last few chapters of the book feature the author's prognostications of the key areas where FDI is to be solicited and the salient features of what China will do in this respect. FDI will continue its massive flow into the Chinese manufacturing industry and play an active role in turning China into a global manufacturing centre for a number of industries. The FDI inflow in the service industry will surge in a sustained fashion, thereby raising its efficiency and improving the services offered. FDI, that from giant transnational corporations in particular, is becoming major strategic investors in transforming and regrouping large and medium-sized state-owned enterprises. In the last section of the book the author presents her idea about the emphasis and trends of the Chinese government when adapting its policies governing foreign investment to an increasingly open economy, and she ponders what administrative policies and measures will be taken in this regard.

The entire book is based on empirical studies as it attempts to provide an all-round and systematic description and analysis of China's effort in soliciting foreign investment since the onset of reform. The data cited in this book are substantial and reliable, and illustrated with large numbers of tables and charts. The controversies surrounding the FDI are also discussed with relative profundity in this work.

INTRODUCTION: FDI AND CHINESE ECONOMY

0-1 FDI'S IMPORTANT ROLE IN THE CHINESE ECONOMY

China began to solicit FDI towards the end of the 1970s. By the end of 2002, the nation had approved the establishment of 424,196 FIEs with a total contractual foreign capital of 828.06 billion US dollars, 447.966 billion US dollars of which were realized. The FDI sector figures prominently in the Chinese economy today.

An Important Source of Funds

FDI made up 10.1% of China's total investment in fixed assets in 2002 and 25.3% of the total investment in the fixed assets of the manufacturing industry.

Expanding Output and Employment

The contributions made by FIEs to output are higher than their share in national total volume of fixed assets. By the end of 2002, FDI accounted for a meager 10.7% of the total stock of assets of the manufacturing industry, whereas FIEs contributed 25.7% of the total value-added of the entire manufacturing industry. By the end of 2002, approximately 22 million were on the payroll of FIEs, or 15.7% of the total number of employees in the Chinese manufacturing industry.

Introducing Advanced Technology

Over 40% of the foreign-invested projects in China use the most advanced technology and products from transnational corporations, and the others are using relatively more advanced technology and products, thereby boosting the technological level of the Chinese industry. In 2002 four fifths of the new projects invested by foreign firms in China adopted the most advanced technology from parent companies and produced products popular on the global market.

Upgrading the Industrial Structure

FDI is most intensively involved in microelectronics, motor vehicles, telecommunications, instruments and meters, cultural and official machinery, medical and pharmaceutical products industries. As all of them are technology- and capital-intensive industries, foreign investment has helped upgrade the Chinese industrial structure. Foreign-invested companies are providing more than half of the output in the microelectronics, cars, telecommunications and office supply manufacturing industries.

Expanding Exports

In 2002, FIEs registered a total imports and exports value of 330.223 billion US dollars, or 53.2% of the national total. Their imports amounted to 169.937 billion US dollars, or 52.2% of China's total exports.

Upgrading The Export Commodities Mix

FIEs export a relatively high percentage of capital- and technology-intensive products and in this way help upgrade the export commodities mix in China. In 2002, these enterprises exported 105.011 billion US dollars worth of machinery and electrical products, or 66.85% of the total exports in this field, and registered a total high-tech export volume of 55.657 billion US dollars, which accounted for 82.20% of national total high-tech exports and 32.75% of the total exports by FIEs.

Increasing Tax Revenue

China's 2002 foreign-related tax revenues amounted to 348.7 billion yuan, 20.52% of national tax revenue. FIEs made up 26.97% of national value-added tax, 1.3 percentage points higher than these enterprises' portion in national value-added industrial outputs.

Promoting Economic Restructuring

In the course of China's progressive reform, FIEs are playing a major role in facilitating the formation of a competitive market structure, a market-oriented legal and macroeconomic management system, as well as corporate management system and philosophy in keeping with the requirements of the market economy.

0-2 Major Controversies on Utilization of Foreign Capital

The controversy about the pluses and minuses of utilizing foreign capital has never subsidized in this country despite of the important position of FDI and FIEs in the Chinese economy. As a matter of fact, the controversy intensified towards the middle and late 1990s. Among the major accusations:

Monopolizing the Market

Because of the transnational corporations' strong financial strength, people are worried that FIEs will become a monopolizing force on the Chinese market, jeopardize the interests of domestic consumers, block the entry of domestic competitors, refuse to introduce sophisticated technology and promote technological renovation, and mar the long-term stability and growth of the Chinese economy.

Aggravating Unemployment and Causing Social Instability

FIEs have absorbed large amounts of labour force. However, if domestic enterprises, state-owned ones in particular, lose the competition to transnational corporations, unemployment will arise in those enterprises that have collapsed in the process, thereby bringing the pressure to bear on social stability.

Onslaught From the Outside

The FDI sector, occupying a large portion of the national economy, help foster close ties between the Chinese economy and the global market. As a result, problems in the world market or the global economy will inevitably find their way into China and cause major economic fluctuations. People are particularly apprehensive that when the global economy sinks into a depression, FIEs -- born "protectors of parent countries' interests" -- may relinquish their investment projects in China to concentrate their resources and efforts on protecting enterprises in their parent countries, thereby dealing a heavy blow on the Chinese economy.

Technological Dependency

For some major Chinese industries, FIEs are a major source of technology. This has prompted many to believe that once the transnational corporations change their strategy on China and stop bringing advanced technology into this country, this will greatly deplete the sources of technology. Moreover, the technological superiority of the transnational corporations may force Chinese enterprises to give up the technological development ability they have already acquired and become dependent on transnational corporations for technology, thereby losing their own abilities for independent technological development.

Drain of Domestic Interests

Some believe that the use of large sums of foreign capital is causing a massive drain of Chinese interests. Firstly, by importing large quantities of component parts and raw materials and exporting massively to the overseas market, the transnational corporations can raise the prices for imported components and raw materials and reduce the prices of their export commodities, thereby gaining colossal profits. Secondly, regarding this country merely as a processing base with low value-added and a market for their products, transnational corporations investing in China will do all they can to minimize worker wages and other costs so as to shift massive amounts of profits to key technological departments in the upper reaches and the sales environment in the lower reaches. Thirdly, a drain of Chinese interests is caused by FIEs in this country that pay parent transnational corporations highly for the use of their technology.

Impact on Government Control

FIEs are intensely market oriented and immune to government regulation and control in the form of state plans or administrative decrees. They are also strongly independent of the government's guidance policies. Therefore, when these enterprises have carved out a large portion of the Chinese market, the government's control of the economy, its direct regulation and control of it in particular, will be restricted.

State Security

Most transnational corporations investing in China are from developed Western countries that differ from China in political and social systems. If many FIEs take the firm political stand of their parent countries or are strongly oriented towards the interests of their motherlands, China's state security is in for hidden troubles. In the event of an unexpected major incident, these enterprises may become a destabilizing force in Chinese economy and society.

Weakening Necessity

In the past, when many major products, technology-intensive ones in particular, were in short supply, China needed to use foreign investment to make up for its huge financial shortage. Since the late 1990s, because China has amassed relatively adequate financial resources in addition to a massive surplus of production capacity, it is unnecessary to continue to incorporate foreign capital on a large scale.

0-3 About this Book: Content, Salient Features and Structure

This book is a study on the FDI sector's role in the Chinese economy. The various aspects mentioned in the foregoing will be analyzed in relevant chapters. In researching and preparing for this book, the author took pains to render the following salient features to this book.

1. Empirical Study

In this book the author adopted the approach of empirical study instead of theoretical deduction and ratiocination. Western economic theories are relatively mature on transnational investment, but, given China's peculiar situation, the mechanical use of Western theories originating in the market economy is inappropriate for an interpretation of Chinese achievements and experience in absorbing foreign capital. The fact that China has been soliciting and utilizing foreign capital for more than two decades has laid a practical foundation with a long time span for the author's empirical studies.

Development of China's foreign economic relations and trade is a challenging issue to researchers, but it also provides a lot of room for creative studies. This is because the Chinese reform and opening-up process are poles apart from the dogmas of mainstream Western economics. Both in reform and in opening up to the outside world, China's progress is gradual. Although state-run foreign trade companies are losing their position, they still figure prominently in the Chinese import and export businesses; it was only recently that manufacturing firms were allowed to engage in foreign trade; fluctuations in foreign exchange rate is still under strong government intervention. However, it is precisely in this "gradual" and "incomplete" process of opening up to the outside world that China has maintained the world's fastest growing volume of exports and highest economic growth rate for the last 20 years. What accounts for these achievements? Of all the reasons, sustained massive FDI inflow is a major one. The FDI sector as a whole has, on the one hand, exploited China's advantages as a developing nation on the verge of an economic takeoff, such as its low-cost manufacturing capacities, immense domestic market, and high-speed economic growth. On the other hand, the FDI sector is able to avoid the disadvantages of China's transition from central planning to a market economy, such as undue government intervention in enterprises, flawed market mechanisms and the low efficiency of state-owned enterprises. The achievements of China over the last two decades and more would be unconceivable without the massive influx of foreign investment.

2. Comprehensive and Systematic Statistics

All the studies featured in this book are based on statistics that are comprehensive and systematic and encompass considerably long periods of time, as the author strives to base her narration, judgment and viewpoints on conclusive facts and avoid deriving general conclusions or theories from a single case or event. Where major statistics were unavailable, such as those on the level of FIEs' use of technology in China, the situation concerning Chinese supplies of accessories for these enterprises, as well as research and development carried out by these enterprises in China, the author organized surveys with sufficiently enough samples, thereby obtaining representative and convincing data.

3. Balanced Analysis

Many fields were involved when the author passed judgment on the influence of foreign investment on a nation's economic development. Therefore her judgment is not limited to capital inflow and introduction of technology that of course command a lot of public attention. This book provides relatively balanced analysis of the impact of foreign capital on the Chinese economy, including its impact on the total investment, economic growth, the upgrading of the industrial structure, technological progress, the expansion of exports and the upgrading of the export commodity mix, tax revenue and profit, the development of regional economies and the gaps between them, and economic restructuring.

4. Addressing Controversial Issues

In her research for this book, the author paid due attention to the most controversial issues concerning China's efforts to solicit foreign investment, and elaborately analyzed, with the support of statistics, such topics as FIEs' local content in China, their behaviours in introducing technology to China, and China's preferential tax payment policies for FIEs and the impact of such policies, the behaviours of FIEs on the Chinese market, and the security of both the FDI sector and the Chinese economy.

5. A Forward-looking Attitude

This book devotes several chapters to the prospects of foreign investment in China and its impact on the Chinese economy. It is the author's belief that the capacity of the Chinese economy to maintain its sustained high-speed growth will continue to hold strong and sustain appeals to foreign investors, that China will rise to become a global manufacturing base for some major manufactured goods, and that the Chinese service industry will markedly sharpen its competitiveness by attracting foreign investment. The author also maintains that the transformation and regrouping of state-owned enterprises will become a major field for attracting foreign investment, and participation of foreign investors in this field will vastly boost the reform of the state-owned enterprises, accelerate the development of the Chinese capital market, and promote the restructuring of the Chinese economic system as a whole. The author also pinpoints a few fields where supervision on the FDI sector has to be tightened up so as to cope with the undesirable aspects of the FDI inflow.

0-4 Introducing the Chapters and Contents

Chapter One analyses the contributions made by FDI to the increase of investment and the improvement of asset quality in this country. From the late 1970s to the mid-1990s, the percentage of FDI in China's total investment in fixed assets grew continuously, but it has a more important and active long-term role to play in increasing the efficiency of financial allocation and improving the quality of the resultant assets. This chapter also takes a brief look at China's position and salient features as a host country for transnational investment.

Chapter Two looks into the contributions made by FIEs to the growth of Chinese industry. Industry has all along been receiving more FDI than any other fields of endeavour in this country. It is also where FIEs have made the most outstanding contributions to output. An analysis is made of the position and role of FIEs in Chinese industry from such perspectives as the percentage of assets, output and profits and taxes, local content, and the development of human resources. The chapter concludes by making a correlation analysis of the relationship between foreign investment and the growth speeds of various industrial fields.

Chapter Three takes a look at FDI's role in promoting China's technological progress and industrial upgrading. FIEs are major suppliers of new products and technology for China, a role they are playing even more visibly in recent years. Foreign investment has contributed to the upgrading of the Chinese industrial structure, and even more impressively so to development of high-tech industries. FIEs' R&D investment in China has been growing robustly in recent years, and the percentage of new technology and new products in their research projects is rising as well.

Chapter Four looks into the behaviours of FIEs in exports and their contributions to increasing Chinese exports and upgrading the mix of Chinese export commodities. FIEs have been quick in increasing their exports in the last dozen years or so, their share in the Chinese total exports is expanding steadily, and they are contributing to more than half of national total exports. By exporting more machinery and electrical products and high-tech products than domestic enterprises, FIEs increase the proportion of commodities with relatively high technological content and value-added in national total exports, upgrade China's export commodities mix, enable China's relative advantage to extend to more industries, and endow Chinese export commodities with more long-term competitiveness on the world market.

Chapter Five dissects the relationship between FDI inflow and development of regional economies. Towards the late 1970s the regional economic pattern of China has seen remarkable changes, with the eastern region outstripping the central and western regions in both growth speed and per-capita income increase. Differences in the amounts of foreign capital incorporated are a major cause for this situation. In this chapter the author analyses the impact of foreign capital on the economic situation of different regions from the perspective of its contributions to investment, output and exports. A correlation analysis is also made on the relationship between the amount of foreign capital incorporated and the growth speeds achieved in different localities.

Chapter Six describes the behaviours of FIEs in financing and in mergers and acquisitions on the Chinese capital market. Investment has been the major behaviour of FIEs in China so far, but a tiny number of them are also engaged in financing on the Chinese capital market. There have been also a few cases of mergers and acquisitions. Since 2000, with the prospects for China's accession to WTO becoming clearer, FIEs have shown increasing desires for financing and mergers and acquisitions on the Chinese market.

Chapter Seven is focused on a study on the competitive behaviour of FIEs in China. In some industries where foreign capital is relatively more concentrated, FIEs are already playing a leading role and the FDI sector has already taken a sizeable market share. Will this situation give rise to monopoly? Generally speaking, some transnational corporations showed a monopolistic tendency when they first set foot in the Chinese market. However, with more and more FIEs coming on the scene, and with domestic enterprises growing in strength steadily, the market structure has been moving towards adequate competition rather than monopoly, a situation that compels FIEs to rectify their market behaviours. In this chapter the author takes the detergent industry as a case in point and provides a detailed description of the changes in FIEs' behaviours in market competition. The last section of this chapter is devoted to an analysis, by taking the global petroleum industry for example, of a relatively common phenomenon in which colossal transnational corporations coexist with a highly competitive global market.

In **Chapter Eight** the author responds to two controversial issues. First, are the preferential policies for FIEs causing unfair competition between FIEs and domestic enterprises, and are these policies major reasons behind FIEs' relatively strong competitiveness? Second, FIEs' net exporting behaviour and their contributions to China's total net exports. The last section of this chapter describes the positive impact of the rising FDI sector on the reform of the Chinese foreign exchange administrative system as a typical case in point for the open policy as the motive force for economic restructuring.

Chapters Nine to Twelve present a forward-looking study on the key fields for foreign investment in the future and their characteristics, and the author's suggestions on what might become the key points of China's strategy for attracting foreign capital. Chapter Nine analyses the new trends of foreign investment in China after the nation's WTO accession, indicating that an improved environment for foreign investors and China's ability to maintain its sustained high-speed economic growth will hold forth sustained appeals for prospective foreign investors. It is expected China will remain a major destination of global FDI inflow.

Chapters Ten and Eleven give some insight into how foreign investment will be distributed in different industries. Chapter Ten is focused on a discussion on new trends of foreign investment in the manufacturing industry. After China's WTO accession, the manufacturing industry remains a key field for FDI, while FIEs continue to improve their technological levels and more and more transnational corporations use the most advanced technology and make the most sophisticated products in this country. This chapter also studies the role of foreign investment in transforming China into the global manufacturing center for a number of industries.

In **Chapter Eleven,** the author looks into the trends and characteristics of foreign investment in the Chinese service industry after the nation acceded to WTO. Since the nation's WTO entry, foreign investment has increased markedly in the Chinese service industry. Some of the services that were only opened marginally before are quickly enhancing their openness, and some of the formerly closed areas are speeding up the opening-up process. A more open service industry has had, and will continue to have, a positive impact on increasing its own efficiency and competitiveness.

Chapter Twelve is a study on the possibility and significance of involving foreign investment in promoting the transformation of all state-owned enterprises in general and the large ones in particular. Judging from the Chinese government's announcements, major progress is likely to be made in encouraging foreign investors to participate in transforming state-owned enterprises, the large ones in particular, in the form of mergers and acquisitions. If this becomes reality, it will have a major and far-reaching impact on both economic restructuring and opening up to the outside world.

Chapter Thirteen looks into the future from a broader prospective by analyzing the relationship between the efforts to absorb foreign investment and mingle with the global economy on the one hand, and the sustained robust growth of the Chinese economy on the other. The Chinese economy has maintained a high-speed growth for the last twenty years and more, and, with its relative advantages changing all the time, the effort to maintain this robust growth will come up against challenges that have never been experienced before. The challenges include the need to accelerate technological upgrading, speed up the effort to raise the enterprises' global competitiveness, be more broadly integrated into the global economy, and so on. To continue absorbing foreign investment will stand China in good stead to meet new challenges in a new environment and achieve the long-term goal of maintaining sustained fast economic growth. In this chapter the author draws the attention of Chinese policymakers to certain key points and directions for policies on supervising foreign investment in an open economy; she also proposes a package of policies and measures to be taken in this regard.

0-5 Acknowledgments

Over the last few years I have devoted mainly efforts on my research of FDI and its impact on the Chinese economy. It took me years to construct this research project and get the documentations and data ready for it. In 2000, my application for a state social science fund was granted, and this prompted me to redouble my efforts for research work associated with this project.

Collecting data and survey was the most time- and energy-consuming part of this research project. At every stage of my research and writing, I have enjoyed the guidance and help from a host of friends working in the academic world, government departments and industrial enterprises. My particular thanks are due to my friends of the Foreign Investment Department and Policy Research Office of the Ministry of Foreign Trade and Economic Cooperation, the Beijing Municipal Commission of Foreign Trade and Economic Cooperation, the Beijing Municipal Science and Technology Commission, the Shanghai Municipal Commission of Foreign Trade and Economic Cooperation, the Shenzhen Municipal Commission of Foreign Investment, the Suzhou Municipal Commission of Foreign Trade and Economic Cooperation, the Ministry of Information Industry, the All-China Federation of Light Industry, the State Office for the Import and Export of Machinery and Electrical products, and the Chinese Detergent Industry Association, for providing me with important data and information and arranging large numbers of enterprises to respond to my surveys and answer questionnaires. My colleagues at the Financial and Trade Economics Institute of the Chinese Academy of Social Sciences also helped me with the collection of information and research work. Ms Li Rui, a Ph.D candidate under my tutelage, helped me collect and sort out data and proofread large amounts of my manuscripts. Without the unstinting help of these people, I would not have accomplished this research project. Once again, my heartfelt thanks to all of them.

Chapter 1

FDI: OUTSIDE FINANCIAL SOURCE AND IMPROVING INVESTMENT QUALITY

To serve as outside financial sources is the most important and direct contributions transnational corporations can make to the economic growth of a developing nation with financial shortages. A transnational corporation can commit itself to investing in a developing country with a high domestic savings deposits rate and a relatively strong investment ability only when it can gain a sharper competitive edge than the enterprises of that country; and absorbing transnational investment stands a better chance than domestic investment behaviors to raise the efficiency of capital allocation and improve the quality of the assets resulting from it. In China's case, the role of transnational investment is apparent in both aspects, but the degree of its impact on these two aspects may change over time.

1-1: POSITION OF FDI IN CHINA'S INVESTMENT AGGREGATES

Financial shortage has been a long-term problem for China. Since the late 1970s, the proportion of FDI as an outside financial source in China's investment in fixed assets has shown a general tendency of remarkable increase. The following two methods are generally used when calculating the ratio of FDI to China's total investment in fixed assets.

1. Calculation According to Realized FDI

This method, which is commonly used in China, involves dividing the total annual investment in fixed assets with realized FDI during the same year. Table 1-1 features the ratio of FDI to the total investment in fixed assets in different years.

Table 1-1: Ratio of realized FDI to national total investment in fixed assets (%)

Year	Total Investment in Fixed Assets in RMB 100 million	Total Investment in Fixed Assets in US$ 100 million	Realized FDI in US$ 100 million	Realized FDI as a Percentage of Total Investment in Fixed Assets %
1991	5508.80	1001.60	43.66	4.36
1992	8080.10	1465.22	110.08	7.51
1993	13072.30	2268.71	275.15	12.13
1994	17042.30	1977.34	337.67	17.08
1995	20019.30	2397.23	375.21	15.65
1996	22974.00	2763.22	417.26	15.10
1997	25300.00	3059.57	452.57	14.79
1998	28457.00	3437.29	454.62	13.23
1999	29876.00	3608.00	403.18	11.17
2000	32619.00	3944.26	407.15	10.32
2001	36898.00	4445.54	468.46	10.54
2002	43202.00	5205.06	527.43	10.13

Source: Department of Foreign Investment of Ministry of Foreign Trade and Economic Cooperation 2002. *Statistics on FDI in China 2002* not for sale figures of 2002 were calculated by the author according to figures provided by National Bureau of Statistics of China.

2. Calculation According to Statistics Derived from Investment in Fixed Assets

China's statistical work concerning investment in fixed assets is done through classifying the financial sources. Foreign capital is one such source, as is shown in Table 1-2.

Table 1-2: Composition of financial sources for investment in fixed assets during the period 1991-2001 (%)

Year	State budgetary appropriation	Domestic loans	Foreign investment	Fundraising and others
1991	6.8	23.5	5.7	64.0
1992	4.3	27.4	5.8	62.5
1993	3.7	23.5	7.3	65.5
1994	3.0	22.4	9.9	64.7
1995	3.0	20.5	11.2	65.3
1996	2.7	19.6	11.8	66.0
1997	2.8	18.9	10.3	67.7
1998	4.2	19.3	9.1	67.4
1999	6.2	19.2	6.7	67.8
2000	6.4	20.3	5.1	68.2
2001	6.7	19.1	4.6	69.6

Source: National Bureau of Statistics of China (2003). *China Statistical Yearbook 2002* (Beijing: China Statistics Press).

Tables 1-1 and 1-2 reveal a similarity in the changes in the percentages derived from the two methods but they also reveal striking differences in statistics. Because the percentages of foreign capital calculated on the basis of financial sources for investment in fixed assets also includes investment using foreign debts, the gap can be still wider if FDI alone is counted.

Convincing empirical analysis is not yet available to account for the glaring differences between these two methods. The probable reasons are, first, as FDI has been put into more extensive uses, realized FDI in China is found in fixed assets and active capital, marketing, technological development and other fields. Second, the profits used by foreign-invested enterprises (FIEs) for re-investment purposes are likely to be counted as "funds raised by enterprises themselves" when statistics about financial sources for fixed assets are collected; as re-investment by foreign-invested enterprises has been increasing quickly over the last couple of years, this may become a major reason behind the yawning gap in the results of calculation using the two different methods since 1999. Third, part of the foreign capital counted as "realized FDI" has not actually been realized for one reason or another.

1-2: A Comparison between FDI in China and Global Transnational Investment

The most direct role of utilizing FDI is in increasing the amount of investment in host economies. In traditional theories on transnational investment, argumentations on the necessity for developing countries to utilize foreign capital are concentrated on the "dual shortages" model, that is, to incorporate foreign capital helps make up for the shortages in both savings deposits and foreign exchange in a developing country and promote its economic growth. Particularly for those low-income countries that are in the initial stage of modern economic growth and have a low domestic ability for savings and investment, foreign capital may well become a major source with which to make up for financial shortages.

Since the early 1990s, China has attracted large amounts of transnational investment. In the 1990s, transnational investment in China approximately accounted for one quarter to one third of the total transnational capital attracted to all the developing economies. The achievement of China in attracting FDI is there for all to see. However, the speed at which foreign capital flew into China and the speed at which the global transnational investment grew in the first half of the 1990s were strikingly different from the second half of that decade. In the first half of that decade, the FDI flow into China was growing far quicker than increases in global transnational investment, with the portion of China-bound FDI in the global volume of investment in fixed assets running as high as more than 19% for four years running between 1993 and 1996 – in 1994, the figure reached an all-time high of 13.5%.

In the second half of the 1990s, however, the FDI inflows into China slowed down considerably while the global transnational investment continued its robust growth. During the period 1996-2000 the realized FDI in China hovered slightly higher than 40 billion US dollars, but the total global transnational investment snowballed from 359 billion US dollars to 1271 billion US dollars. The high-speed growth in global transnational investment and the standstill in China's absorption of FDI dropped this country's speed in FDI utilization way below the growth speed of global transnational investment. The percentage of FDI attracted to China in the global transnational investment had kept going down steadily, so much so that it dropped to 3.2% in 2000, an all-time low since 1992 or less than one quarter of what it was in 1994.

The year 2001 saw the FDI inflow pick up speed in China, with remarkable increases in both contractual and realized volumes. That year China registered 69.191 billion US dollars in total contractual volume of FDI and 46.846 billion US dollars in the volume of realized FDI, 10.43% and 14.9% respectively more than the 2000 figures. That year also witnessed a major reduction in global transnational investment. The increase in the volume of FDI utilized in China, coupled with a major reduction in the total global transnational investment, boosted the proportion of foreign capital utilized in China in 2001 in the total global transnational investment by three percentage points to 6.1%. In 2002, while China saw FDI inflow continue to grow by big margins, the total global transnational investment kept on a decline. According to UNCTAD's estimate, global transnational investment amounted to only 540 billion US dollars in 2002 and only 45 billion US dollars of it ended up in the United States. That year China replaced the United States as the leading recipient of FDI among all the countries in the world -- China's share in the global transnational investment rose to 9.98%.

In Table 1-3 and Figures 1-1 and 1-2 the amount and growth rates of the global transnational investment are compared with the amount of it attracted to China and with the Chinese speed in attracting foreign capital.

Table 1-3: Global transnational investment and FDI growth rate in China
(Unit: US$ 100 million %)

Year	Global FDI inflow	Growth Rate %	Realized FDI in China	Growth Rate %	Realized FDI in China as a percentage of Global FDI inflow %
1991	1981		43.66		2.26
1992	2015	1.72	110.08	152.13	5.46
1993	2391	18.66	275.15	149.95	11.51
1994	2511	5.02	337.67	22.72	13.45
1995	3387	34.89	375.21	11.12	11.08
1996	3590	6.00	417.26	11.20	11.62
1997	4640	29.25	452.57	8.46	9.75
1998	6440	38.79	454.62	0.5	7.06
1999	8655	34.39	403.18	-11.3	4.66
2000	12710	46.85	407.15	0.99	3.20
2001	7600	- 40.20	468.46	15.1	6.16
2002	5400	-27.00	528.00	13.1	9.98

Sources: Statistics about China are quoted from the *China Statistical Yearbook* of corresponding years, but the figures for 2002 are estimates; global statistics are quoted from the *World Investment Report*, but the figures for 2002 are UNCTAD estimates.

Figure 1-1: Comparisons between the FDI growth rate in China and the growth rate of global transnational investment

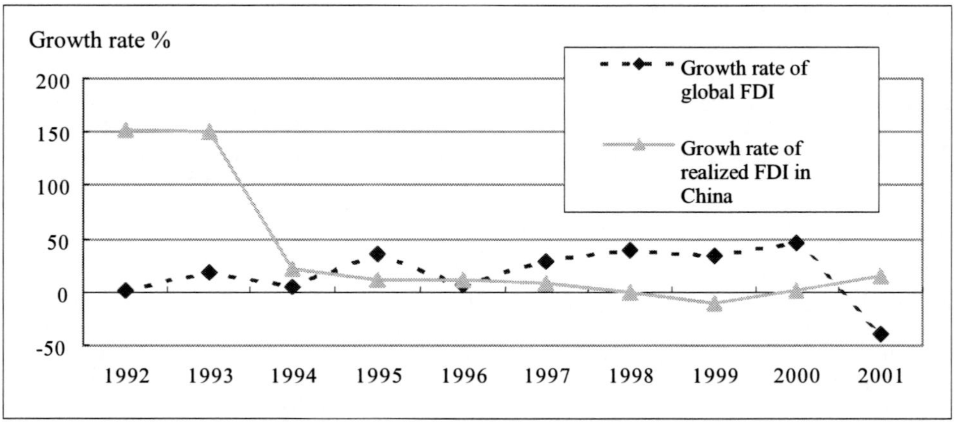

Figure 1-2: Ratio of foreign capital utilized in China to global transnational investment

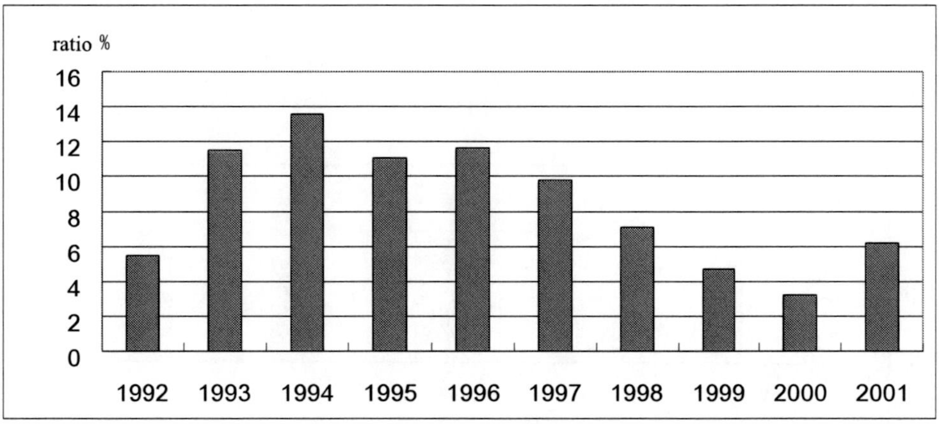

1-3: CHINA'S INTERNATIONAL POSITION AS A REPOSITORY OF GLOBAL TRANSNATIONAL INVESTMENT

In the early and mid-1990s, China's utilization of foreign capital increased much higher than global transnational investment. The share of FDI in China's total investment in fixed assets outstripped the average levels of both developed and developing countries as well as the Central and Eastern European countries.

Towards the end of the 1990s, global transnational investment rose dramatically and raised its percentage in the total volumes of investment of various types of countries, but in China it was at a standstill, so much so that FDI lost its prominent position as an outside financial source. During that period, FDI's share in the country's capital aggregates was only slightly higher than the average level of developing countries and about the same as that of the Central and Eastern European countries in economic transition. China's position as a FDI recipient country declined. Table 1-4 and Figure 1-3 features a comparison between foreign capital's position in China and in other countries and the changes that have taken place in the process.

Table 1-4: Percentages of FDI in total investment in fixed assets in various types of countries

Year	All countries	Developed countries	Developing countries	Central and Eastern European Countries	China
1991-1997 average	5.0	4.1	7.1	7.6	12.3
1998	11.1	10.9	11.5	12.9	13.23

Sources: Statistics concerning China are calculated on the basis of figures provided in the Foreign Investment Department of the Ministry of Foreign Trade and Economic Cooperation (2001). *Statistics on FDI in China 2001*; the 1991-1997 figures concerning the other countries are based on the tables and figures in UNCTAD Department of Transnational corporations and Investment (1999). *World Investment Report 1999: Foreign Direct Investment and the Challenge for Development* (Geneva and New York: United Nations), United Nations publication and the 1998 figures are quoted from UNCTAD (2000). *World Investment Report 2000: Cross-border Mergers and Acquisitions and Development* (Geneva and New York: United Nations), United Nations Publication.

* With the exception of China, the ratio of FDI to the total capital formation of all the domestic industries is used in this table.

Figure 1-3: Ratio of foreign capital to the total investment in fixed assets in various types of countries (1991-1998)

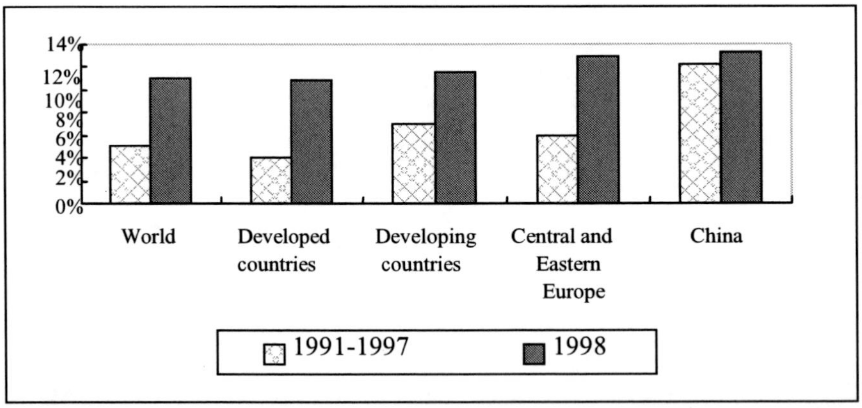

However, generally speaking, large nations are heavily dependent on domestic resources. As a result, the ratio of foreign capital to the total capital formation is relatively low. Because China is the largest developing country, a comparison between China and the average world level is of limited significance. If China is compared only with other large developing countries, then its position as a recipient country is outstanding because it leads all these nations in the ratio of foreign capital to the total capital formation. Table 1-5 sheds some light on the utilization of foreign capital utilized in large nations each with a population of upwards of 50 million. The left column of this table features the situation of large developing nations, where the shares of foreign capital in the total investment in fixed assets average 6.1%; the right column features large developed countries, where the figure stands at 6.0%. For China, it stands at 14.8%, which means that the share of FDI in the total investment in fixed assets of China as the leading developing nation is much higher than the average levels of other large developing and developed countries, ranking second among all large developing countries and third among all the large countries. Among the nine countries each with a population of more than 100 million, China ranked number one in this field. See Figure 1-4.

Table 1-5: Comparisons between large nations in terms of relative levels in utilization of foreign capital (1997)

Large developing country				Large developed country			
Country	**Population (million)**	**FDI inflow (in US$ 100 million)**	**FDI inflow as a percentage of total capital formation (%)**	**Country**	**Population (million)**	**FDI inflow (in US$ 100 million)**	**FDI inflow as a percentage of total capital formation (%)**
India	979.1	34.0	3.2	United Kingdom	59.1	630.0	15.4
Indonesia	203.7	47.0	7.5	United States	270.0	1930.0	7.5
Brazil	165.9	290.0	7.6	France	58.8	280.0	8.9
Bangladesh	125.6	1.4	1.1	German	82.1	159.6	2.0
Nigeria	121.3	15.4	12.2	Italy	57.6	25.0	2.0
Pakistan	131.6	7.0	8.3	Japan	126.3	32.0	0.1
Mexico	95.9	103.0	20.6				
Philippines	75.1	12.3	7.5				
Turkey	63.5	8.0	1.8				
Russia	146.9	22.0	4.3				
Ukraine	50.3	7.5	4.5				
Thailand	61.1	37.4	3.0				
Vietnam	77.6	34.0	…				
Egypt	61.4	10.7	5.5				
Iran	61.9	4.0	0.5				
Ethiopia	61.3	1.8	4.0				
Average of countries above mentioned			6.1	Average of countries above mentioned			6.0
China	1250.0	452.0	14.8				

Source: Figures on population were from Table 3 in World Bank (1999). *World Development Report 1999/2000: Entering the 21st Century* (Oxford: Oxford University Press). FDI inflow and its share in total capital formation were calculated on the basis of related figures and tables in UNCTAD (1999). *World Investment Report 1999: Foreign Direct Investment and the Challenge for Development* (Geneva and New York: United Nations), United Nations Publication.

Note: The definition for "large nation" is one with a population of upwards of 50 million people.

Figure 1-4: Percentages of foreign capital in the total capital formation in countries each with a population of more than 100 million (1997)

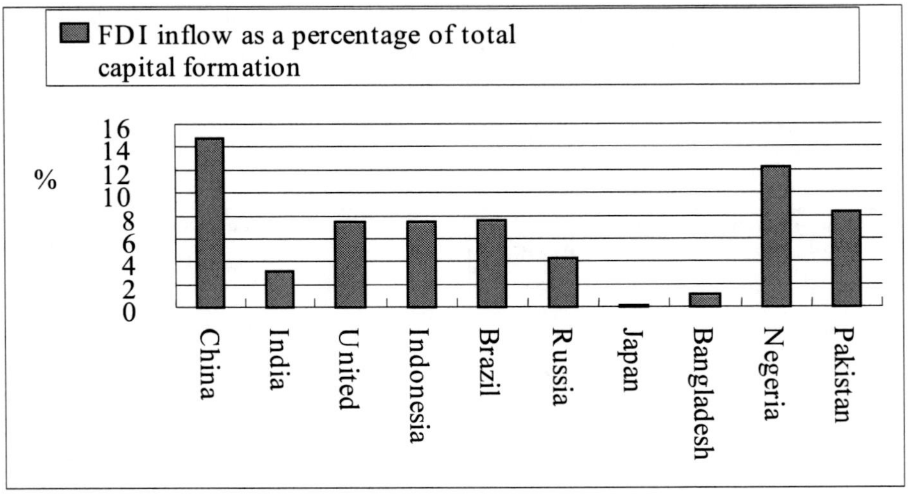

1-4: ATTRACTING FDI AND IMPROVING INVESTMENT QUALITY

Beginning from the latter half of the 1990s, domestic financial shortage in China was gradually ameliorated, and banks acquired considerable surpluses for several consecutive years, a situation that was never seen before. During this period, the aggregate supply of most commodities outstripped the aggregate demand, market competition was intensifying as never before, and the economic results of domestic enterprises kept sliding. In the meantime, the volume of foreign investment in China kept at the level of more than 40 billion US dollars, foreign-invested enterprises were steadily expanding their shares in the Chinese market and reached high percentages in some industries. These problems combined to fuel the controversy: Why is it necessary to use large amounts of foreign investment in a sustained way when domestic savings deposits are going strong and there is no longer a financial shortage on the home front?

Generally speaking, after the strain on domestic financial resources is eased, the most important significance for attracting FDI lies in its ability to increase the efficiency of financial allocation and promote the improvement in the quality of assets. This is because labor capital, technological level, capabilities for technological development and application and for opening up the world market, managerial ability, the capacity to understand clients' demand – these and other creative resources needed for improving asset quality will be brought into China along with investments by transnational corporations. From this point of view, domestic capital can by no means replace foreign capital.

The role of FDI inflow in improving asset quality manifests itself in the following three aspects:

1. Cultivating New Assets of High Quality

The low output-investment ratio is a persistent problem in China's industrial development that had never been properly tackled. Since the founding of the People's Republic, China's investment rate has been one of the highest among all the countries in the world. However, low investment efficiency affected the quality of newly added assets and resulted in massive waste of money. Since reform came under way in China, state-owned enterprises have attached more importance to profits, market demand and the tightening up of domestic management, but little has been done to tackle the "soft constrains" on enterprise finance, and it has been a chronic problem for enterprises to scramble for investment at the expense of economic returns. In the meantime, domestic enterprises' flawed abilities for technological development, marketing and management are responsible for the fact that the products of large numbers of newly built construction projects are not competitive on the market and that many new enterprises began losing money as soon as they started production. That is why the high domestic savings deposits rate and the "adequate" or even "abundant" investment capital can meet the quantitative demand for investment but cannot improve the quality of investment, nor can they help shift the nation's economic growth from an extensive mode to an intensive mode.

Foreign capital can cultivate value-added assets of high quality by establishing new enterprises or using new investment to set up joint ventures with domestic enterprises. Prior to 1992, most of the foreign-invested enterprises originated in Hong Kong, Macao and Taiwan. Although most of them belonged to labor-intensive industries and were lacking technologically, they brought in a good variety of new products in short supply, introduced new concepts on product quality, designs, sales method and management for domestic enterprises, and supplied quite a few new products to meet the domestic consumer demand. After 1992, transnational corporations from developed countries began to make large-scale investment in China, and FDI obviously contains better technology than what is used in domestic industries, and a considerable portion of FIEs have found their way into technology- and capital-intensive industries, thereby upgrading the Chinese industrial structure and markedly improving the quality of the newly added assets. The idea that the entry of FDI has improved the quality of China's assets will run consistently through this and other chapters of this book, and will be further analyzed from the perspectives of technological progress, structural upgrading, and export commodities' improved competitiveness.

2. Raising the Quality of Stock Assets

Large amounts of stock assets in China today are of a low quality. Some are based on outdated and backward production capacities. Some are in the possession of advanced technology and equipment but their products lack competitiveness due to poor management or inability to use such technology and equipment. It is possible for transnational corporations to use investment to transform these stock assets into high-quality ones. Some of our case studies indicate that rather than increasing their financial input, foreign investors have successfully made up for the enterprises' financial losses simply by changing such "software" as management, marketing expertise and the interior distribution methods. Transnational investment is called "one package of creative investment" because with the shift of the funds, concepts, technology, management expertise, marketing strategy and marketing networks will all be shifted to the recipient of the investment. Without the transnational transfer of these comprehensive factors, it will be impossible for many enterprises suffering financial losses or having management difficulties to markedly improve their stock assets and the quality of their newly added assets even if they continue to spend massive amounts of money on technological and product updating.

3. Spurring on Relevant Industries to Improve the Quality of their Assets

A foreign-invested enterprise invariably comes into multifarious contacts with Chinese enterprises. For example, when buying accessories and raw materials from domestic enterprises, it will set high requirements for quality, technology and properties, and it may also provide technological standards and assistance to help these enterprises raise their technological levels and improve the quality of their products. A survey of 74 foreign-invested enterprises[1] that get their supply of accessories from domestic firms indicates that 51, or 69%, of them set requirements for these firms and provide assistance for them. The main methods used by these 51 foreign-invested enterprises to help domestic accessory-supplying firms raise their competitiveness are, in the order of frequency of mentions made of them, setting new quality standards, providing technological help, investing in shares and developing the needed technology, and joint investment in development. See Table 1-6.

Table 1-6: Major methods used by foreign-invested enterprises to help domestic accessory-supplying firms

(Number of samples: 51)

Method	Number of firms that responded (duplicated choices)	Percentage in the total number of samples (%)
Setting quality standards	40	78.4
Providing technical assistance	33	64.7
Investing in shares and developing needed technology	12	23.5
Joint investment in developing technology	6	11.7

Source: A series of surveys presided over by the author. For details about these surveys, see Section 3-1 of Chapter Three.

When a foreign-invested enterprise uses a local commercial system to sell its products, it may impart a more advanced distribution system and marketing expertise to local enterprises. The investment from transnational corporations in the service industry has had a positive impact on the improvement of the quality of assets of many industries in China. For instance, the entry of foreign banks into China has provided foreign-invested enterprises and domestic enterprises with quality financial services and made it convenient for them to make prompt financing efforts at low costs. Using their high reputation on the international capital market,

1 The survey covers accessory and materials suppliers only; it does not include power and water supply, transportation and other firms in the infrastructure, nor does it include those providing various services.

these foreign banks also raise funds from the world market to loan to domestic enterprises; without these banks' help, it would be impossible for domestic enterprises to gain access to such funds.

The relationship between Coco-cola and its suppliers is a good case in point. In the early 1980s, Coco-cola was looking for glass bottle suppliers in order to bring it bottling lines into China. According to its technical and safety standards, Coco-cola demanded that their glass bottles be sturdy enough to stand a 32-atmosphere pressure, but the best China could produce at that time could only sustain 16 atmospheres. To cultivate qualified suppliers, technical and management experts from the Coco-cola headquarters went on an inspection tour of several glass manufacturing factories in China and provided advice on technological process and equipment in order to help them improve the quality of their products. Coco-cola also supplied part of the equipment and molds free. As a result, these enterprises were able to measure up to Coco-cola's quality standards and became its accessory suppliers in China.

4. Investment, Output and Economic Results of Foreign-Invested Enterprises: A Series of Aggregate Indicators

The quality of assets may be appraised in many ways. However, increases in technological content, the upgrading of the industry structure and improvement in other fields – all these find concentrated expression in high economic returns. In this chapter the author takes a look at the impact of utilizing foreign capital on the effort to improve asset quality from the perspective of improving the quality of the formation of assets in the most ordinary sense of the term, that is, the achievement of relatively more output and better economic returns from a given amount of financial input. More detailed analyses of its impact on upgrading the industrial structure, enhancing international competitiveness, promoting technological progress, and accelerating economic restructuring will be presented in other chapters of this book.

Statistics show that foreign-invested enterprises in Chinese industry account for only 10.18% of national total industrial assets, but they provide 27.39% of the gross industrial output value, 23.98% of the total value-added, 26.79% of the total industrial sales revenue, 29.19% of the total industrial profits, and 21.81% of the total value-added tax payable. A comparison of this cluster of statistics indicates that foreign-invested enterprises have a far better investment-output efficiency than the domestic enterprises as a whole. In the entire Chinese industry, foreign-invested enterprises use one tenth of the assets to create one fifth of the value-added tax payments, one quarter of the output value and sales revenue, and one third of the profits. See Table 1-7 and Figure 1-5 for detail.

Table 1-7: Major economic indicators for foreign-invested enterprises (2000)

	Total Industry	FIEs	FIEs as a percentage of total Industry
Total Assets	126211.24	12849.54	10.18
Gross Industrial Output Value	85673.66	23464.55	27.39
Value-added	25394.80	6090.35	23.98
Sales Revenue	84151.75	22545.74	26.79
Total Profits	4393.48	1282.48	29.19
Value-added Tax Payable	3685.20	738.88	20.05

Source: Calculated on the basis of figures of Table13-13, 13-14, 13-15 and 13-16 in National Bureau of Statistics of China (2002). *China Statistical Yearbook 2001* (Beijing: China Statistics Press).

Figure 1-5: The share of major economic indicators for foreign-invested enterprises in Chinese industry as a whole (2000)

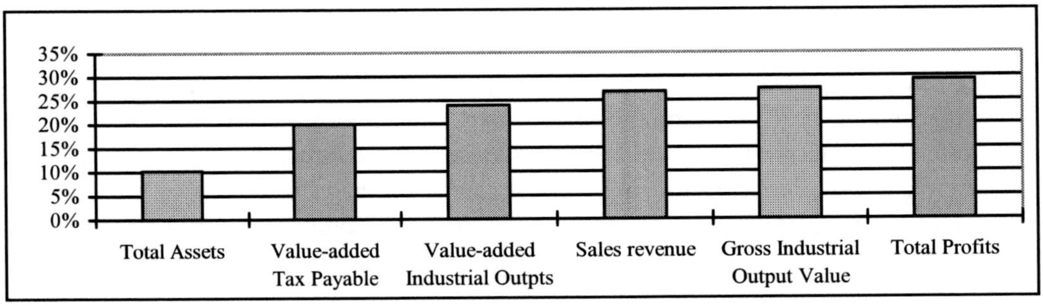

Chapter 2

Contributions of Foreign-Invested Enterprises to Industrial and GDP Growth in China

2-1: Status of Foreign-Invested Enterprises (FIEs) in Chinese Industry

1. Status of Foreign Investment in Chinese Industrial Assets Formation

Industry was the earliest to be opened to FDI, and the widest at that, after China adopted the policy of reform and opening up to the outside world. Today, industry is where most of the FDI that has found its way into China is gravitated. By the end of 2001, FDI in industry had accounted for 61.3% of national total contractual FDI value. See Figure 2-1.

Figure 2-1: Percentages of FDI in different fields

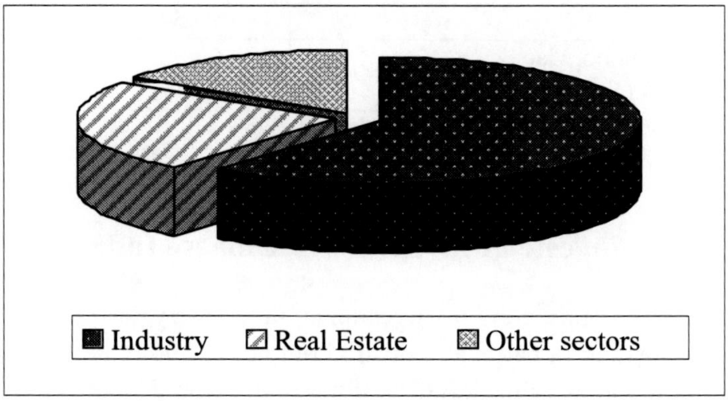

FDI's concentrated share in China's total industrial investment is higher than its share in China's total investment in fixed assets. In 2000 the national investment in fixed assets totaled 3291.773 billion RMB, of which 29.1%, or 957.906 billion RMB, was gravitated to industry; during that year, the realized FDI in Chinese industry reached 27.765 billion US dollars, equivalent to 230.45 billion RMB, according to which FDI made up 24.06% of China's total industrial investment[1].

The concentration of FDI in industry enables foreign-invested enterprises to carve out a considerable share in the total industrial assets. In 2000, these enterprises combined to comprise 10.18% of the total industrial assets, whereas in the industries of electronic and telecommunications, cultural, educational and sports articles, leather, furs, down and related products, foreign-invested enterprises accounted for more than one third of the total assets. Table 2-1 features the 10 fields where foreign-invested enterprises have the highest share in the total assets. For a look at the detailed statistics concerning the ratios of foreign-invested enterprises to the total assets in various industrial fields, see Annex Table 2-1 of this chapter.

Table 2-1: Ten industries where foreign-invested enterprises have the highest shares of assets (2000)

Unit: RMB 100 million

Industry	Total Assets of Total Industry	Total Assets of FIEs	FIEs' share in total assets of Total Industry
All industry	126211.24	12849.54	10.18
Electronic and Telecommunications	7518.79	2814.99	37.44
Cultural, Educational and Sports Articles	516.01	178.98	34.69
Leather, Furs, Down and Related Products	939.10	319.43	34.01
Garments and Other Fiber Products	1758.77	493.78	28.08
Furniture Manufacturing	363.48	97.25	26.76
Instruments, Meters, Cultural and Official Machinery	984.52	237.10	24.08
Plastic Products	2052.16	453.64	22.11
Metal Products	2545.63	547.88	21.52
Food Manufacturing	1684.43	296.54	17.60
Timber Processing, Bamboo, Cane, Palm Fiber and Straw Products	694.94	121.17	17.44

Source: Calculated on the basis of the figures in Table 13-13, 13-14, 13-15 and 13-16 in National Bureau of Statistics of China (2002). *China Statistical Yearbook 2001* (Beijing: China Statistics Press).

2. Status of Foreign-invested Enterprises in Chinese Industrial Output

Sustained and large-scale foreign investment in industry has earned foreign-invested enterprises a major position in national industrial output. In 2000, they accounted for 27.39% of the gross industrial output value, 23.98% of the total value-added, and 26.79% of the total industrial sales revenue –foreign-invested enterprises made up 25% or even a larger

[1] The national volumes of investment in fixed assets are quoted from the China Statistical Yearbook 2001, the ratio of industry to the total investment in assets are provided by the National Bureau of Statistics of China, and the volumes of realized FDI in industry are provided by the Department of Foreign Investment of the Ministry of Foreign Trade and Economic Cooperation.

percentage in all these three aspects. In some industries where FDI takes up a high percentage, foreign-invested enterprises have a more important position. In electronic and telecommunications, for instance, they account for 71.57%, 65.39% and 72.21% respectively of the gross industrial output value, value-added and sales revenue. They also make up more than 40% of each of these three categories in a number of other industries, including cultural, educational and sports articles, leather, furs, down and related products, instruments, meters, cultural and official machinery, garments and other fiber products, plastics products and furniture manufacturing. In metal products, electrical equipment and machinery, and transportation equipment manufacturing, foreign-invested enterprises contributed 30% of their value-added. Tables 2-2, 2-3 and 2-4 list the industries where foreign-invested enterprises make up more than 30% of their industrial output value, value-added and sales revenues respectively. For detailed statistics concerning the shares of foreign-invested enterprises in the above-mentioned indicators of various industries, see Annex Tables 2-2, 2-3 and 2-4 of this chapter.

Table 2-2: Industries where foreign-invested enterprises have large shares in their gross industrial output value (2000)

Unit: RMB 100 million

Industry	Gross Industrial Output Value by Total Industry	Gross Industrial Output Value by FIEs	FIEs' share in Gross Industrial Output Value by Total Industry
All industry	85673.66	23464.55	27.39
Electronic and Telecommunications	7549.58	5403.41	71.57
Cultural, Educational and Sports Articles	617.94	368.73	59.67
Instruments, Meters, Cultural and Official Machinery	867.91	492.51	56.75
Leather, Furs, Down and Related Products	1345.17	759.40	56.45
Garments and Other Fiber Products	2291.16	1112.06	48.54
Furniture Manufacturing	370.18	166.17	44.89
Plastic Products	1899.70	828.86	43.63
Food Manufacturing	1442.52	564.06	39.10
Metal Products	2539.76	964.98	37.99
Rubber Products	812.70	286.75	35.28
Chemical Fibers	1243.07	436.46	35.11
Electric Equipment and Machinery	4834.68	1603.06	33.16
Printing and Record Pressing	616.71	198.21	32.14
Timber Processing, Bamboo, Cane, Palm Fiber and Straw Products	656.77	207.76	31.63
Papermaking and Paper Products	1590.36	502.23	31.58
Transportation Equipment Manufacturing	5364.83	1624.85	30.29

Source: Ibid.

Table 2-3: Industries where FIEs have large shares in their total value-added (2000)

Unit: RMB 100 million

Industry	Value-added by Total Industry	Value-added by FIEs	FIEs' share in Value-added by Total Industry
All industry	25394.80	6090.35	23.98
Electronic and Telecommunications	1824.31	1192.97	65.39
Cultural, Educational and Sports Articles	155.30	92.34	59.46
Leather, Furs, Down and Related Products	323.62	176.77	54.62
Instruments, Meters, Cultural and Official Machinery	214.36	105.88	49.39
Garments and Other Fiber Products	592.02	289.07	48.83
Plastic Products	464.43	205.84	44.32
Furniture Manufacturing	94.86	41.62	43.88
Chemical Fibers	295.78	116.17	39.28
Rubber Products	218.98	77.92	35.58
Metal Products	609.46	212.24	34.82
Electric Equipment and Machinery	1231.50	421.69	34.24
Transportation Equipment Manufacturing	1323.61	408.25	30.84

Source: Ibid.

Table 2-4: Industries where foreign-invested enterprises have shares in their total sales revenues (2000)

Industry	Sales Revenue by Total Industry	Sales Revenue by FIEs	FIEs' share in Sales Revenue by Total Industry
All industry	84151.75	22545.74	26.79
Electronic and Telecommunications	7363.27	5317.06	72.21
Cultural, Educational and Sports Articles	588.09	355.58	60.46
Instruments, Meters, Cultural and Official Machinery	849.59	488.35	57.48
Leather, Furs, Down and Related Products	1238.19	708.98	57.26
Garments and Other Fiber Products	2133.01	1046.25	49.05
Furniture Manufacturing	344.59	158.38	45.96
Plastic Products	1799.73	791.66	43.99
Food Manufacturing	1353.07	552.17	40.81
Metal Products	2369.79	930.72	39.27
Rubber Products	731.78	261.77	35.77
Chemical Fibers	1192.80	423.39	35.50
Electric Equipment and Machinery	4527.29	1532.97	33.86
Timber Processing, Bamboo, Cane, Palm Fiber and Straw Products	621.00	203.47	32.76
Printing and Record Pressing	588.00	191.21	32.52
Papermaking and Paper Products	1503.09	473.74	31.52
Transportation Equipment Manufacturing	5229.58	1613.32	30.85

Source: ibid.

3. Status of Foreign-invested Enterprises in Industrial Profit and Tax

Foreign-invested enterprises have made outstanding contributions to the profit and tax revenue of Chinese industry. They contribute more to profit than to industrial output, indicating that their economic returns are better than the general level of the Chinese industry. Table 2-5, which lists industries where foreign-invested enterprises account for more than 30% of their total profit, indicates that these enterprises make up 29.19% of the profit of the entire Chinese industry, as compared with 26.79% of its total sales revenue, and that there are 19 industry where these enterprises account for more than 30% of their total profit, and 16 industries where they account for more than 30% of their sales revenues. For detailed statistics concerning the ratios of foreign-invested enterprises to various industries, see Annex Table 2-5 of this chapter.

Table 2-5: Industries where foreign-invested enterprises have a high profile in total profit

Industry	Total Profits by Total Industry	Total Profits by FIEs	FIEs' share in Total Profits by Total Industry
All industry	4393.48	1282.48	29.19
Petroleum Processing and Coking Products	2.38	7.22	303.36
Electronic and Telecommunications	497.13	350.23	70.45
Instruments, Meters, Cultural and Official Machinery	38.21	25.67	67.18
Transportation Equipment Manufacturing	194.76	127.85	65.64
Cultural, Educational and Sports Articles	22.79	12.85	56.38
Garments and Other Fiber Products	86.44	43.54	50.37
Plastic Products	70.82	34.32	48.46
Leather, Furs, Down and Related Products	34.86	16.17	46.39
Chemical Fibers	63.53	29.15	45.88
Food Manufacturing	54.79	24.04	43.88
Ordinary Machinery Manufacturing	96.76	42.05	43.46
Furniture Manufacturing	15.96	6.86	42.98
Printing and Record Pressing	47.31	20.33	42.97
Coal Mining and Processing	0.50	0.21	42.00
Metal Products	71.65	29.63	41.35
Electric Equipment and Machinery	195.40	80.74	41.32
Papermaking and Paper Products	59.52	22.96	38.58
Special Purpose Equipment Manufacturing	60.89	22.18	36.43
Raw Chemical Materials and Chemical Products	170.95	56.62	33.12

Source: Ibid.

By 2000, the share of foreign-invested enterprises in the total value-added tax payable by the Chinese industry as a whole had been lower than their share in the total value-added. In 2000, these enterprises made up 23.98% of the total value-added and 20.05% of the total value -added tax, indicating that they enjoyed certain preferential treatment in taxation.

However, the share of foreign-invested enterprises in the total value-added tax payments is slightly lower than their share in the total value-added, which means the preferential treatment they received was only marginal. Table 2-6 introduces the industries where foreign-invested enterprises paid more than 30% of the value-added tax. For detailed statistics concerning the shares of value-added tax payable by foreign-invested enterprises in various industries, see Annex Table 2-6 of this chapter.

Table 2-6: Industries where foreign-invested enterprises account for a large share of value-added tax payable

Industry	Value-added Tax Payable by Total Industry	Value-added Tax Payable by FIEs	FIEs' share in Value-added Tax Payable by Total Industry
All industry	3685.20	738.88	20.05
Electronic and Telecommunications	179.69	103.30	57.49
Food Manufacturing	64.34	32.24	50.11
Furniture Manufacturing	9.89	4.55	46.00
Leather, Furs, Down and Related Products	26.40	11.98	45.38
Chemical Fibers	42.16	17.67	41.91
Garments and Other Fiber Products	55.11	22.53	40.88
Plastic Products	50.46	20.15	39.93
Transportation Equipment Manufacturing	202.50	78.45	38.74
Instruments, Meters, Cultural and Official Machinery	23.89	9.02	37.76
Timber Processing, Bamboo, Cane, Palm Fiber and Straw Products	20.83	7.41	35.57
Cultural, Educational and Sports Articles	13.05	4.60	35.25
Rubber Products	26.97	9.08	33.67
Beverage Manufacturing	108.06	33.93	31.40
Metal Products	68.50	21.48	31.36

Source: Ibid.

By 2001, the share of value-added tax paid by foreign-invested enterprises in the Chinese industry had exceeded their share in the total value-added. In 2001, the total value-added were 2695 billion RMB, and 662.2 billion RMB or 24.57% of it was contributed by foreign-invested enterprises. During that year, national value-added were 709.1 billion RMB, 183.7 billion RMB or 25.91% of which was paid by foreign-invested enterprises, or 1.34 percentage points higher than their contribution to the total value-added[2].

[2] The statistics are provided by the Foreign Investment Department of the Ministry of Foreign Trade and Economic Cooperation.

2-2: Industrial Linkages between Foreign-invested Enterprises and Chinese Domestic Industry

In the early days of China's utilization of foreign capital, foreign investors regarded China mainly as a low-cost processing and assembling base that relied on imports of component parts, and their contributions to domestic manufacturing and value-added were low, indicating that foreign-invested enterprises had a low level of coordination with the domestic industry. This situation was not unique to China alone. Studies on transnational investment show that poor correlation between the industries of a host country and foreign-invested enterprises is a long-standing problem that has drawn widespread attention.

There were three main causes behind this problem in China. First, transnational corporations strategically regarded China as a processing and assembling base; second, given its low technical level, the domestic industry lacked the ability to provide up-to-standard accessory products for foreign-invested enterprises; and third, few overseas enterprises entered China to supply accessories for foreign-invested enterprises, which means their investment in the manufacturing of accessories in China was rather limited.

The situation has improved a great deal in recent years. Domestic industry is continuously enhancing its ability to supply accessories for foreign-invested enterprises, thereby raising the degree of correlation between foreign-invested enterprises and domestic industry.

Figure 2-2 features changes in the rate of correlation between Japanese-invested enterprises and Chinese industry, which stood as low as 20% in 1992. By contrast, the rate of correlation of Japanese-invested enterprises in ASEAN countries ran as high as 46.7% that year. However, Japanese enterprises' rate of correlation kept increasing in the 1990s, and by 1999, it had risen to 47.3%; during the same period, the rate showed little change in ASEAN countries.

The reasons why foreign-invested enterprises have been increasing their rate of correlation with domestic enterprises and their correlation with the Chinese industry over the last few years are as follows:

1. The Ability of Domestic Industry to Supply Accessories Enhanced

Thanks to more than 20 years of reform and development, and spurred on by fierce market competition, a considerable number of enterprises in China have, through technological innovation and introduction of advanced technology, quickly raised the technical level and quality of their products, enhanced their competitiveness, and emerged as suppliers of accessories for famous brands and products both at home and abroad. The efforts of foreign-invested enterprises in finding qualified accessory enterprises in China have also helped raise the domestic enterprises' ability to supply accessories for the products of foreign-invested enterprises. Of Motorola's 700-odd suppliers in China, for instance, more than 400 are domestic ones; in 2000, the domestic accessory industry for Motorola exceeded 7.5 billion RMB in output value.

Figure 2-2: Rate of local content of Japanese-invested enterprises in China[3]

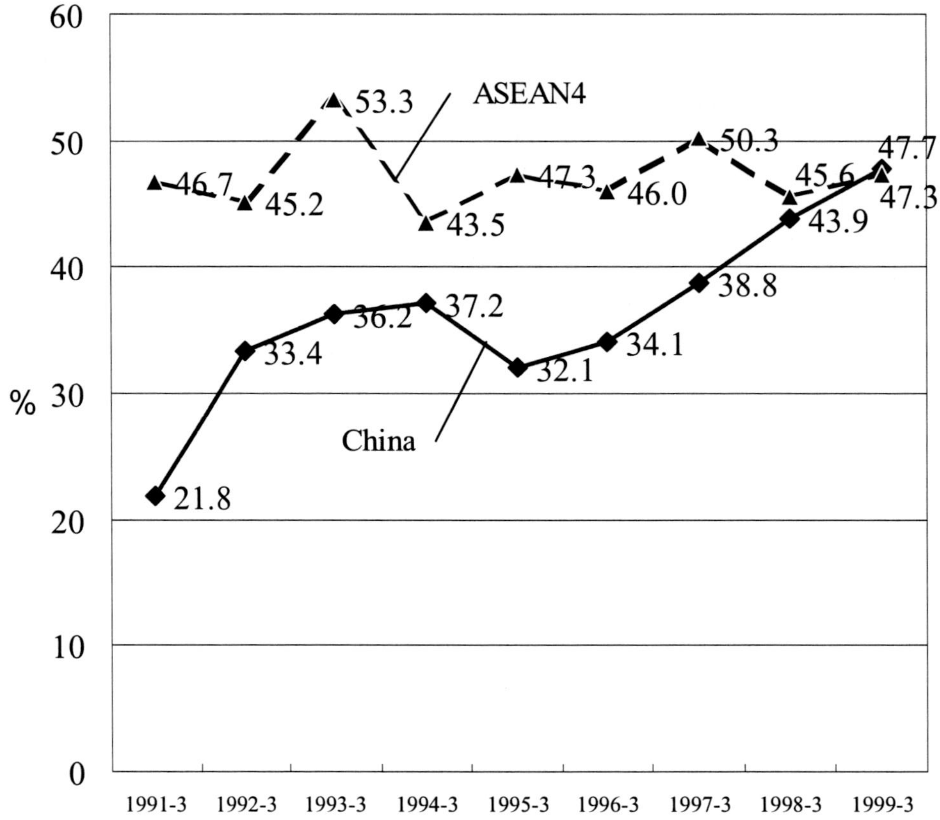

2. FDI in Accessory Supplies Increased

FDI generally begins in China from a single product or a single technological process. Only after its operation has been running smoothly for a period of time, and confidence has been gained in the prospects of development in China, will the foreign investor invest more in accessory supplies. Toshiba of Japan, for instance, started its business in China by investing in electronic component projects, such as the one producing components for television sets in Dalian. After a period of operation, it established joint ventures in Shanghai and Wuxi, and thus acquired a complete network for the supply of components for the manufacturing of

[3] The author is grateful to Mr. Imai of the Asian Economy Research Institute of Japan for providing this chart and associated information. The rate of local purchases =(the volume of local purchases of raw materials and components)/(the total volume of purchases of raw materials and components). The statistics originated from the *Overseas Enterprising Activity of Japanese Enterprises* compiled by the International Enterprise office of the Industrial Policy Bureau of the Japanese Ministry of International Trade and Industry based on a survey of Japanese enterprise headquarters with overseas legal entity status and overseas legal entities (2,151 headquarters and 13,017 overseas legal entities, not including finance and real estate industries.

color television sets. Then Toshiba set up a color television set manufacturing company in Dalian, thereby forming a complete production system in this country.

The example of Toshiba provides one pattern followed by transnational corporations acquiring a complete production system by steadily expanding investment in China. Another important way to improve a company's accessory-supply ability is to follow up the investment made by other foreign-invested enterprises. When a transnational corporation invests in China, its overseas suppliers of intermediary products and correlated services often come to invest in this country too in order to continue to supply their client with highly competitive accessory products. This kind of follow-up investment takes place on a large scale in many countries, particularly in developing countries. Because these developing countries lack suppliers of high-quality intermediary products and correlated services, transnational corporations that have set up shop there will encourage their overseas accessory suppliers to come and invest. China is a typical case in this regard. For instance, after Volkswagen started a joint venture in Shanghai, more than 100 of the enterprises across the globe that supplies accessories for it responded by investing in China. When General Motors started investing in Shanghai, 44 of its auto component suppliers arrived and invested a total of 2.23 billion US dollars. After Isuzu set up a joint venture in Chongqing, a number of its accessory suppliers came to China too, including Hatsujo, Coa, Jidosha Imono, and Tokyo Tanzo from Japan, and Yinjian from Hong Kong, and invested in an impressive number of factories in Chongqing. So far, more than half of the global largest auto accessory manufacturing companies has established joint ventures in China to coordinate the manufacturing of automobiles in China.

Over the last couple of years, localized production of accessories has picked up speed to back up joint ventures manufacturing products in China. The world's three leading mobile telecommunications manufacturers have all raised the portion of their purchases in China. The purchases made by Motorola in 2001 exceeded 12 billion RMB. Ericsson quadrupled its purchases in China in recent years, reaching 14.9 billion RMB in 2000; more than 60% of the production of some of its cell phones has been localized in China, while the production of Ericsson battery chargers and batteries have been completely localized. Ericsson is also buying large amounts of cell phone accessories for export, and its production of wireless base stations reached a 51% rate of localization. Nokia purchased more than 1 billion US dollars worth of accessories in China in 2000, and bought even more in 2001. The increased purchases in China were made by foreign-invested enterprises in accessory-supply services. Nokia, for instance, established the Xingguang Industrial Garden to attract more accessory makers to invest in China and cultivate a foreign-invested enterprise group with the production of mobile telecommunications products at the core.

2-3: Foreign-invested Enterprises and Development of Domestic Human Resources

The important role of developing human resources in economic growth is universally recognized. Human resources are imbued with a special kind of creativity. All the ways and means for raising productivity and the output of production elements cannot be developed, disseminated and utilized without human resources. In that sense, human resources are the most fundamental motive force behind changes in the mode of economic growth.

Transnational corporations are in the possession of abundant human resources. Because of this they are able to develop complicated technical and management systems that can ensure their competitiveness. Human resources are constantly accumulating, transforming and upgrading the knowledge needed for the technology and managerial expertise, so that transnational corporations can keep improving their advantage in market competition. This dynamic competitiveness based on high-quality human resources can hardly be imitated, nor can it be transferred by such hardware as books, reference materials and operational manuals. Herein lies the secret whereby transnational corporations are able to maintain their technological advantage.

Precisely because their competitiveness cannot be completely materialized in the form of equipment and technology in the absence of human resources, transnational corporations are bound to combine themselves with China's development of human resources so that their investment projects can run effectively. Our studies indicate that, first, almost all the transnational corporations operating large investment projects in China have set up training centers in this country, and many of them are providing Chinese employees with almost the same training opportunities and facilities as employees in their parent companies; second, transnational corporations are spending far more on developing human resources than their Chinese counterparts, and the higher the technological level is for their investment projects in China, the more they spend on development of human resources; third, the global manufacturing and managerial networks of transnational corporations and their global information systems have resulted in high abilities and efficiency in the development of human resources, and the employees in the companies they have invested in have the opportunities to receive training in their headquarters or other overseas subsidiaries or engage in systematic studies in the education or training centers inside the companies; and fourth, to provide selected Chinese employees with training in their headquarters and other subsidiaries is, for many enterprises invested by transnational corporations, not only a major part of their human resource development plans but also an effective measure for encouraging their Chinese employees to work hard.

More importantly, the efforts of transnational corporations to develop human resources in China are playing an indispensable role in helping local managers and technicians improve their ability to grasp business opportunities and judge the merits of knowledge or skills. In the present-day world, where knowledge and information are exploding, the knowledge provided by regular education at home and abroad is often divorced from such pragmatic goals as developing business opportunities and meeting market demand, while the training provided by domestic enterprises, too, is often lacking in adequate understanding and grasp of global trends. Therefore, regular school education, and domestic enterprise training cannot help a learner to judge if any one kind of the knowledge at his choice is important for him to enhance his business acumen. Because their products, technology and management embody the trend of development in their respective fields, transnational corporations can ensure high uniformity of their training plans with their employees' demand for self-development. The content and method of training provided by transnational corporations to their employees are exemplary for Chinese enterprises training their own employees.

Specifically, the positive impact of investment from transnational corporations on the development of human resources in China is asserted mainly in the following forms:

1. Cooperating with Chinese Scientists and Technicians in Technological Research and Development

Some of the transnational corporations which regard China as a major strategic market and have invested in multiple technology-intensive projects in China are, for their strategic purposes of making use of China's abundant scientific and technological human resources, fostering a fine image in China, and cultivating a positive attitude among senior Chinese researchers towards their own technology and products, engaged in scientific research, technological development by establishing research centers, laboratories and management colleges in cooperation with universities and research institutes in China. Some of them are doing so by establishing technology development departments in the enterprises. This behavior of transnational corporations not only serves their own strategic goals but also helps training many professional talents for China. For instance, in cooperation with the Beijing University of Posts and Telecommunications, Nortel Networks established China's first foreign-invested R&D centre, the BUPT-Nortel Networks Posts and Telecommunications R&D Center. Before it established a joint venture in China, General Motors had already established a research institute together with Tsinghua University. This kind of cooperative project is not uncommon between famous Chinese universities and transnational corporations. By the end of 2000, Tsinghua University had established 18 training centers and four research institutes in cooperation with transnational corporations. Since 1997, Tsinghua University has engaged in more than 100 research projects in cooperation with foreign organizations. These institutes conduct basic research projects and provide Chinese universities with assistance for certain urgent research projects, but their main efforts are devoted to R&D projects needed by the transnational corporations. Cooperative research serves to give full play to the potential talents of those scientists and technicians who are strong in research but weak in industrializing and marketing their own research results, and cultivate a contingent of high-caliber scientific and technological personnel who can meet the requirements of a market economy.

2. Training Local Talents into High-level Managers for Foreign-invested Enterprises in China

When investing in enterprises in China, virtually all the large transnational corporations have been training senior managers and technicians in their headquarters or their global training centers. Some of the enterprises that have been operating in China for a long time have already sent all of their middle-level technical and managerial personnel abroad for training. This kind of training has helped these senior technical and managerial personnel understand and master the global strategy, management philosophy, technological requirements, managerial characteristics, and marketing methodology of the transnational corporations, and enabled them to open up their horizons and master the most advanced management and technical expertise in the world. Take Motorola for instance. Towards the end of 2000, native Chinese had accounted for 72% of all the senior and middle-level managers of Motorola's companies in China; by contrast, the figure was a meager 12% in 1994, when Motorola had just started operation in China.

3. Providing Multi-layered Training for Employees Inside Enterprises

It is not uncommon for transnational corporations to provide multi-layered training for the personnel in the enterprises they are operating in China. This includes professional training for various levels of managers and those in accounting, marketing, production, quality control, and personnel affairs. There are also classes for ordinary workers and staff members. All the training programs have well-defined goals. It is the belief of the managers of transnational corporations that the competitive advantage of a company manifests itself in the behavior of the entire work force. In other words, it is high-quality human resources that count, instead of equipment and technology. This is particularly the case with accounting, management, marketing and quality control. In these fields it is impossible to keep "high-quality" work to the parent companies and shift "mediocre" or "low-level" work to subsidiaries in China, and because of this, all the managerial expertise and professional knowledge and secrets have to be shared with the subsidiaries. The training provided by these transnational corporations is rich and practical, and highly efficient, and it not only raises the quality of the companies' own workforce, but also provides practical methods and textbooks for personnel training in domestic enterprises.

4. Supporting Local Enterprises in Training their Own Personnel

Some of the transnational corporations also provide training services for local Chinese enterprises. Motorola, for instance, established an enterprise optimization centre in cooperation with the State Planning Commission to supply various ways and means of training and applicable rules and regulations for state-owned enterprises in China. By the end of 2001, Motorola had trained more than 1,400 high-level managers and technicians for 400-odd enterprises in this country.

2-4: Quantitative Analysis: Foreign-Invested Enterprises and the Industrial Growth Speed

The analyses made in this chapter show that FDI has carved out a major niche in the growth of Chinese industry. These analyses were made from the perspective of aggregates. In this section, the author will make a quantitative analysis of the correlation between the growth speed of an industry and the ratio of foreign-invested enterprises in this industry's value-added.

Table 2-7: Industries with the highest growth speeds and foreign-invested enterprises' shares in value-added (1991-2000)

Industry	Annual Growth speed %	FIEs' share in Value-added of Total Industry %
Ordinary Machinery Manufacturing	25.18	22.18
Electronic and Telecommunications	22.37	65.39
Transportation Equipment Manufacturing	18.61	30.84
Petroleum Processing and Coking Products*	14.77	5.70
Instruments, Meters, Cultural and Official Machinery	13.59	49.39
Special Purpose Equipment Manufacturing	13.40	14.92
Chemical Fibers	13.17	39.28
Electric Equipment and Machinery	12.29	34.24
Beverage Manufacturing	12.21	27.86
Medical and Pharmaceutical Products	11.91	24.56

Sources: National Bureau of Statistics of China (1992, 1994, and 2001). *China Statistical Yearbook* (Beijing: China Statistical Press)[4].

Note: The mark "*" indicates that the average growth speed of an industry is calculated on the basis of statistics for the seven years since 1993, when a different method was adopted for classifying industries in China.

Figure 2-3: Correlation between industrial growth speed and FDI

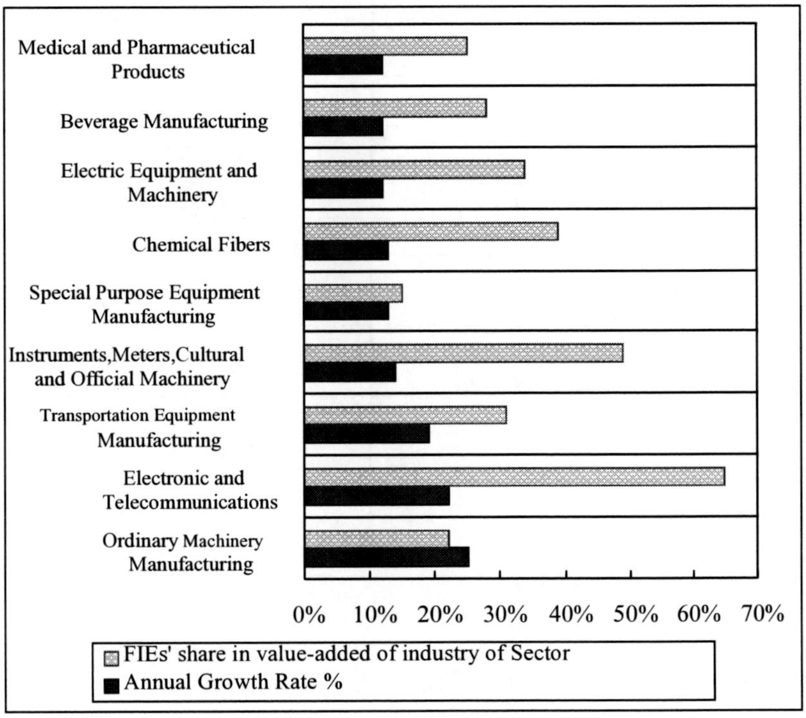

[4] The petroleum processing and coking products industry ranks fifth in growth rate, but it is not included here because it has been opened only marginally to foreign investors and is therefore meaningless for comparisons.

Table 2-8: Growth speed and share of foreign-invested enterprises in value-added of different industries (1991-2000)

Industry	Annual Growth Speed %	FIEs' share in Value-added of Total Industry %
Ordinary Machinery Manufacturing	25.18	22.18
Electronic and Telecommunications	22.37	65.39
Transportation Equipment Manufacturing	18.61	30.84
Petroleum Processing and Coking Products*	14.77	5.70
Instruments, Meters, Cultural and Official Machinery	13.59	49.39
Special Purpose Equipment Manufacturing	13.40	14.92
Chemical Fibers	13.17	39.28
Electric Equipment and Machinery	12.29	34.24
Beverage Manufacturing	12.21	27.86
Medical and Pharmaceutical Products	11.91	24.56
Smelting and Pressing of Ferrous Metals	11.01	4.71
Smelting and Pressing of Nonferrous Metals	10.18	11.15
Raw Chemical Materials and Chemical Products	8.68	21.54
Coal Mining and Processing	7.61	0.15
Papermaking and Paper Products	5.45	28.77
Timber Processing, Bamboo, Cane, Palm Fiber and Straw Products	5.42	27.99
Ferrous Metals Mining and Processing	4.82	0.55
Plastic Products	4.55	44.32
Leather, Furs, Down and Related Products	4.52	54.62
Rubber Products	4.46	35.58
Cultural, Educational and Sports Articles	4.15	59.46
Nonferrous Metals Mining and Processing	4.08	0.88
Nonmetal Mineral Products	4.07	17.30
Printing and Record Pressing	2.85	29.36
Metal Products	2.16	34.82
Nonmetal Minerals Mining and Processing	1.94	4.13
Textile Industry	0.62	20.73
Food Manufacturing*	0.39	4.19
Food Processing*	-2.96	20.68
Furniture Manufacturing	-3.80	43.88
Garments and Other Fiber Products*	-9.15	48.83

Source and note were the same as Table 2-7.

2. Weak Correlation between FDI and All Industries

However, the growth speeds of various industries would show a weak correlation to foreign-invested enterprises' shares in value-added if all the industry were taken into consideration rather than a few fast-growing industries. In Table 2-8 the growth speeds of various industries are arranged in a sequence, and so are the ratios of foreign-invested enterprises to national total value-added as a whole in Table 2-9.

Table 2-9: Shares of foreign-invested enterprises in value-added of different industries and growth speeds of these industries (1991-2000)

Industry	FIEs' share in Value-added of Total Industry %	Growth speed of Total Industry %
Electronic and Telecommunications	65.39	22.37
Cultural, Educational and Sports Articles	59.46	4.15
Leather, Furs, Down and Related Products	54.62	4.52
Instruments, Meters, Cultural and Official Machinery	49.39	13.59
Garments and Other Fiber Products*	48.83	-9.15
Plastic Products	44.32	4.55
Furniture Manufacturing	43.88	-3.80
Chemical Fibers	39.28	13.17
Rubber Products	35.58	4.46
Metal Products	34.82	2.16
Electric Equipment and Machinery	34.24	12.29
Transportation Equipment Manufacturing	30.84	18.61
Printing and Record Pressing	29.36	2.85
Papermaking and Paper Products	28.77	5.45
Timber Processing, Bamboo, Cane, Palm Fiber and Straw Products	27.99	5.42
Beverage Manufacturing	27.86	12.21
Medical and Pharmaceutical Products	24.56	11.91
Ordinary Machinery Manufacturing	22.18	25.18
Raw Chemical Materials and Chemical Products	21.54	8.68
Textile Industry	20.73	0.62
Food Processing*	20.68	-2.96
Nonmetal Mineral Products	17.30	4.07
Special Purpose Equipment Manufacturing	14.92	13.40
Smelting and Pressing of Nonferrous Metals	11.15	10.18
Petroleum Processing and Coking Products*	5.70	14.77
Smelting and Pressing of Ferrous Metals	4.71	11.01
Food Manufacturing*	4.19	0.39
Nonmetal Minerals Mining and Processing	4.13	1.94
Nonferrous Metals Mining and Processing	0.88	4.08
Ferrous Metals Mining and Processing	0.55	4.82
Coal Mining and Processing	0.15	7.61

Source and note were the same as Table 2-7.

As Tables 2-8 and 2-9 indicate, the growth speed of an industry fails to show a clear correlation to the share of foreign-invested enterprise in its value-added. In Table 2-8, in which the average growth speeds of various industries are arranged in a sequence, the growth speed of the industry, with the exception of a few that lead the list, do not show obvious correlation to the foreign-invested enterprises' shares in value-added. In ordinary machinery manufacturing and special purpose equipment manufacturing industries, the growth speeds are high, but the shares of foreign-invested enterprises in their value-added are low. In Table 2-9, in which the shares of foreign-invested enterprises in value-added of various industries are also arranged in a sequence, the industries in which FDI accounted for high ratios to value-added, such as the cultural, educational and sports articles, garment and other fiber products, furniture manufacturing industries, do not show a high growth speed except the electronic and telecommunications, instruments, meters, cultural and official machinery and other industries that lead the list; by contrast, industries in which FDI has a low ratio to value-added, such as coal mining and processing, smelting and pressing of ferrous metals, petroleum processing and coking products industries, are marked by high growth speeds.

The following is a correlation analysis of a cross-section of the average annual growth speeds of various industries during the ten-year period from 1990 to 2000 in relation to foreign-invested enterprises' share in national total value-added.

In this correlation analysis, we have deleted six industries – petroleum and national gas extraction, logging and transport of timber and bamboo, tobacco processing, electric power, steam and hot water production and supply, gas production and supply, tap water production and supply – because they are not open to FDI or are marginally opened to it and therefore would render our analysis meaningless.

After deleting these six industries, the growth speeds of various industries and the ratios of foreign-invested enterprises to their value-added are subjected to a linear regression analysis by using the method of the minimum squares for the fitting of a straight line. The coefficient of correlation derived from our calculations stands at 0.0285, meaning a feeble correlation (with $r<0.3$ being feeble correlation, r being the coefficient of correlation).

3. An Analysis of the Causes behind the Feeble Correlation

The feeble correlation between industrial growth and the shares of foreign-invested enterprises fails to a large measure to justify people's direct perception of it, and it does not accord with the achievements made by Chinese industry since the adoption of the policy of reform and opening up to the outside world. Therefore, it merits further study and analysis. The following are the hypotheses that can be raised in this regard:

(1) Access Barriers

In certain industry that enjoy high-speed growth but where foreign-invested enterprises have a small share of the value-added, there may exist barriers against the entry of FDI. Such barriers may be natural or related with government policies. For instance, the petroleum processing and coking products industry develops robustly, but foreign-invested enterprises take up a low percentage in its value-added because government policies have resulted in barriers for FDI. For a long period of time, the tapping of natural resources in China is generally not opened to FDI, and even if some of the fields are open to it, the room given is rather limited. Among the enterprises engaged in the tapping of domestic resources, most are large state-owned enterprises, while petroleum imports are basically government controlled.

This has resulted in a shortage of competitive crude oil resources, which makes it hard for foreign-invested enterprise to enter the petroleum processing and coking products industry. The situation is similar for coal and other mining industries. The ordinary machinery manufacturing industry ranks first in growth speed, but the share of foreign-invested enterprises in its value-added is low because this industry has a sound industrial foundation, and the medium- and low-grade products of domestic enterprises are rather competitive.

(2) The Crowding-out Effect

The crowding-out effect may be felt in those industries where the growth speed is low but the shares of foreign-invested enterprises are high. That is to say, in these fields FDI has acquired a conspicuous competitive edge, and their entry has crowded out domestic enterprises and new domestic investors and thereby replaced domestic investment, leading to a branch-wise low growth speed. The cultural, educational and sports articles industry, for instance, does not have a high growth speed but has a high ratio of foreign-invested enterprises probably because the products of this industry enjoy a high export rate and because, with famous brands and international marketing networks, foreign-invested enterprises have more advantages than their domestic counterparts.

(3) Inactivity of Transnational Investment in Certain Industry

Judging from the aggregates, transnational investment figures prominently in the global manufacturing industry, but the situation varies from industry to industry. Generally speaking, the processing and assembling industry is where transnational investment is the most active. The characteristics of processing and assembly work enable transnational corporations to formulate global manufacturing systems under which a product can be manufactured in a number of countries. The electronic and telecommunications and the instruments, meters, cultural and official machinery industries are typical of the processing and assembling industry. However, in some other industries, transnational investment is inactive and its importance is far smaller than in the processing and assembling industry. The metallurgical industry is a typical case in point; in this industry transnational investment is far from active because in virtually all the countries domestic enterprises form its backbone, and it is particularly true with the metallurgical industries of large nations. In the last decade, the growth speeds of several metallurgical industries in China are by no means low, but foreign-invested enterprises account for a low ratio to their output due probably to the fact that transnational investment in the global metallurgical industry as a whole is not active enough.

2-5: Contributions of Foreign-Invested Enterprises to the Growth of Chinese GDP

In 2001 China recorded a 7.3% GDP growth rate. Industrial growth contributed 3.8% to it, with the rate of contribution standing at 52%. According to the calculations made in the foregoing, the rate of contribution of foreign-invested enterprises to the Chinese industrial growth stands at 39.1%. After discounts are made, foreign-invested industrial enterprises' rate of contribution to the GDP of China is 20.3%, or one fifth.

Available statistics do not list the percentages of foreign-invested enterprises in the output of the tertiary industry. A probable method of estimation is to suppose the investment/output ratio of FDI in the tertiary industry is the same as FDI's input/output ratio in industry, derive the rate of contribution of foreign-invested enterprises to the tertiary industry, and then convert this rate into their rate of contribution to the GDP. Accordingly, foreign-invested enterprises' 2001 rate of contribution to the tertiary industry was 17.6%, and their rate of contribution to GDP was 5.9%.

Because foreign investment's share in the primary industry is so low as to be negligible, the sum total of the rates of contribution of foreign-invested enterprises to industry and the tertiary industry can be regarded as their rate of contribution to GDP. Thus their rate of contribution to GDP was 26.2%. That is to say, foreign-invested enterprises contributed 1.9 percentage points to the 7.3% growth of the Chinese GDP in 2001. Statistics show that foreign-invested enterprises have emerged as major contributors to the growth of the national economy of China.

ANNEX TABLES

Annex Table 2-1: FIEs as a percentage of Total Assets in Industries in 2000

Unit: RMB 100 Million

Industry	Total Assets of Total Industry	Total Assets of FIEs	FIEs' share in Total Assets of Total Industry
National Total	126211.24	12849.54	10.18
Coal Mining and Processing	3868.51	5.70	0.15
Petroleum and Natural Gas Extracting	4088.12		
Ferrous Metals Mining and Processing	326.00	0.45	0.14
Nonferrous Metals Mining and Processing	548.93	2.10	0.38
Nonmetal Minerals Mining and Processing	669.14	9.98	1.49
Logging and Transport of Timber and Bamboo	401.53		
Food Processing	3078.22	360.07	11.70
Food Manufacturing	1684.43	296.54	17.60
Beverage Manufacturing	2742.77	296.49	10.81
Tobacco Processing	1973.82	6.40	0.32
Textile Industry	5917.01	610.22	10.31
Garments and Other Fiber Products	1758.77	493.78	28.08
Leather, Furs, Down and Related Products	939.10	319.43	34.01
Timber Processing, Bamboo, Cane, Palm Fiber and Straw Products	694.94	121.17	17.44
Furniture Manufacturing	363.48	97.25	26.76
Papermaking and Paper Products	2511.99	383.22	15.26
Printing and Record Pressing	973.73	148.52	15.25
Cultural, Educational and Sports Articles	516.01	178.98	34.69
Petroleum Processing and Coking Products	3785.91	61.40	1.62
Raw Chemical Materials and Chemical Products	8688.03	649.42	7.47
Medical and Pharmaceutical Products	2798.90	289.86	10.36
Chemical Fibers	1808.44	159.58	8.82
Rubber Products	1118.81	187.21	16.73
Plastic Products	2052.16	453.64	22.11
Nonmetal Mineral Products	6113.11	461.67	7.55
Smelting and Pressing of Ferrous Metals	9228.25	187.43	2.03
Smelting and Pressing of Nonferrous Metals	2866.65	151.04	5.27
Metal Products	2545.63	547.88	21.52
Ordinary Machinery Manufacturing	4787.90	509.63	10.64
Special Purpose Equipment Manufacturing	3255.29	255.35	7.84
Transportation Equipment Manufacturing	8129.68	995.29	12.24
Electric Equipment and Machinery	5260.20	917.43	17.44
Electronic and Telecommunications	7518.79	2814.99	37.44
Instruments, Meters, Cultural and Official Machinery	984.52	237.10	24.08
Electric Power, Steam and Hot Water Production and Supply	18626.94	421.58	2.26
Gas Production and Supply	610.91	18.74	3.07
Tap Water Production and Supply	1523.19	5.36	0.35

Source: Calculated on the basis of figures of Table 13-13, 13-14, 13-15 and 13-16 in National Bureau of Statistics of China (2002). *China Statistical Yearbook 2001* (Beijing: China Statistics Press).

Annex Table 2-2: Outputs by FIEs as a percentage of Total Outputs in Industries in 2000

Unit: RMB 100 Million

Industry	Gross Industrial Output Value of Total Industry	Gross Industrial Output Value by FIEs	FIEs' share in Gross Industrial Output Value of Total Industry
National Total	85673.66	23464.55	27.39
Coal Mining and Processing	1276.81	6.81	0.53
Petroleum and Natural Gas Extracting	3130.11		
Ferrous Metals Mining and Processing	164.86	1.26	0.76
Nonferrous Metals Mining and Processing	405.36	3.27	0.81
Nonmetal Minerals Mining and Processing	356.94	18.00	5.04
Logging and Transport of Timber and Bamboo	121.09		
Food Processing	3722.70	859.81	23.10
Food Manufacturing	1442.52	564.06	39.10
Beverage Manufacturing	1752.37	514.68	29.37
Tobacco Processing	1451.29	7.28	0.50
Textile Industry	5149.30	1094.13	21.25
Garments and Other Fiber Products	2291.16	1112.06	48.54
Leather, Furs, Down and Related Products	1345.17	759.40	56.45
Timber Processing, Bamboo, Cane, Palm Fiber and Straw Products	656.77	207.76	31.63
Furniture Manufacturing	370.18	166.17	44.89
Papermaking and Paper Products	1590.36	502.23	31.58
Printing and Record Pressing	616.71	198.21	32.14
Cultural, Educational and Sports Articles	617.94	368.73	59.67
Petroleum Processing and Coking Products	4429.19	239.81	5.41
Raw Chemical Materials and Chemical Products	5749.02	1183.87	20.59
Medical and Pharmaceutical Products	1781.37	403.73	22.66
Chemical Fibers	1243.07	436.46	35.11
Rubber Products	812.70	286.75	35.28
Plastic Products	1899.70	828.86	43.63
Nonmetal Mineral Products	3692.85	647.92	17.55
Smelting and Pressing of Ferrous Metals	4732.90	339.32	7.17
Smelting and Pressing of Nonferrous Metals	2180.23	293.15	13.45
Metal Products	2539.76	964.98	37.99
Ordinary Machinery Manufacturing	3046.95	652.68	21.42
Special Purpose Equipment Manufacturing	2192.63	334.59	15.26
Transportation Equipment Manufacturing	5364.83	1624.85	30.29
Electric Equipment and Machinery	4834.68	1603.06	33.16
Electronic and Telecommunications	7549.58	5403.41	71.57
Instruments, Meters, Cultural and Official Machinery	867.91	492.51	56.75
Electric Power, Steam and Hot Water Production and Supply	4611.39	714.13	15.49
Gas Production and Supply	170.30	47.82	28.08
Tap Water Production and Supply	325.53	6.46	1.98

Source: Ibid.

Annex Table 2-3: Value-added by FIEs as a Percentage of Total Value-added in Industries in 2000

Unit: RMB 100 Million

Industry	Value-added of Total Industry	Value-added by FIEs	FIEs' share in Value-added of Total Industry
National Total	25394.80	6090.35	23.98
Coal Mining and Processing	583.09	0.88	0.15
Petroleum and Natural Gas Extracting	2209.02		
Ferrous Metals Mining and Processing	62.31	0.34	0.55
Nonferrous Metals Mining and Processing	139.77	1.23	0.88
Nonmetal Minerals Mining and Processing	122.64	5.06	4.13
Logging and Transport of Timber and Bamboo	61.49		
Food Processing	835.29	172.76	20.68
Food Manufacturing	415.81	174.43	4.19
Beverage Manufacturing	618.90	172.41	27.86
Tobacco Processing	935.80	4.55	0.49
Textile Industry	1272.84	263.80	20.73
Garments and Other Fiber Products	592.02	289.07	48.83
Leather, Furs, Down and Related Products	323.62	176.77	54.62
Timber Processing, Bamboo, Cane, Palm Fiber and Straw Products	157.53	44.10	27.99
Furniture Manufacturing	94.86	41.62	43.88
Papermaking and Paper Products	412.62	118.71	28.77
Printing and Record Pressing	201.39	59.13	29.36
Cultural, Educational and Sports Articles	155.30	92.34	59.46
Petroleum Processing and Coking Products	787.99	44.94	5.70
Raw Chemical Materials and Chemical Products	1415.81	305.00	21.54
Medical and Pharmaceutical Products	633.88	155.71	24.56
Chemical Fibers	295.78	116.17	39.28
Rubber Products	218.98	77.92	35.58
Plastic Products	464.43	205.84	44.32
Nonmetal Mineral Products	1126.72	194.88	17.30
Smelting and Pressing of Ferrous Metals	1299.29	61.25	4.71
Smelting and Pressing of Nonferrous Metals	512.69	57.18	11.15
Metal Products	609.46	212.24	34.82
Ordinary Machinery Manufacturing	840.75	186.46	22.18
Special Purpose Equipment Manufacturing	580.97	86.70	14.92
Transportation Equipment Manufacturing	1323.61	408.25	30.84
Electric Equipment and Machinery	1231.50	421.69	34.24
Electronic and Telecommunications	1824.31	1192.97	65.39
Instruments, Meters, Cultural and Official Machinery	214.36	105.88	49.39
Electric Power, Steam and Hot Water Production and Supply	2328.62	359.88	15.45
Gas Production and Supply	34.74	7.32	21.07
Tap Water Production and Supply	150.88	3.13	2.07

Source: Ibid.

Annex Table 2-4: Sales Revenue by FIEs as a percentage of Total Sales Revenue in Industries in 2000

Unit: RMB 100 Million

Industry	Sales Revenue of Total Industry	Sales Revenue by FIEs	FIEs' share in Sales Revenue of Total Industry
National Total	84151.75	22545.74	26.79
Coal Mining and Processing	1213.77	7.29	0.60
Petroleum and Natural Gas Extracting	2914.99		
Ferrous Metals Mining and Processing	152.84	1.10	0.72
Nonferrous Metals Mining and Processing	375.18	3.12	0.83
Nonmetal Minerals Mining and Processing	323.20	16.43	5.08
Logging and Transport of Timber and Bamboo	108.50		
Food Processing	3477.52	846.38	24.34
Food Manufacturing	1353.07	552.17	40.81
Beverage Manufacturing	1647.47	489.88	29.74
Tobacco Processing	1430.76	7.40	0.52
Textile Industry	4810.45	1017.86	21.16
Garments and Other Fiber Products	2133.01	1046.25	49.05
Leather, Furs, Down and Related Products	1238.19	708.98	57.26
Timber Processing, Bamboo, Cane, Palm Fiber and Straw Products	621.00	203.47	32.76
Furniture Manufacturing	344.59	158.38	45.96
Papermaking and Paper Products	1503.09	473.74	31.52
Printing and Record Pressing	588.00	191.21	32.52
Cultural, Educational and Sports Articles	588.09	355.58	60.46
Petroleum Processing and Coking Products	4571.03	249.70	5.46
Raw Chemical Materials and Chemical Products	5422.06	1143.62	21.09
Medical and Pharmaceutical Products	1627.48	365.83	22.48
Chemical Fibers	1192.80	423.39	35.50
Rubber Products	731.78	261.77	35.77
Plastic Products	1799.73	791.66	43.99
Nonmetal Mineral Products	3364.17	594.42	17.67
Smelting and Pressing of Ferrous Metals	4887.05	329.70	6.75
Smelting and Pressing of Nonferrous Metals	2087.59	282.31	13.52
Metal Products	2369.79	930.72	39.27
Ordinary Machinery Manufacturing	2839.72	621.85	21.90
Special Purpose Equipment Manufacturing	2003.48	321.61	16.05
Transportation Equipment Manufacturing	5229.58	1613.32	30.85
Electric Equipment and Machinery	4527.29	1532.97	33.86
Electronic and Telecommunications	7363.27	5317.06	72.21
Instruments, Meters, Cultural and Official Machinery	849.59	488.35	57.48
Electric Power, Steam and Hot Water Production and Supply	6819.67	676.79	9.92
Gas Production and Supply	234.65	49.60	21.14
Tap Water Production and Supply	308.07	7.11	2.31

Source: Ibid.

Annex Table 2-5: Profits by FIEs as a percentage of Total Profits in Industries in 2000

Unit: RMB 100 Million

Industry	Total Profits of Total Industry	Total Profits by FIEs	FIEs' share in Total Profits of Total Industry
National Total	4393.48	1282.48	29.19
Coal Mining and Processing	0.50	0.21	42.00
Petroleum and Natural Gas Extracting	1148.42		
Ferrous Metals Mining and Processing	6.54	0.03	0.46
Nonferrous Metals Mining and Processing	30.84	0.15	0.49
Nonmetal Minerals Mining and Processing	10.69	1.03	9.64
Logging and Transport of Timber and Bamboo	1.13		
Food Processing	68.74	13.28	19.32
Food Manufacturing	54.79	24.04	43.88
Beverage Manufacturing	97.51	19.61	20.11
Tobacco Processing	142.58	0.44	0.31
Textile Industry	136.88	33.70	24.62
Garments and Other Fiber Products	86.44	43.54	50.37
Leather, Furs, Down and Related Products	34.86	16.17	46.39
Timber Processing, Bamboo, Cane, Palm Fiber and Straw Products	17.75	2.92	16.45
Furniture Manufacturing	15.96	6.86	42.98
Papermaking and Paper Products	59.52	22.96	38.58
Printing and Record Pressing	47.31	20.33	42.97
Cultural, Educational and Sports Articles	22.79	12.85	56.38
Petroleum Processing and Coking Products	2.38	7.22	303.36
Raw Chemical Materials and Chemical Products	170.95	56.62	33.12
Medical and Pharmaceutical Products	136.58	32.86	24.06
Chemical Fibers	63.53	29.15	45.88
Rubber Products	10.35	2.18	21.06
Plastic Products	70.82	34.32	48.46
Nonmetal Mineral Products	97.50	26.82	27.51
Smelting and Pressing of Ferrous Metals	158.09	12.57	7.95
Smelting and Pressing of Nonferrous Metals	63.52	6.29	9.90
Metal Products	71.65	29.63	41.35
Ordinary Machinery Manufacturing	96.76	42.05	43.46
Special Purpose Equipment Manufacturing	60.89	22.18	36.43
Transportation Equipment Manufacturing	194.76	127.85	65.64
Electric Equipment and Machinery	195.40	80.74	41.32
Electronic and Telecommunications	497.13	350.23	70.45
Instruments, Meters, Cultural and Official Machinery	38.21	25.67	67.18
Electric Power, Steam and Hot Water Production and Supply	457.16	120.32	26.32
Gas Production and Supply	-3.69	1.34	
Tap Water Production and Supply	9.27	2.06	0.22

Source: Ibid.

Annex Table 2-6: Value-added Tax Payable as a percentage of Total Value-added Tax Payable in Industries in 2000

Unit: RMB 100 Million

Industry	Value-added Tax Payable of Total Industry	Value-added Tax Payable by FIEs	FIEs' share in Value-added Tax Payable of Total Industry
National Total	3685.20	738.88	20.05
Coal Mining and Processing	98.11	0.24	0.24
Petroleum and Natural Gas Extracting	297.41		
Ferrous Metals Mining and Processing	7.09	0.04	0.56
Nonferrous Metals Mining and Processing	12.90	0.10	0.78
Nonmetal Minerals Mining and Processing	16.43	0.44	2.68
Logging and Transport of Timber and Bamboo	2.61		
Food Processing	70.25	14.52	20.67
Food Manufacturing	64.34	32.24	50.11
Beverage Manufacturing	108.06	33.93	31.40
Tobacco Processing	143.95	0.72	0.50
Textile Industry	158.41	25.85	16.32
Garments and Other Fiber Products	55.11	22.53	40.88
Leather, Furs, Down and Related Products	26.40	11.98	45.38
Timber Processing, Bamboo, Cane, Palm Fiber and Straw Products	20.83	7.41	35.57
Furniture Manufacturing	9.89	4.55	46.00
Papermaking and Paper Products	62.91	18.51	29.42
Printing and Record Pressing	31.02	9.23	29.75
Cultural, Educational and Sports Articles	13.05	4.60	35.25
Petroleum Processing and Coking Products	118.37	6.13	5.18
Raw Chemical Materials and Chemical Products	213.78	54.02	25.27
Medical and Pharmaceutical Products	115.43	30.13	26.10
Chemical Fibers	42.16	17.67	41.91
Rubber Products	26.97	9.08	33.67
Plastic Products	50.46	20.15	39.93
Nonmetal Mineral Products	172.58	28.66	16.60
Smelting and Pressing of Ferrous Metals	247.76	10.03	4.05
Smelting and Pressing of Nonferrous Metals	82.31	5.27	6.40
Metal Products	68.50	21.48	31.36
Ordinary Machinery Manufacturing	122.96	26.07	21.20
Special Purpose Equipment Manufacturing	73.57	10.88	14.79
Transportation Equipment Manufacturing	202.50	78.45	38.74
Electric Equipment and Machinery	156.39	45.73	29.24
Electronic and Telecommunications	179.69	103.30	57.49
Instruments, Meters, Cultural and Official Machinery	23.89	9.02	37.76
Electric Power, Steam and Hot Water Production and Supply	532.19	61.99	11.65
Gas Production and Supply	6.82	0.52	7.62
Tap Water Production and Supply	18.44	0.34	1.84

Source: Ibid.

Chapter 3

Transnational Investment, Technological Progress and Industrial Upgrading

3-1: Transnational Corporations: Important Suppliers of New Products and Technology

Technological progress is a major reason why transnational corporations are gaining increasing importance in the global economy. These companies are spending several hundred millions or even billions of US dollars, and for a small number of large companies, the figure exceeds one hundred billion US dollars. The importance of transnational corporations has something to do with their control of development and utilization of technology. Worldwide flow of technology is becoming increasingly more dependent on transnational corporations' investment as a vehicle. Transnational corporations control upwards of 85% of transnational transfers of advanced technology.

In the entire 1980s, foreign investors were mainly medium-level and small investors from Hong Kong, Macao and Taiwan, who accounted for around 75% of the total FDI in China. Investment in China by enterprises from the United States, Japan and European Union went mainly into medium-sized and small projects. Generally speaking, the technological level of these enterprises was not necessarily higher than the average level of Chinese enterprises, state-owned ones in particular. In the late 1980s, only 2% of the foreign-invested enterprises (FIEs) in China were regarded as technologically advanced, and enterprises using advanced technology made up a meager 5% of the total FDI in this country[1]. A generally low technological level was a major feature of FDI in China during this period. For this reason foreign-invested enterprises were often criticized for their low technological level and their failure to serve this country's purpose of introducing foreign capital.

Since the mid-1990s, investment by large transnational corporations has been fast growing. By the end of 2001, more than 400 of the world's top 500 transnational manufacturing companies had invested in China. By replacing medium-sized and small enterprises as major investors in China, large transnational corporations have markedly raised the technological level of foreign-invested enterprises in China.

[1] Jiang Xiaojuan: *A Study on the relationship between Chinese Industrial Development and Foreign Trade*, Economic Management Publishing House, Beijing, 1996.

The practice of transnational corporations investing in China indicates that almost all the transnational investment is linked with a certain form of technological transfer. Transnational investment introduces technology mainly through the following channels:

First, introducing capital goods and processing craft with relatively high technological content, and using them with high efficiency, thereby raising the technological level of the domestic industry. In the 1990s, capital goods imported for investment purposes by foreign-invested enterprises accounted for 11-14% of the realized FDI in China[2], most of which were advanced processing equipment.

Second, introducing new products, which help boost the shares of products that meet the market demand and have high technological content and high incremental value in the Chinese manufacturing industry. For instance, foreign-invested enterprises have made outstanding contributions to the increased share of cars in the Chinese auto industry.

Third, introducing R&D capabilities, which is a new change in global investment. China is one of the developing countries having received more transnational investment in R&D. Over the last few years, transnational corporations have invested in a considerable number of projects with designing, R&D functions, many of which are independent global R&D centers. The introduction of R&D capacities not only raises the technological level of existing enterprises in China but also increased the nation's R&D ability.

Fourth, introducing managerial capacities that facilitate the highly efficient use of advanced technology. While introducing advanced technology, transnational corporations also introduce managerial capacities to put such technology to effective use. The enterprises invested by transnational corporations in many industries lead their Chinese counterparts in technological and managerial levels. Their advanced managerial expertise not only enables them to efficiently use the advanced technology they have brought into China, but also provides their Chinese counterparts with practical learning opportunities and enables them to know the ways and means of advanced managerial expertise for improving enterprise efficiency -- for instance, from the perspective of internal management, the ways and means to integrate the production, marketing and technological developmental networks scattered around the globe into a highly efficient whole so as to reduce the costs and expanding market shares; and from the perspective of enterprise strategy for development, how to seek new low-cost expansion opportunities, new intellectual sources and innovational ideas on a global scale, and how to make effective use of service systems such as financial, accounting and global databases, and research and consultancy services. With their exemplary role, transnational corporations are both eye openers and fine examples for domestic enterprises.

Most of the global mains IT manufacturing companies have begun to build up advanced manufacturing capacities in China. The global major notebook computer manufacturers are building large-scale and most sophisticated production capacities. China will become the global most advanced notebook computer production center. The world's major chip producers have also started large-scale investment in China. Semiconductor Manufacturing International (Shanghai) Corporation, a joint venture with American and Taiwan capital, produced its first batch of chips in August 2002 to become the first semi-conductor company to be able to batch-produce 0.18-micro 8-inch wafers in China. According to estimates based on those projects that are under construction, nine newly built semi-conductor factories will

[2] For detailed statistics, see Table 8-9, Chapter Eight.

be marketing first-generation Chinese-made chips by 2007, thereby turning China into the world's second largest chip producing country behind the United States.

Apart from the IT industry, transnational corporations in other industries are also actively shifting their most advanced products and technology to China. The new factory invested in and built in the Zhangjiang Hi-tech Park in Shanghai's Pudong New Area by Boehringer Ingelheim of Germany, one of the world's top 20 pharmaceutical companies, is first rate and up to the GMP standard in both technology and production facilities. Other transnational pharmaceutical companies have also begun to product their newest products in China. GlaxoSmithKline has placed China on its first global list of countries where it will market its new pharmaceuticals, and built a raw materials factory in Tianjin. Bristol-Myers Squibb China recently released five new drugs. In Hangzhou, Sanofi-Synthelabo will release its latest anticoagulant this year, and GlaxoSmithKline and Novo Nordisk of Denmark have begun producing new drugs for treating diabetes. The protection of intellectual property rights provided by China's accession to WTO has rid foreign companies of their misgivings for unfair competition and encouraged them to introduce new products to China.

Those transnational corporations that started early and invested considerably in China are increasing their investment and introducing more advanced products. In 2000, Volkswagen of Germany announced that it would speed up its development in China in three fields, and would invest an additional 2.5 billion euro in the next three to five years, so that its total investment in this country will amount to 5.5 billion euro. Du Pont announced that it will invest an additional 90 million US dollars for the expansion of a Lycra factory in Qingpu, Shanghai, so that when the factory is completed in September next year, the Lycra fiber's annual production capacity in China will be expanded from 4,000 tons to 10,000 tons.

Since 2002, one foreign-invested enterprise after another has chosen China as the initial market for global sales of their products. Three companies did so in August that year: Compaq Evo, the first new product developed since the founding of the new Hewlett Packard, rolled off the production line in a Shanghai factory; a new model of washing machine that represents the latest Hitachi technology landed in the Chinese market four months earlier than in Japan and way ahead of European and American competitors; and China was Sony's first market for a model of television sets that represents a new breakthrough in the high-definition technology.

3-2: A Survey on the Technical Level of Foreign-Invested Enterprises

From 2000 to 2001 the author presided over a series of surveys involving 127 enterprises invested in China by transnational corporations in Beijing, Shanghai, Shenzhen and Suzhou. Managers of 67 of these enterprises were interviewed, and the others responded by filling in questionnaires. The technological level is one major aspect of our surveys. We established two reference systems, one for China and the other for foreign countries, with which we studied the relative technical level of these enterprises. The following are our findings:

1. The Overwhelming Majority of Transnational Corporations Have Provided Advanced or Relatively Advanced Technology from their Parent Companies

Using the foreign parent companies as the reference system, we classified the technology the foreign-invested enterprises have introduced from their parent companies into three ranks: advanced, relatively advanced and ordinary. Advanced technology refers to the kind of technology or product that has been adopted or marketed by the parent company for less than three years; relatively advanced technology refers to technology or product that has been in use or production for more than three years but is still being used or produced; and ordinary technology refers to technology or product that is no longer in use or production in the parent company. If an enterprise is using or producing two or three categories of such technology or product, then its main product counts; if several products produced at these three categories of technological level are roughly the same in sales volume, then the one with the largest sales volume counts.

Our survey reveals that 57 of these enterprises are using relatively advanced technology from parent companies, 53 are advanced technology, and 17 are ordinary technology.

2. A Considerable Number of Transnational Corporations Have Provided Technology that Filled in Blanks in China

When domestic enterprises are used for reference, the technology of these foreign-invested enterprises is classified also into three categories: technology that fills in blanks in China, that is, never before had any enterprise in China had used this kind of technology or produced this kind of products; advanced technology in China, that is, technology or product that is advanced in China but is already being used or produced by domestic enterprises; and ordinary technology in China, that is, technology that is no longer regarded in China as being advanced. If an enterprise is using two or three types of technology, our study will focus on its major product; if several products produced at different technical levels are roughly the same in sales volume, our study will focus on the product with the highest sales volume.

Of all the enterprises surveyed, 83, or 65%, are using technology that has filled in blanks in China; 44, or 35%, are using advanced technology; and no enterprise is using the kind of technology deemed ordinary in China.

The technical levels of foreign-invested enterprises, calculated on the basis of the aforementioned reference systems are listed in Table 3-2.

Table 3-1: Technical levels of enterprises invested by transnational corporations (127 samples)

	Number of enterprises	**% in sampled enterprises**
Compared with parent companies		
Using most advanced technology	53	42
Using relatively advanced technology	57	45
Using ordinary technology	17	13
Compared with domestic enterprises		
Using technology that filled in blanks in China	83	65
Using advanced technology	44	35

Some other surveys have come to similar conclusions. A study on the projects invested in China by 33 famous transnational corporations indicates that 17 enterprises, or 52% of the sampled ones, have provided technology that filled in blanks in China. Another study of 40 Japanese-invested enterprises shows that most of them use advanced technology and are producing competitive products; altogether, 39 enterprises are using new technology, technology that filled in blanks in China, and advanced technology, accounting for over 95% of the enterprises sampled during the study[3].

The aforementioned studies indicate that not only the technology used by enterprises of transnational corporations in China is generally higher than the technical level of their Chinese counterparts, but a considerable number of them are using advanced technology from parent companies and filled in technical blanks in China as well.

3-3: The Technological Spillover Effect of Transnational Corporations

The positive role of investment in China by transnational corporations in technological progress and industrial upgrading manifests itself not only in the projects invested but also in the "spillover" effect of their technology on their Chinese counterparts.

1. Mayor Channels for Technological Spillovers

The technological spillover effect refers to the impact of the advanced technology adopted by enterprises invested in China by transnational corporations on the improvement of the technological level of China as a whole. Major channels for such spillovers are technological diffusion, exemplary and application effects. These three channels are having a major impact on the technological level of Chinese enterprises as a whole.

[3] These two surveys were organized by Mr. Wang Zhile. For the results of the first survey, see *Investment in China by the World's Famous Transnational corporations* compiled by Wang Zhile, China Economic Publishing House, Beijing, 1995; for the results of the second survey, see *Investment in China by Japanese Enterprises* edited by Wang Zhile, China Economic Publishing House, Beijing, 1998.

1) Technological Diffusion

This refers to the diffusion of technological capabilities of transnational corporations from within foreign-invested enterprises. Major forms of such diffusion are as follows:

-- Personnel flow: The flow of talented people between foreign-invested enterprises and domestic enterprises is a major channel for the diffusion of technology from transnational corporations. South Korea, Thailand and Malaysia and China's Taiwan Province successfully increased the technological level of their enterprises by introducing advanced technology, and the flow of professionals between foreign-invested and domestic enterprises is their major experience in technological diffusion. In China, with the environment and enterprising conditions for domestic enterprises improving constantly, an important measure for promoting the diffusion of technology of transnational corporations is to foster systems and formulate policies to facilitate the flow of professionals between enterprises.

-- Localizing supply of accessories: The technological capabilities of transnational corporations can be shifted to Chinese enterprises by localizing the supply of accessories. When a transnational corporation with a high technological standard purchases components and raw materials from Chinese enterprises, it invariably raises high requirements for the quality, technology and functions of accessory products. It may also provide relevant technological standards and assistance. Sometimes it will invest in joint development so as to ensure that the technology and products of accessory enterprises measure up to its demands.

-- Technological exchange: The technological level of foreign-invested enterprises is way higher than that of domestic enterprises. As the technology of foreign-invested enterprises is hard to be imitated, they tend to be open to their Chinese counterparts and are willing to receive visitors, train technicians for them and sponsor academic symposiums, which are effective forms of disseminating technology.

-- Technological cooperation: Some transnational corporations have established R&D organizations in cooperation with research institutes and universities in China. These include a telecommunications R&D center run jointly by the Beijing University of Posts and Telecommunications and Nortel Networks of Canada, a SMC pneumatic laboratory named after the SMC and Tsinghua and two other Chinese universities, a joint laboratory run by Rockwell in cooperation with Tsinghua and nine other Chinese universities. Research topics for these cooperative R&D centers are decided jointly by the partners, and they are engaged in researches of development projects needed by enterprises as well as research into fundamental disciplines of learning.

-- Technological demonstration: When a transnational corporation using advanced technology invests in an enterprise in a country, its technology will have an impact on its counterparts and enterprises using similar technology in that country through such tangible and intangible forms as equipment, products, personnel contacts and technical reference materials provided for clients. The effectiveness of these forms of technological demonstration depends to a large degree on the ability of the local enterprises in understanding and applying the technology involved. The technological demonstration of transnational corporations is playing a remarkable role in some industries where Chinese enterprises are well established in technology.

2) Technological Competition

When confronted with competition from enterprises invested by transnational corporations, domestic enterprises that are advanced in technology or monopolizing will speed up technological development and raise their technological level so as to maintain their competitiveness on the market. The pressure of competition from transnational corporations provides an important motive force for Chinese enterprises in electronic and telecommunications, motor vehicles, machinery manufacturing, power station equipment industry, etc. to keep raising their technological levels. In some service industries that are only marginally opened to the outside world, domestic enterprises are less pressured to improve their services and raise their efficiency and are therefore lagging far behind the advanced level in the world. In the last couple of years, as banking, insurance, telecommunications, wholesaling and retailing are obviously quickening up their speed in improving their efficiency and services as they become increasingly more open to FDI.

3) Application of Technology

Some of Chinese industries have reached a fairly high level or even the world's most advanced level in designing and assembling final products, but the quality and grades of such products are deteriorating because the accessories and raw materials and technological processes provided by domestic enterprises fail to measure up to the standards. If they rely on massive imports of accessories and raw materials, this can boost the costs and is therefore infeasible from an accountant's point of view. The entry of foreign-invested enterprises into accessory industries and their supplies of components and raw materials with high quality and at low costs make it possible for the technology China has possessed for the manufacturing of certain final products to become applicable, thereby raising the technological level of the domestic industry.

2. How Do Local Content Increase the Level of Domestic Enterprises: A Case in Point Concerning Technological Spillover

Another major item in the aforementioned survey of 127 foreign-invested enterprises is to look into the situation of transnational corporations getting accessory supplies from domestic enterprises.

Of all the enterprises sampled during the survey, 74 have domestic enterprises supply them with accessories[4], and 51, or 69%, of them set requirements on these accessory enterprises and help them in various ways. The major means and ways by which these 51 foreign-invested enterprises help domestic accessory enterprise raise their technology level and product competitiveness are, according to the sequence in which they appear, 1) setting new quality standards, 2) providing technological assistance, 3) investing in the development of technology, 4) setting up joint ventures for development purposes. See Table 3-2.

[4] The study covers only important suppliers of components and raw materials and does not include accessory on electric power and water production and supply, transportation and other infrastructure facilities and services.

Table 3-2: Major ways and means by which foreign-invested enterprise help accessory enterprises in China

(Number of samples: 51)

Form of help*	Number of enterprises that responded	% in the number of enterprises sampled
Setting quality standards	40	78.4
Providing technological assistance	33	64.7
Investing in technological development	12	23.5
Running joint ventures for technological development	6	11.7

*These forms of help could be repeatedly chosen in the survey.

3-4: Transnational Investment and the Upgrading of the Chinese Industrial Structure

Another major role of transnational corporations' investment in China is in accelerating the upgrade of the domestic industrial structure.

Since the early 1990s, most of the projects invested by large transnational corporations have been found in labor-intensive processing industries, which have no vigorous promotion on the Chinese industrial restructuring. The microelectronics, motor vehicles, household electrical appliance, telecommunications, instruments, meters, cultural and official machinery, medical and pharmaceutical products and chemicals industries are where transnational investment has been most concentrated.

In 2000 the International Investment Research Center of the Chinese Academy of Social Sciences sponsored a survey of enterprises invested by the global Top 500 transnational corporations for an analysis of the behaviors and influence of these companies' investment in China. The Top 500 refer to the *Fortune* magazine's 1998 list of the 500 largest transnational corporations in the world. During this survey data were collected on 1,196 enterprises invested in China by these transnational corporations, with a total volume of foreign investment of 30.232 billion US dollars[5].

The survey indicates that the investment in China by the Top 500 is concentrated mainly on four capital- and technology-intensive industries, that is, the electronic and telecommunications, machinery manufacturing, transportation equipment manufacturing, raw chemical materials and chemical products industries. The Top 500 have invested in 486 projects in these four industries, accounting for 40% of the total number of projects they have invested. The investment in these projects totals 16.61 billion US dollars, or 55% of the Top 500's total investment in China. Little of the Top 500 investment has been found in the textile, garments and other labor-intensive industries; their investment in the textile and garments industry amounts to less than 600 million US dollars, or 2% of their total in China.

[5] For a general introduction to a report on this survey, see Jiang Xiaojuan's "Investment by Large Transnational corporations: Its Impact on China's Industrial Structure, Technological Progress and Economic Globalization" in the *China Foreign Investment Report 2000 – Investment in China by Large Transnational corporations* edited by Wang Luolin, China Financial and Economic Publishing House, Beijing, 2000.

Surveys of certain industries and countries also confirm the fact that transnational investment in China is densely concentrated in capital- and technology-intensive industries. Of the 231 projects invested by 30 large transnational corporations from Germany and Japan, 48, or 21%, are found in the electronics industry; the auto industry comes second with 28 such projects, or 12% of the total; and the household electrical appliance industry comes third with 23 projects, or 10% of the total. The electric and telecommunications, machinery manufacturing, electric equipment and machinery, and chemical industries are where there are relatively more transnational-invested projects, whereas few such projects are found in the textile, garments and light industries where there were many enterprises invested by medium-sized and small foreign companies. See Table 3-3. These surveys indicate that investment from transnational corporations is playing a remarkable role in promoting the upgrade of the Chinese industrial structure.

Table 3-3: Distribution of enterprises invested by 30 Japanese and German companies in China

Industry	Number of Projects	Industry	Number of Projects
Farming, Forestry, Animal Husbandry and Fishing	0	Telecommunication	17
Energy, Mining and Processing	5	Machinery and Equipment	17
Food/Tobacco	3	Motor Vehicles	28
Textile/Garments	2	Electrical Equipment	16
Light Industry	15	Scientific Research and Design	17
Personal Computer	23	Trade and Services	7
Chemical, Rubber and Plastic Products	18	Investment Management	11
Medical and Pharmaceutical Products	4	Total	231
Electronics	48		

Source: Wang Zhile (ed.) (1996). *Famous Transnational Corporations' Investment in China* (Beijing: China Economy Publishing House).

The information and auto industries are two most typical cases in point. In the last couple of years, the Chinese information industry has been growing three times faster than GDP. The exports of electronic information products are the largest of all the export commodities by China, and accounts for 28% of national total exports. China leads the world in the output of program-controlled switchboards, cell phones, color television sets, DVD players and tape-recorders. The auto industry has also maintained a high-speed growth, which is something China has been striving for. In 2002, China produced 3.2 million automobiles, which included 1.1 million cars, with an average increase of nearly 40% in both regards as compared with the previous year. The robust growth in the production capacities of these industries as well as the fast increase in the technological level of their products are directly related to massive input of foreign capital. Take the auto industry for instance. A study of the nine large auto groups that have resulted from global M&As over the last few years shows that by the end of 2001, all these nine auto groups had invested on a large scale and established auto-making joint ventures in China.

3-5: Transnational Investment and the Development of Chinese High-Tech Industries

1. Robust Growth of Chinese High-Tech Industries

Judging from the general scale of industrialization in the world, China is in a period in which the industrial structure is experiencing the most drastic changes. Whether or not the Chinese industry can maintain its fast growth depends to a large degree on whether industrial upgrade can proceed smoothly and whether enterprises can quicken their technological progress. The quick development of high-tech industry is a major indicator in this regard. Transnational corporations are in the possession of major shares of funds for global R&D of high technology and are playing a leading role in technological transfers. To attract their investment can help quickly revamp the Chinese industrial structure and upgrade its technological level, and speed up development of the Chinese high-tech industry.

The high-tech industry in China has been growing rapidly over the last few years. During the period 1996-2000, this industry registered an average annual growth of 21.2%, which was 11 percentage points higher than the growth rate of national total industrial output value during the same period.

2. Foreign-invested Enterprises are a Staunch Force Promoting the Development of Chinese High-Tech Industry

Investment from a considerable number of transnational corporations is a major factor behind the robust growth of the high-tech industry in this country, where foreign-invested high-tech enterprises have emerged as a staunch force behind the development of the high-tech industry. In 2000, the foreign-invested high-tech enterprises in Beijing, Shanghai, Shenzhen and Suzhou accounted for 65% and 79% respectively of the total output value and profits of the nation's high-tech industry[6].

Foreign-invested enterprises are major contributors to remarkable growths in China's exports of high-tech products in the last few years. In 2002, the high-tech exports by these enterprises totaled 55.657 billion US dollars, 46.98% more than in the same period of the previous year, and accounting for 82.20% of national total high-tech exports, 32.75% of the total exports by foreign-invested enterprises at 169.936 billion US dollars.

3. Foreign-invested Enterprises' Important Contributions to the Development of Chinese High-Tech Gardens

The high-tech industry of China is mainly distributed in the nation's 52 high-tech gardens. The statistics collected from these gardens give a detailed expression to the overall situation of the Chinese high-tech industry. We have designed a comprehensive index, that is, the rate of comprehensive contribution by foreign-invested enterprises, to appraise the important role foreign-invested enterprises play in the Chinese high-tech industry.

[6] Source: a research into the high-tech industry presided over by the author in 2001.

The rate of contribution to the general revenue from trade in high-tech products = the total revenue of foreign-invested enterprises from high-tech trade/the total revenue of high-tech gardens from high-tech trade

The rate of contribution to product sales revenue = the revenue of foreign-invested enterprises from product sales/the high-tech gardens' total product sales revenue

The rate of contribution to production = the industrial output value of foreign-invested enterprises/the gardens' total industrial output value

The rate of contribution to exports = the total exports of foreign-invested enterprises/the gardens' total exports

The rate of contribution to R&D = the input of foreign-invested enterprises in R&D/the gardens' total input in R&D

The rate of comprehensive contributions by foreign-invested enterprises = (The rate of contribution to the general revenue from trade in high-tech products + the rate of contribution to product sales revenue + The rate of contribution to production + the rate of contribution to exports + the rate of contribution to R&D)/5

Table 3-4 takes a look at the individual rates of contribution of foreign-invested high-tech enterprises in China's high-tech gardens and their rate of comprehensive contribution in 2001.

Table 3-4: Degree of internationalization of high-tech industry in China's high-tech development zones (2001) %

Year	The rate of contribution to the general revenue from trade in high-tech products	The rate of contribution to product sales revenue	The rate of contribution to production	The rate of contribution to exports	The rate of contribution to R&D	The rate of comprehensive contributions by foreign-invested enterprises
1991	12.64	-	16.06	16.67	-	15.12
1992	0.43	0.46	0.43	9.76	1.32	2.48
1993	19.33	28.03	23.71	61.11	12.50	28.94
1994	24.71	31.47	27.55	64.57	19.72	33.60
1995	26.88	33.30	30.22	65.87	14.71	34.20
1996	31.35	37.09	36.37	73.72	22.60	40.23
1997	31.85	36.81	34.54	77.31	24.74	41.05
1998	31.78	35.80	35.26	66.47	26.49	39.16
1999	36.41	40.87	41.72	76.07	28.60	44.73
2000	41.97	46.90	46.41	79.39	-	53.67

Note: the figures are derived from the Torch High-tech Industrial Development Center of the Ministry of Science and Technology (2001). *A statistical report on the ten-year development of national high-tech industrial development zones* (Beijing: Scientific and Technical Documents Publishing House). Because statistics on sales revenue and R&D for 1991 are unavailable, the comprehensive internationalization index for that year is calculated on the basis of the formula (the degree of dependence on the total revenue from high-tech product trade + the degree of dependence on production + the degree of dependence on exports)/3. Because the statistics concerning 2000 lack the figures on the input in R&D, the comprehensive internationalization index for that year is calculated on the basis of the formula (the degree of dependence on the total revenue from high-tech product trade + the degree of dependence on product sales revenue + the degree of dependence on production + the degree of dependence on exports) / 4.

3-6: From Manufacturing to R&D: The Latest Trend[7]

1. A General Introduction to R&D Institutions Founded by Transnational Corporations in China

During the past years, foreign investors had been criticized for their failure to bring their technological developmental abilities into China while their investment enabled them to acquire considerable manufacturing capacities in this country. The situation is no longer the same in recent years. Since the mid-1990s, the number of R&D institutions established by foreign investors in China has been increasing fairly quickly and their R&D efforts have been on a rise in scale and level.

In 1994, the Canadian company Nortel Networks invested in Beijing to establish a joint venture R&D center in cooperation with the Beijing University of Posts and Telecommunications, which was the first of its kind ever established in China by a transnational corporation. In the same year SMC cooperated with Tsinghua University and set up a pneumatic laboratory. Since transnational corporations have been establishing more and more R&D centers in this country. By the end of 2002, more than 180 such centers had been established across the country, but most of the independent R&D institutes established by transnational corporations are found in Beijing and Shanghai. According to incomplete statistics, by the end of 2001 transnational corporations were operating 44 independent R&D centers in Beijing and 41 such centers in Shanghai, 14 of which are global R&D centers. There are also 18 such centers in Shenzhen and 7 in Suzhou.

Most of the independent R&D centers established in China by transnational corporations are wholly foreign-owned institutions and are mainly distributed in the information and telecommunication, bioengineering pharmaceutical, refined chemical, and transportation equipment manufacturing industries. The transnational corporations involved include Microsoft, Intel, IBM, Nokia, Motorola, Ericsson, Lucent, Fujitsu, Procter & Gamble, Hewlett Packard, Unilever, Novo Nordisk, SUN, General Motors, Volkswagen, Matsushita, Toshiba, Nortel Networks, Nestles, Alcatel, Microsoft, Bell and Michelin Tyres.

2. Salient Features of Transnational Corporations that Established R&D Centers in China

1) Most of the Transnational Corporations Engaged in R&D in China Have Been Investing in China for at Least Five Years

The overwhelming majority of the transnational corporations operating R&D centers in China are among the earliest investors in China. About one third of them were already investing in enterprises in China prior to 1995.

[7] Except where noted, all the information and statistics provided in this section are derived from the research on "Issues Concerning Promoting the Transfer of Advanced Technology from Transnational corporations to China", a soft science topic raised by the State Scientific and Technological Commission. A total of 38 foreign-invested R&D institutions responded to the research by receiving interviews or answering the questionnaires. For a report on this research, see Jiang Xiaojuan's "A Study on the Behaviors of Foreign-invested Enterprises in R&D", *Science and Technology Review*, issue No. 9, 2000, Beijing.

2) Most of the Transnational Corporations Engaged in R&D Have Developed Large-Scale Operations in China

Most of the transnational corporations that have established R&D centers in China own several enterprises, have developed considerable manufacturing capacities and have a lot of interests in this country. Most of them have invested in five to twenty enterprises in China. Matsushita, for instance, owns 43 subsidiary companies in this country and their products are found in virtually all the household electrical appliance manufacturing industries. A considerable number of these transnational corporations have established regional or national headquarters in China; they carry out long-term development strategies in this country, and the R&D centers they have established in this country are part of such strategies.

3) The Transnational Corporations Adopt a Shareholding Structure that Enables them To Control their Enterprises

When conducting R&D activities, transnational corporations have to consider such issues as technological confidentiality and economic returns for their advanced technology. For this reason they are in favor of wholly owned enterprises and structures in which they hold controlling shares, joint ventures being the most frequently used structure. In our survey, foreign-controlled enterprises comprise 52.6% of the enterprises sampled; wholly foreign-owned enterprises come second at 23.7%; this is followed by joint ventures with the Chinese side controlling the majority shares at 13.2%; and enterprises in which the shares are split fifty-fifty between Chinese and foreign partners come last at 10.5%. Thus wholly foreign-owned enterprises and foreign-controlled joint ventures make up 76.1% of the total number of enterprises sampled during the survey. See Table 3-5. It is thus clear that when transnational corporations operating R&D activities invest in enterprises, they are in favor of shareholding structures that put them in control. An obvious phenomenon is that the more technologically advanced an enterprise is, the more it is inclined to adopt wholly owned forms of enterprise.

Table 3-5: Shareholding structures of enterprises invested by transnational corporations (Based on 38 sample enterprises)

	Wholly Foreign-Owned Enterprises	Joint ventures with dominating shares of foreign partners	Joint ventures with dominating shares of Chinese partners	Joint ventures with equal shares
Percentage %	23.7	52.6	13.2	10.5
The ratio between FIEs and JVEs with dominating shares of foreign partners	76.1			

Source: see Footnote 3.

3. Reasons for Transnational Corporations to Establish R&D Centers in China

Recent years have witnessed an increase in the number of R&D institutions established by transnational corporations in China. The major reasons behind this phenomenon are as follows:

1) The Importance of the Chinese Market

Investment of transnational corporations is growing quickly in China, so much so that this country has become some of the famous transnational corporations' major overseas market. For some, China is already a major part of the global market. Because of this it is all the more necessary for them to carry out R&D activities in order to adapt their products and technology to the technological structures and demand of the Chinese market.

2) Technological Progress Makes it Possible to Globalize R&D Activities

Progress achieved so far in information and telecommunications technology has made it possible for the global system of a transnational corporation to swap information promptly with any of its subsidiary companies no matter where it is located, thereby enabling R&D activities to be carried out in different parts of the world. An overseas R&D institute can, through the interior network of a transnational corporation, obtain R&D resources, statistics and expertise from its parent company, keep abreast with clients' demands for products and services, ensure that the products it has developed and designed will meet the requirements of overseas clients, and produce such products in any one of the enterprises within the framework of the parent company.

3) Utilizing China's Research Ability and Intellectual Resources

An important reason why transnational corporations establish R&D institutions in China is because among developing nations, China has a relatively high level in science and technology and holds an advantage in intellectual resources. Beijing, for example, is where high-level scientists and technicians are concentrated. There is the Chinese Academy of Sciences, top-calibre institutions of higher education such as Peking and Tsinghua universities, and Zhongguancun, the nation's Silicon Valley with the backing of the Chinese Academy of Sciences and a cluster of universities. Beijing's dense populace of talented people is highly appealing for foreign investors looking for opportunities to run R&D centers. Just as Bill Gates has said, he chose China as the venue for Microsoft's first research institute in Asia because of its many outstanding people. The Microsoft Research Institute in China plans to invest in 80 million US dollars to enroll 100 researchers in six years' time.

4) Fostering a Fine Public Image

As some transnational corporations see it, to go in for manufacturing without bringing in technological development capabilities is detrimental to their long-term development in China, and they have been keenly aware of the need to change the situation. To gain the trust of the Chinese government and foster a good public image has become a major driving force behind some transnational corporations' decision to set up R&D centers in China. When Rockwell decided to foster cooperative ties with some universities in China, one of its major purposes was to foster a fine image in the Chinese community, win public trust, and achieve long-term success.

5) The Guiding Role of Government Policies

Over the last few years the Chinese government has come to realize the importance of encouraging transnational corporations to engage in R&D in China, and has formulated a package of preferential policies to woo these companies to this country to set up regional or national headquarters and R&D centers.

4. Organizational Forms of Foreign-invested R&D Institutions

Independent R&D centers are but one form of organization adopted by transnational corporations engaged in R&D activities in China. There are other forms. When we look into foreign-invested enterprises' activities in R&D, we need to take all kinds of such activities into consideration. According to our findings, the enterprises invested by transnational corporations mainly use three organizational forms to conduct R&D work in this country.

1) As an Organizational Branch

Some enterprises invested by transnational corporations run R&D bodies as part of their daily operations. For instance, Lucent Technologies Fiber Optic Co., Ltd. (Beijing), ABB Beijing Drive Systems Co., LTD, JVC (Beijing) Co., Ltd., Mitsubishi Stone Semiconductor Co., Ltd., and Beijing Suohong Electronic Company[8] have all set up R&D centers inside themselves. Such development centers are generally established after a company has been set up, and most of them are small in scale, hiring two to 30 researchers.

2) As Independent Organizations

Some enterprises invested by transnational corporations do not run R&D bodies as part of their organizational structures, but their parent companies have independent R&D institutes in China or R&D departments in headquarters situated elsewhere in the service of enterprises invested in China. The Novo Nordisk (China) Co., Ltd. runs a special R&D organization in Beijing, so that its subsidiaries in other parts of the country do not need to run their own research centers. Procter & Gamble Technology Center Beijing Limited is an independent R&D center established by its parent company in China to serve its subsidiaries in China. Motorola has set up several independent research departments in China to serve its enterprises in this country. NEC (Beijing) Co., Ltd. offers technological support for its enterprises in China. Fujitsu of Japan also runs a development centre in China to serve its enterprises in this country. The parent companies of these research institutes have large-scale operations in China, and for this reason they hire teams of researchers ranging from 30 to 200 in number.

3) Cooperative R&D Centers

Some enterprises invested by transnational corporations in China do not have research departments inside them, nor have their parent companies established independent R&D centers in China either. However, they are running special R&D organizations together with Chinese research institutes or colleges to meet their own needs. Examples are a telecommunications R&D center run by Canada's Nortel Networks together with the Beijing University of Posts and Telecommunications, a pneumatic laboratory run by the SMC (China) Co., Ltd. in cooperation with Tsinghua and two other universities, and a joint laboratory run by Rockwell China Company along with ten universities including Tsinghua. These cooperative R&D centers choose research topics through joint discussion; some of the research projects are in the service of their enterprises, and some are for basic research purposes.

Some Wholly Foreign-owned Enterprises serve concurrently as R&D organizations. Motorola, for instance, not only runs independent research centers but also operates

---

[8] The company has no English name and we give this English name to it according to its Chinese name.

cooperative research centers as well as research departments as part of its organizational structure.

5. Types of R&D Activities Conducted by Foreign-invested Enterprises

Our study reveals that foreign-invested enterprises' R&D activities generally fall into three categories: creative R&D, adaptive R&D, and R&D of special technology.

1) Creative R&D

This refers to R&D projects that are of a creative nature within the framework of a parent company. The results of such projects serve the purpose of raising the technical level of a transnational corporation in a specific field, or the purpose of developing new products or new technological processes.

2) Adaptive R&D

This refers to R&D activities designed to transform the technology introduced from the parent company and adapt it to the level and structure of the Chinese demand. This kind of activity is often designed to localize the production of a certain product, such as studies of English software in a Chinese context and the development of a Chinese platform.

3) Development of Special-purpose Technology

This refers to research and development of technology with the peculiar characteristics of the Chinese market in mind. For instance, consumers of developed countries are in the habit of washing laundry with warm water because the enzyme contained in the detergent works better in warm water. The Chinese consumers, however, use cold water in washing machines and for this reason R&D institutes of some transnational corporations are searching for enzymes that work well in cold water.

6. R&D Activities of Transnational Corporations in China: Salient Features and the Reasons behind Them

The following salient features mark the R&D behaviors of transnational corporations operating in China:

1) R&D of Applicable and Special-purpose Technology Constitutes the Major Part of their Work

Almost all the foreign-invested R&D organizations oriented to the Chinese market are engaged in R&D of applicable and special technology for the Chinese market, a characteristic that is determined by the salient features of the Chinese market. This is particularly so in telecommunications, software, integrated optical, machinery and electrical equipment, refined chemicals, and equipment for environmental protection. Adaptive research and development of special-purpose technology are imperative because Chinese demand and technical platforms are different from the parent countries of the transnational corporations.

2) Some Enterprises are Working Concurrently on Creative R&D Projects

Almost none of the foreign-invested R&D organizations are engaged mainly in creative R&D work. However, some of them are working concurrently on all three categories of research projects. Such organizations generally have the following two hallmarks:

Firstly, they regard China as one of their most important markets. For some transnational corporations, China is their most important overseas market or even the largest part of their global market, and they have developed production scales that are not only very large but also most advanced in technology, and, what is more, they have established national or regional headquarters in this country. This kind of R&D centers are often among their parent companies' leading global research centers, and their R&D activities in China have become an integral part of their global operations. Motorola, for instance, operates two R&D departments under its mobile phone and cell phone departments, and it has established a man-machine telecommunications technology laboratory in cooperation with the Computer Institute of the Chinese Academy of Sciences. Some of the research projects of this laboratory are highly creatively and getting close to the front ranks of the world. The R&D center run by Procter & Gamble, which has a large share of the Chinese market and regards China as its major overseas market, is engaged in the research of new formulas, new technology and new products that are partly oriented to the global market.

Secondly, competition on the Chinese market is intensifying. When competition is intensifying among enterprises invested in China by transnational corporations, they are forced to adopt the most advanced technology and engage in creative research work to strive for favorable positions in such competition. Examples in this regard are a dime and a dozen. When a foreign-invested enterprise is monopolizing the Chinese market, it tends to keep its products and technology intact for a long time, and such products and technology, far from being advanced in the world, are often the ones that have been phased out in foreign markets. However, once the monopoly is threatened by the entrance of other transnational corporations, it will hurriedly release new products and technology, and its R&D efforts will be brought to a new level.

Since 2001, foreign-invested enterprises have markedly raised their investment in R&D projects in China. Firstly, there is an increase in the level of their R&D projects. In the past almost all the R&D organizations of these enterprises were engaged in developing applicable technology and products for the Chinese market. In recent years, they have been engaged in increasing numbers of projects for creative or universal purposes. The video-frequency technology, basic system software, and coders developed by the Intel's Chinese software laboratory, for instance, became the company's 2002 line of major products. Secondly, the position of their R&D institutes is rising. With their position on the increase, transnational corporations' R&D centers in China have also enhanced their position in transnational corporations' global R&D networks. Some of them have become the global R&D center, some have emerged as transnational corporations' only research centers in Asia or serve as their research headquarters, and a tiny number of them have become their companies' only overseas research centers outside their parent countries. Nokia's research centre in Hangzhou, for instance, is the company's third global research centre along with one centre in Finland and another in the Silicon Valley in the United States. Dell's China Research Centre is the company's first overseas research organizations. The new product research centre of Japan's Omron in Shanghai is its first overseas research institute. LG opened the headquarters of its China Electronics R&D Center towards the end of 2002; situated in the Wangjing Science and Technology Garden of Beijing and serving as LG's largest research centre for its overseas market, this research centre not only develops products for the Chinese market – it also develops new products for the global market as well.

Chapter 4

CONTRIBUTIONS OF FOREIGN-INVESTED ENTERPRISES TO EXPORTS

Over the last decade and more, exports by foreign-invested enterprises (FIEs) have been growing a lot faster than national total exports, and their share in total exports is rising steadily as well. These enterprises have exported a higher percentage of machinery and electrical products and high-tech products, thereby increasing the portion of commodities with relatively high technological content and incremental values in total exports, and upgrading the export commodities mix as a whole. The changes in the export commodities mix show that China's comparative advantage is extending towards more industries, and Chinese export commodities have acquired more long-term competitiveness on the world market.

This chapter discusses foreign-invested enterprises' behaviors in export and their contributions to the growth of exports and the upgrading of the export commodities mix in China.

4-1: CONTRIBUTIONS OF FOREIGN-INVESTED ENTERPRISES TO CHINA'S TOTAL EXPORTS

In the 1990s, China's foreign trade maintained a high speed of growth. The total exports and imports raised from 135.7 billion US dollars in 1991 to 620.785 billion US dollars in 2002, with the exports and imports increasing from 71.91 billion US dollars to 325.569 billion US dollars and from 63.79 billion US dollars to 295.216 billion US dollars respectively. See Table 4-1.

The remarkable growth in the exports of China in the 1990s was attributed to a large extent to the robust growth of exports by foreign-invested enterprises and the remarkable growth in their percentage in national total exports. The exports by foreign-invested enterprises grew from 12.047 billion US dollars in 1991 to 169.937 billion US dollars in 2002, and their portion in national total exports increasing from 15.75% to 52.2% during the same period. See Table 4-1 and Figure 4-1 for detail.

Table 4-1: Foreign-invested enterprises' imports and exports and their percentage in national total imports and exports

(Unit: US$ 100 million)

Year	Imports and Exports			Imports			Exports		
	National	**FIEs**	**Share**	**National**	**FIEs**	**Share**	**National**	**FIEs**	**Share**
1991	1357.01	289.55	21.34	637.91	169.08	26.51	719.10	120.47	16.75
1992	1655.25	437.47	26.43	805.85	263.87	32.74	849.40	173.60	20.44
1993	1957.03	670.70	34.27	1039.59	418.33	40.24	917.44	252.37	27.51
1994	2366.21	876.47	37.04	1156.15	529.34	45.78	1210.06	347.13	28.69
1995	2808.48	1098.19	39.10	1320.78	629.43	47.66	1487.70	468.76	31.51
1996	2899.04	1371.10	47.29	1388.38	756.04	54.45	1510.66	615.06	40.71
1997	3250.60	1526.20	46.95	1423.60	777.20	54.59	1827.00	749.00	41.00
1998	3239.23	1576.79	48.68	1401.66	767.17	54.73	1837.57	809.62	44.06
1999	3606.49	1831.33	50.78	1657.18	858.84	51.83	1949.31	886.28	45.47
2000	4743.08	2367.14	49.91	2250.97	1172.23	52.10	2492.12	1194.41	47.93
2001	5097.68	2590.98	50.83	2436.13	1258.63	51.67	2661.55	1332.35	50.06
2002	6207.85	3302.23	53.19	2952.16	1602.86	54.29	3255.69	1699.37	52.20

Source: provided by Customs General Administration People's Republic of China.

Figure 4-1: Changes in the shares of foreign-invested enterprises in China's total exports

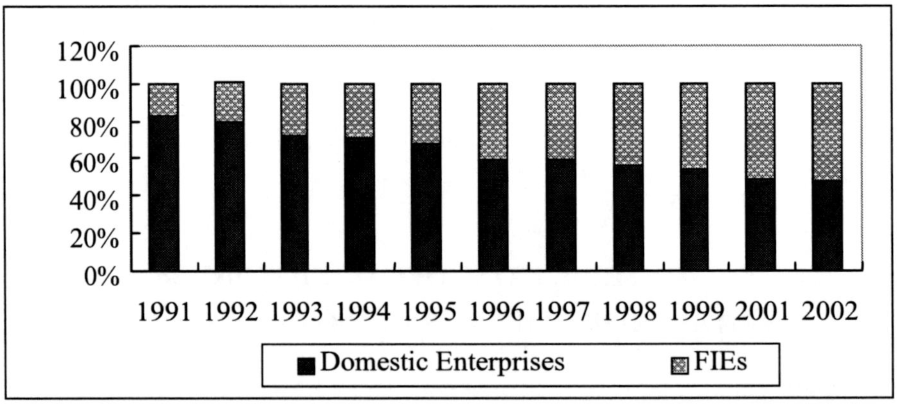

If the volume of increase in exports alone is taken into account, then foreign-invested enterprises contributed the major share in the growth in China's annual exports. During the 11-year period from 1992 to 2002, foreign-invested enterprises accounted for as high as 62% of the increase in national exports, and these enterprises' contribution exceeded 100% in 1993, 1996 and 1998. That is to say, without the contributions of foreign-invested enterprises, the exports of China would have recorded negative growths during these three years. See Table 4-2

Table 4-2: Foreign-invested enterprises' volume of increases in imports and exports and share in national volume of increases in the 1990s

(Unit: US$ 100 million)

Year	Increases in Imports and Exports			Increases in Imports			Increases in Exports		
	National	FIEs	Share	National	FIEs	Share	National	FIEs	Share
1992	298.24	147.92	49.60	167.94	94.79	56.44	130.30	53.13	40.78
1993	301.78	233.23	77.28	233.74	154.46	66.08	68.04	78.77	115.77
1994	409.18	205.77	50.29	116.56	111.01	95.24	292.62	94.76	32.38
1995	442.27	221.72	50.13	164.63	100.09	60.80	277.63	121.63	43.81
1996	90.56	272.91	301.36	67.60	126.61	187.29	22.96	146.30	637.20
1997	351.56	155.10	44.12	35.22	21.16	60.08	316.34	133.94	42.34
1998	-11.37	50.59	*	-21.94	-10.03	45.72	10.57	60.62	573.51
1999	367.26	254.54	69.31	255.52	91.67	35.88	111.74	76.66	68.61
2000	1136.59	535.81	47.14	593.79	313.39	52.78	542.81	308.13	56.77
2001	354.60	223.84	63.12	185.16	86.40	46.67	169.43	137.94	81.41
2002	1110.00	711.10	64.06	515.90	344.09	66.70	594.10	367.01	61.78
Total	4850.67	3012.53	62.11	2314.12	1433.64	61.95	2536.54	1578.89	62.25

Source: provided by Customs General Administration People's Republic of China.

*In 1998, national total imports and exports recorded a negative growth, while that of foreign-invested enterprises showed a positive growth. This indicates that these enterprises made outstanding contributions to the growth to national imports and exports. Without them, national imports and exports would have shown considerable negative growths.

Foreign-invested enterprises are able to make outstanding contributions to Chinese exports due mainly to two factors. First, their production aggregates are growing steadily; second, exports make up a higher percentage in the total output by the foreign-invested enterprises than that by domestic enterprises. During the period 1996-1999, exports accounted all along for lower than one tenth of the output value by the domestic enterprises, whereas the figure ran more than 40% for foreign-invested enterprises. In 2001, despite an impressive growth, the exports by domestic industrial enterprises made up a meager 16.17% of their industrial output value, whereas the exports by foreign-invested enterprises accounted for 40.62% of their industrial output value. See Table 4-3.

Table 4-3: A comparison of the export tendencies between foreign-invested and domestic enterprises

(Unit: RMB 100 million %)

Year	Domestic Industrial Enterprises			Foreign Invested Industrial Enterprises		
	Gross Industrial Output Value RMB 100 mil.	**Exports RMB 100 mil.**	**Exports as a percentage of Gross Industrial Output Value %**	**Gross Industrial Output Value RMB 100 mil.**	**Exports RMB 100 mil.**	**Exports as a percentage of Gross Industrial Output Value %**
1996	87478	7431.82	8.50	12117	5105.33	42.13
1997	99334	8954.87	9.01	14399	6216.70	43.17
1998	101298	8536.55	8.43	17750	6719.68	37.86
1999	106033	8822.90	8.32	20078	7356.29	36.64
2000	62209	10721.68	17.23	23464	9913.52	42.25
2001	68228	11032.36	16.17	27221	11058.51	40.62

Source: Calculated on the basis of figures in correspondent National Bureau of Statistics of China (1997-2002). *China Statistical Yearbook* (Beijing: China Statistics Press).

Note One: The gross industrial output value by domestic enterprises is derived from national gross industrial output value minus the gross industrial output value by foreign-invested enterprises, while the exports by domestic enterprises is derived from national total exports minus the exports of foreign-invested industrial enterprises, with one US dollar converted into 8.3 RMB.

Note Two: The reductions in the 2000 volumes of total industrial output value by both domestic and foreign-invested industrial enterprises are caused by changes in the statistical methodology. The total industrial output value for the year 2000 refers to that by state-owned industrial enterprises plus that by non-state enterprises above the prescribed scale, whereas previously it referred to all the industrial enterprises.

4-2: Contributions of Foreign-invested Enterprises to the Upgrading of the Export Commodities Mix

Increasing the exports of commodities with high incremental value and high technological content and upgrading the export commodities mix have been the long-term and profound contributions made to China's exports by foreign-invested enterprises. The reason why these enterprises are able to upgrade the export commodities mix by a remarkable margin is because they can introduce elements that are unavailable in China, such as technology and the ability to use such technology, and marketing abilities on the world market, thereby changing China's makeup of production elements and comparative advantage.

After the mid-1990s, investment by large transnational companies with powerful technological capabilities has been growing robustly in China and provided a great impetus for the growth of manufacturing industries with high incremental value and technological content in this country. This resulted in remarkable improvements in the Chinese export commodities mix during the middle and late 1990s, major indications of which were increases in the shares of industrial manufactures, machinery and electrical products, and high-tech products in the total export commodities. The contributions of foreign-invested enterprises to these increases were impressive.

1. Foreign-invested Enterprises' High Share in the Exports of Industrial Manufactures

In the 1990s, the share of industrial manufactures in China's total exports rose from 77.5% in 1991 to 91.3% in 2002, while the share of primary products decreased steadily from 22.5% to 8.7%. See Table 4-4.

Table 4-4: Changes in the Chinese export commodities mix in the 1990s

(Unit: US$ 100 million)

Year	Total Exports	Primary products		Industrial Manufactures	
		Value	Share %	Value	Share %
1991	718.4	161.5	22.5	556.9	77.5
1992	849.4	170.0	20.0	679.4	80.0
1993	917.6	166.7	18.2	750.9	81.8
1994	1210.4	197.1	16.3	1013.3	83.7
1995	1487.7	214.9	14.4	1272.8	85.6
1996	1510.7	219.3	14.5	1291.4	85.5
1997	1827.9	239.3	13.1	1587.7	86.9
1998	1837.6	206.0	11.2	1631.6	88.8
1999	1949.3	199.3	10.2	1750.0	89.8
2000	2492.1	254.6	10.2	2237.5	89.8
2001	2661.6	263.5	9.9	2398.0	90.1
2002	3255.7	284.8	8.7	2970.9	91.3

Source: Customs General Administration People's Republic of China (1991-2002). *Customs Statistical Almanac of the People's Republic of China* (Beijing: *Customs Statistics* Editorial Department of the Customs General Administration People's Republic of China).

Industrial manufactures made up upwards of 90% of the total exports of commodities by foreign-invested enterprises during the 1990s save for a few years. Because of the impressive growth of their exports and the remarkable expansion of their shares in national total exports, foreign-invested enterprises whose major business is exporting industrial manufactures are having a positive impact on the growth of China's exports of industrial manufactures. See Table 4-5.

Table 4-5: Changes in the composition of commodities exported by foreign-invested enterprises in the 1990s

(Unit: US$ 100 million)

Year	Total Exports	Primary products		Industrial Manufactures	
		Value	Share %	Value	Share %
1992	173.60	10.49	6.00	163.07	93.90
1993	252.37	18.32	7.20	233.96	92.70
1994	347.13	26.20	7.50	320.89	92.40
1995	468.76	29.99	6.30	438.93	93.60
1996	615.06	116.45	18.93	497.15	80.83
1997	749.00	140.77	18.79	606.29	80.95
1998	809.62	47.13	5.82	762.48	94.18
1999	886.28	52.21	5.89	834.03	94.10
2000	1194.41	200.07	16.75	991.26	82.99
2001	1332.35	226.53	17	1105.82	83
2002	1699.36	94.8	5.58	1605.1	94.4

Source: National Bureau of Statistics of China (1991-2002), *China Statistical Yearbook* (Beijing: China Statistics Press).

2. Foreign-invested Enterprises' High Share in the Exports of Machinery and Electrical Products

Steady increases in the share of machinery and electrical products in total exports was another major indication of a vastly ameliorated Chinese export commodities mix in the 1990s. Foreign-invested enterprises have a remarkably higher share in the export of machinery and electrical products than the average national level, and their contributions to the growth of exports in this field are outstanding. In 2002, these enterprises exported 105.011 billion US dollars worth of machinery and electrical products, up 37.0% from the previous year. The share of foreign-invested enterprises in national total volume of machinery and electrical product exports (157.08 billion US dollars) rose from 31.2% in 1992 to 66.85%, and their share in total exports by foreign-invested enterprises (169.936 billion US dollars) amounted to 61.79%.

Table 4-6: National exports of machinery and electrical products and those by foreign-invested enterprises

(Unit: US$ 100 million %)

Year	National		FIEs		
	Exports of machinery and electrical products	Share in national total exports	Exports of machinery and electrical products	Share in total exports by FIEs	Share in national total exports of machinery and electrical products
1992	195.5	23.0	61.0	35.1	31.2
1993	227.1	24.7	83.9	33.2	37.0
1994	320.0	26.4	132.8	38.3	41.5
1995	438.6	29.5	206.2	44.0	47.0
1996	482.1	31.9	269.1	43.8	55.8
1997	593.2	32.5	343.3	45.8	57.9
1998	665.4	36.2	401.2	49.6	60.3
1999	769.7	39.5	464.2	52.4	60.3
2000	1053.1	42.3	667.3	55.9	63.4
2001	1187.9	44.6	766.6	57.5	64.5
2002	1570.8	48.2	1050.1	61.8	66.9

Source: Provided by National Office of Machinery and Electrical Products Exports.

Figure 4-2: FIEs as a percentage in the national total machinery and electrical products exports

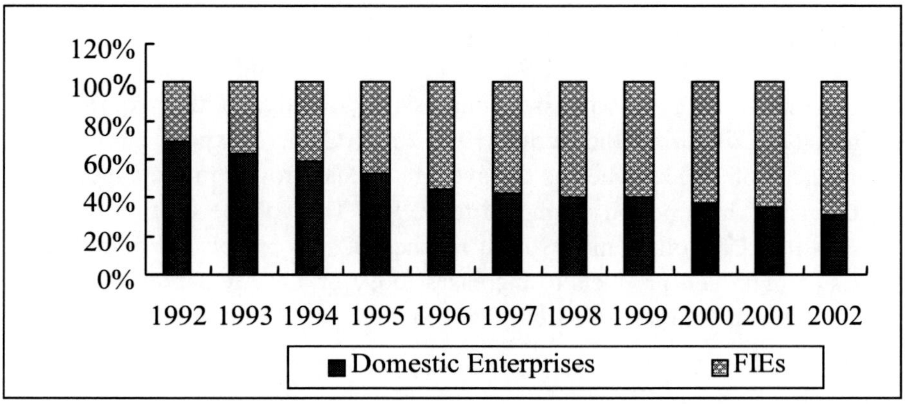

In the 1990s as a whole, foreign-invested enterprises all along accounted for a major share in China's annual machinery and electrical product exports. During the ten years from 1993 through 2002, the shares of these enterprises in national annual increases in machinery and electrical product exports exceeded 50% on an annual basis, and exceeded the 70% mark for six years. The contributions of these enterprises are there for all to see. See Table 4-7.

Table 4-7: Increases in national total machinery and electrical product exports, and the increases and shares of foreign-invested enterprises in this regard

(Unit: US$ 100 million %)

Year	National		FIEs		
	Increases in exports of machinery and electrical products	**Share in national total increases in exports**	**Increase in exports of machinery and electrical products**	**Share in total increases in exports by FIEs**	**Share in national total increases in exports of machinery and electrical products**
1993	31.56	45.6	22.9	29.0	72.6
1994	92.94	31.7	48.9	52.0	52.6
1995	118.57	43.2	73.4	60.2	61.9
1996	43.49	177.7	62.9	43.2	144.6
1997	111.11	35.4	74.2	54.9	66.8
1998	72.27	552.1	57.9	97.6	80.1
1999	104.26	94.5	63.0	81.8	60.4
2000	283.40	52.4	203.1	66.0	71.7
2001	134.8	79.6	99.3	72.0	73.7
2002	382.9	64.5	283.6	77.3	74.1
Total	1393.3	54.9	989.2	62.7	71.0

Source: Calculated on the basis of figures provided by National Office of Machinery and Electrical Products Exports and the figures in Table-4-2 .

3. Robust Growth in the Exports of High-Tech Products[1]

The last few years have witnessed impressive growths in the exports of high-tech products from China. During the period 1996-2002, China's exports grew at an average annual growth rate of 13.7%, whereas the average annual growth in the exports of high-tech products during the same period amounted to 32.3%. The volume of high-tech exports was only 12.663 billion US dollars in 1996 but reached 67.865 billion US dollars in 2002. The contributions of high-tech products to increases in exports are remarkable, as their share in exports of all the commodities rose from 8.4% in 1996 to 20.8% in 2002. See Table 4-8 and Figure 4-3 for detail.

[1] Most of the high-tech products are high-tech machinery and electrical products and are therefore counted in the category of machinery and electrical products. With a view to the special importance of high-tech products over the last few years, as well as the importance of foreign-invested enterprises in the export of high-tech products, high-tech products are singled out in this chapter for an analysis.

Table 4-8: A comparison between the export of high-tech products and national total exports

(Unit: US$ 100 million, %)

Year	National Total Exports		National Exports of High-tech products		High-tech products as a percentage of National Total Exports
	Exports	Change from the previous year	Exports	Change from the previous year	
1996	1510.5		126.63		8.4
1997	1827.9	21.0	163.10	28.80	8.9
1998	1837.1	0.1	202.51	24.16	11.0
1999	1949.3	6.1	247.04	21.99	12.7
2000	2492.0	27.9	370.43	49.95	14.9
2001	2661.6	6.8	464.57	25.41	17.5
2002	3255.7	22.3	678.65	46.08	20.8
Average Annual Growth Rate from 1996 to 2002		13.7		32.29	

Source: Figures about National Total Exports were quoted from National Bureau of Statistics of China (2003). *China Statistical Yearbook 2002* (Beijing: China Statistics Press). Figures about the exports of High-tech products were provided by Ministry of Science and Technology of the People's Republic of China.

Figure 4-3: A comparison of growths in total exports with the growths in high-tech products exports

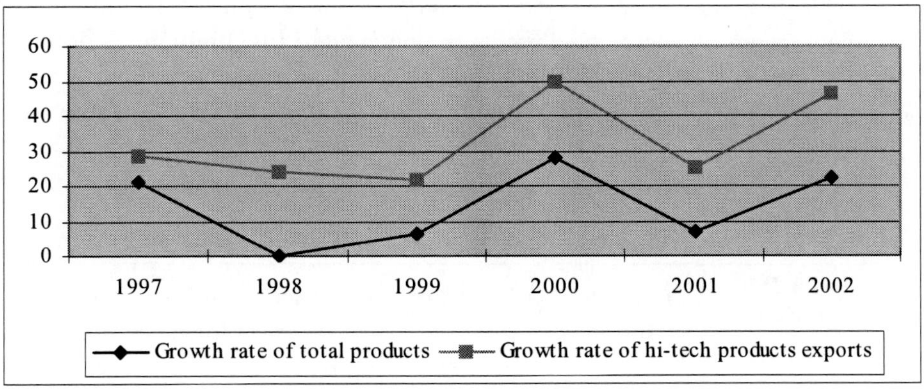

From Figure 4-3, we can see that the growth rate of total products is much lower than that of hi-tech products exports. It is obvious that since 1999 the above two growth rates rise and fall in same degree at the same time, that is to say, the double growth rates change in same regulation.

Foreign-invested enterprises have all along been a staunch force in China's high-tech product exports and maintained a high-speed growth. Their high-tech product exports was 7.421 billion US dollars in 1996, but it rose to 55.657 billion US dollars in 2002 and accounted for 82.20% of national total high-tech product exports of 67.708 billion US dollars and 32.75% of total exports by foreign-invested enterprises of 169.936 billion US dollars of the same year. During these seven years, foreign-invested enterprises' share showed impressive increases in national total high-tech product exports as it rose from 58.6% in 1996 to 82.0% in 2002. See Table 4-9.

Table 4-9: The position of foreign-invested enterprises as a staunch force in China's high-tech product exports

(Unit: US$ 100 million, %)

Year	Total Exports of High-tech products	Of Which, Exports of High-tech products by FIEs	FIEs as a percentage of Exports of High-tech products
1996	126.63	74.21	58.6
1997	163.10	109.15	66.9
1998	202.51	149.39	73.7
1999	247.04	187.75	76.0
2000	370.43	299.67	80.9
2001	464.57	378.81	81.5
2002	678.65	556.57	82.0

Source: figures from 1996 to 1999 were provided by Ministry of Science and Technology of the People's Republic of China, figures from 2000 to 2002 were provided by Customs General Administration People's Republic of China.

Computers and mobile telecommunications are the two high-tech industries with the highest growth rates in development and in the growth of exports. In both industries foreign-invested enterprises are making outstanding contributions to production and exports.

The production and export of computers in China registered a sustained fast growth during the 1990s. In 2000, this industry reported a total output value of 280 billion RMB, and the export of computers and associated products amounted to 17.53 billion US dollars. During the ten years from 1991 through 2000, computer exports averaged an annual growth rate of 44.23%, and their share in national total exports rose from 0.6% to 7%. See Table 4-10.

Table 4-10: Exports of computers and parts from China in the 1990s

(Unit: US$ 100 million; %)

Year	Exports of computers and parts	Growth Rate	National Total Exports	Computers and parts as a percentage of National Total Exports
1991	4.5	55.0	718.4	0.6
1992	10.7	137.7	849.4	1.2
1993	15.6	45.8	917.4	1.7
1994	28.0	79.5	1210.3	2.3
1995	49.6	77.1	1487.7	3.3
1996	64.7	30.4	1510.7	4.8
1997	87.3	34.9	1827.0	4.8
1998	68.9	-21.1	1837.6	3.7
1999	122.9	78.5	1949.3	6.3
2000	175.3	42.6	2492.1	7.0

Source: Qu Weizhi et al (2001). *Report on the research of Exports of Chinese IT products* (Beijing: China Economy Publishing House).

Foreign-invested enterprises are the staunch force in the export of computers. In 2000, they accounted for 84% of national total computer exports and 92.5% of the exports of assembled computers. The top five computer exporters are all foreign-invested enterprises: TG Computer Shenyang Co., Ltd., International Information Products (Shenzhen) Co., Ltd., Shenzhen Fujin Precision Industry Co., Ltd., Dell Computer (China) Co., Ltd. and Xiamen Overseas Chinese Electronic CO., Ltd.

In 2000, China exported 2.83 billion US dollars worth of mobile telecommunications equipment, or 3.47 times of that in the previous year, of which foreign-invested enterprises accounted for 2.73 billion US dollar, or 96.4%. The top five exporters are all foreign-invested enterprises: Beijing Nokia Mobile Telecommunications Co., Ltd., Motorola (China) Electronics Limited, Dongguan Nokia Mobile Phones Co., Ltd., Beijing Ericsson Mobile Telecommunications Co., Ltd., and Nanjing Ericsson Panda Communication Co., Ltd.[2]

Foreign-invested enterprises are the staunch force in those cities where the export of high-tech products is burgeoning. In Guangdong Province, where labor-intensive products constituted the lion's share of local exports in the past, the export commodities mix has been upgraded rather quickly over the recent years and the export of machinery and electrical products in general and IT products in particular is rising steadily by big margins. In 2001, exports in this province slowed down due to the influence of international factors, but the total exports of a good variety of computer-associated products were 30% up the previous year and accounted for 32% of the province's total exports, an increase of four percentage points. Thus computers replaced such traditional products as garments and toys to become one of the major export products in Guangdong. The growth of computer exports in Guangdong originated mainly from large foreign-invested enterprises – nine of the top ten major computer-dealing enterprises in this province are foreign-invested ones that contribute 53% of the province's computer exports.

4-3: Transnational Corporations' Global Manufacturing Systems and Foreign-Invested Enterprises' Exports in Processing Trade

Throughout the 1990s, growths of processing trade contributed tremendously to the growth of China's total exports, as its share in total exports rose from 45% in 1991 to 55% in 2002. See Table 4-11. This was a result of continuous China's involvement in the global industrial division of labor. The Chinese manufacturing industry is gradually rising as a component part of the global manufacturing industry.

[2] The information about the export of mobile telecommunications equipment is derived from the *White Paper on China's Foreign Trade and Economic Cooperation 2001* compiled by the Ministry of Foreign Trade and Economic Cooperation of the People's Republic of China, China Society Press, Beijing, 2001

Table 4-11: Ratio of processing trade exports to total exports

(Unit: US$ 100 million)

Year	Total Exports	Exports of Processing Trade	Processing Trade as a percentage of Total Exports (%)
1991	718.4	324.6	45.1
1992	849.4	396.1	46.6
1993	917.6	442.5	48.2
1994	1210.1	569.8	47.1
1995	1487.8	737.0	49.5
1996	1510.5	843.4	55.8
1997	1827.0	996.6	54.5
1998	1837.6	1044.7	56.9
1999	1949.3	1108.8	56.9
2000	2492.1	1376.6	55.2
2001	2661.6	1474.4	55.4
2002	3255.7	1799.6	55.3

Source: Customs General Administration People's Republic of China (1991-2001). *Customs Statistical Almanac of the People's Republic of China* (Beijing: *Customs Statistics* Editorial Department of Customs General Administration People's Republic of China. Figures of 2002 were provided by Customs General Administration People's Republic of China.

The growing processing business of foreign-invested enterprises is a major factor in the growth of China's processing trade. The ratio of processing trade to foreign-invested enterprises' total exports is markedly higher than the average national level, and these enterprises occupy a major share in national total processing trade, as is indicated in Table 4-12. The share of processing trade by foreign-invested enterprises in their exports has shown a slow tendency of reduction; nationwide, however, processing trade still takes up a rather high share in exports.

Table 4-12: Ratios of exports by FIEs in processing trade to total exports

(Unit: US$ 100 million, %)

Year	Imports of Processing Trade by FIEs	Exports of Processing Trade by FIEs	FIEs as a percentage of National Total Exports of Processing Trade	Processing Trade as a percentage of Exports by FIEs
1995	370.7	420.7	57.1	89.7
1996	415.1	530.9	62.9	86.3
1997	476.9	638.5	64.1	80.4
1998	483.3	691.8	66.2	85.5
1999	527.6	745.6	68.1	84.1
2000	687.4	972.3	70.6	81.4
2001	703.0	1066.0	72.3	80.0
2002	941.5	1346.1	74.8	79.2

Source: figures of Table 4-1, 4-10 in Customs General Administration People's Republic of China (1991-2001). *Customs Statistical Almanac of the People's Republic of China* (Beijing: *Customs Statistics* Editorial Department of Customs General Administration People's Republic of China). Figures of 2002 were provided by Ministry of Foreign Trade and Economic Cooperation.

The fact that foreign-invested enterprises have a high share in processing trade has something to do with the position of their parent companies in the global division of labor. The enterprises invested by many transnational companies in China are part of their parent companies' global manufacturing systems, and their products, markets and accessory systems are intimately associated with their parent companies' global systems. For this reason, they depend on imports for a considerable portion of their equipment, raw materials and the imports of other intermediary products.

We have conducted a systematic survey of the relationship between the imports and exports of transnational companies and their parent companies' global manufacturing systems[3]. Among the samples are 117 enterprises which deal in export businesses; exports are the main business for 52 of them, and the other enterprises do business mainly on the home market or on both home and world markets. Our survey indicates that a foreign-invested enterprise with good exporting performance is often backed by a parent company that has a high level of globalization and operates manufacturing enterprises in many places in the world – these enterprises supplement each other to form a global manufacturing system.

In our survey we divide these foreign-invested enterprises that are devoted mainly to exports into two categories: those exporting final products, and those exporting intermediary products. The enterprises in either category are highly dependent on their mother companies' global sales networks; 72% of them use their parent companies' original sales outlets, and in some cases their sales are directly handled by parent companies.

Approximately 52% of the foreign-invested enterprises manufacturing final products sell a considerable percentage of their products back to their parent countries. About 61% of those manufacturing intermediary products supply accessories for the other enterprises belonging to the same transnational company.

The transnational companies' strategy of global division of labor also manifests itself in the purchasing behaviors of foreign-invested enterprises, as 47% of those foreign-invested enterprises that depend mainly on import of component parts get their supplies from counterparts under the same parent transnational company.

Table 4-13 is about the degree of linkage between foreign-invested enterprises in China and their parent transnational companies' global manufacturing systems.

Table 4-13: The degree of linkage between foreign-invested enterprises and the global manufacturing systems of their parent transnational companies (based on a sampling of 52 enterprises)

Mode of linkage	% in the number of enterprises sampled
Using parent companies' overseas sales outlets for exports	72
Exporting intermediary products as components for other enterprises belonging to the same parent company	61
Selling a considerable portion of final products to parent companies	52
Importing most of the component parts needed from within a transnational company	47

[3] See Section 3-1 of Chapter Three for a description of the timing and scale of this survey.

Figure 4-4 gives some idea about major indicators for the position of foreign-invested enterprises in China's total exports in 2002, and shows, in a succinct way, the major contributions foreign-invested enterprises are making to the growth of China's exports and the upgrade of China's export commodities mix.

Figure 4-4: Position of foreign-invested enterprises in China's exports (2002)

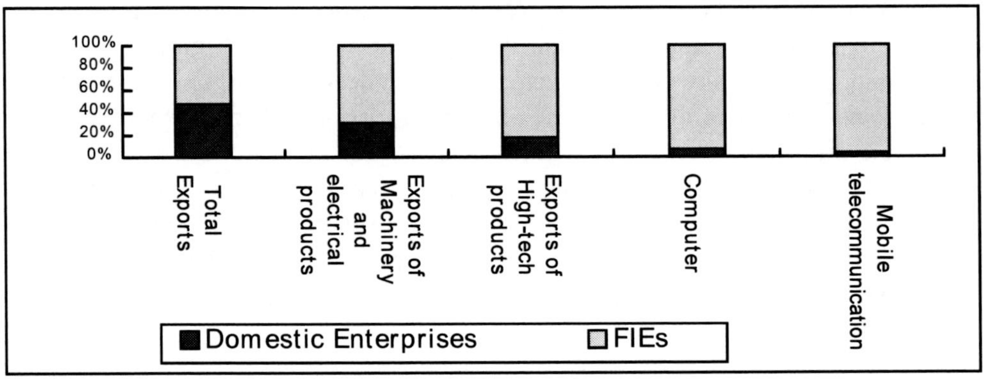

Chapter 5

GEOGRAPHICAL DISTRIBUTION OF FDI AND ITS IMPACT ON LOCAL ECONOMY

Remarkable changes have taken place in the pattern of local economies in China since the adoption of the policy of reform and opening up to the outside world towards the end of the 1970s, with the eastern region outstripping the central and western regions in terms of economic growth speed and increase in per-capita income. Differences in the volume of FDI inflow are a major reason behind this situation. The distribution of FDI in China is rather uneven, and the lion's share of it is concentrated on the eastern coastal region. This chapter describes the geographical distribution of FDI and its impact on local economies and discusses a possible FDI shift to the hinterland in the days to come.

5-1: REGIONAL ECONOMIC GAP IN CHINA

1. Central and Western Regions Trailing Far Behind Eastern Coastal Region in the Level of Economic Development

The Chinese economy can be divided into three regions: eastern coastal region, central region and western region. The eastern region encompasses eight coastal provinces and three municipalities directly under the central government -- Liaoning, Beijing, Tianjin, Hebei, Shandong, Jiangsu, Zhejiang, Shanghai, Fujian, Guangdong and Hainan; the central region consists of eight provinces – Shanxi, Jilin, Heilongjiang, Anhui, Jiangxi, Henan, Hubei and Hunan; and the western region comprises six provinces, five autonomous regions and one municipality directly under the central government – Chongqing, Sichuan, Guizhou, Yunnan, Tibet, Shaanxi, Gansu, Ningxia, Xinjiang, Inner Mongolia and Guangxi.[1] See Figure 5-1.

---

[1] Inner Mongolia and Guangxi belonged to central and east China respectively prior to 1998, and they became part of the western region after China adopted the strategic to develop the western region in a big way. The statistics featured in Tables 5-2 and 5-2 are used for an analysis of the changes that took place in the last two decades of the 20th century. To maintain the continuity and comparability of the statistics, these two tables follow the old ways of geographical division, and as a result Inner Mongolia is listed as part of central China and Guangxi as part of east China.

Figure 5-1. Three Regions

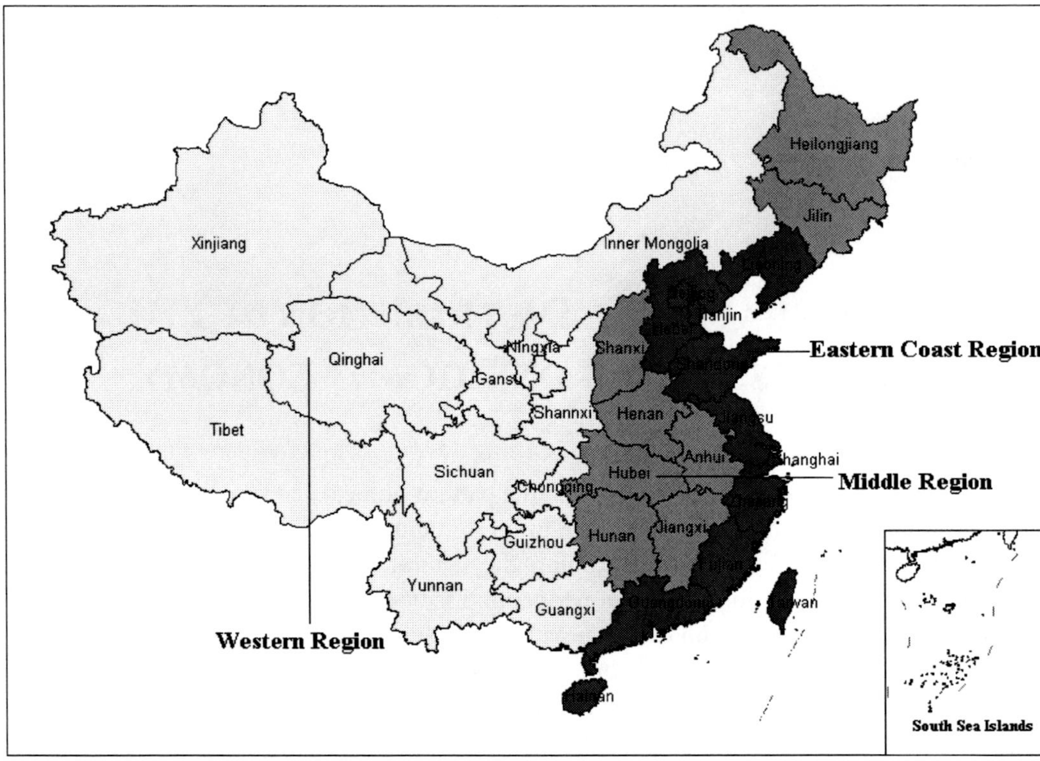

Uneven regional distribution has been an outstanding problem in the development of the Chinese economy in the last 20 or so years. In terms of developmental level, the eastern region is the most developed, the central region comes second, and the western region is relatively backward. In 2000, China's GDP amounted to 8940.4 billion RMB – 5752.7 billion RMB for the eastern region, 2625.0 billion RMB for the central region, and 1309.1 billion RMB for the western region. The eastern region accounts for 13.5% of the national territory and 42% of the national population but it contributes 64.3% of the nation's GDP. Take the average per-capita income in the eastern region as 1, then the average per-capita income of the central region is 56.2% of what it is in the eastern region and that of the western region is only 41.3%. The tremendous gap between these three regions in economic development is there for all to see. See Table 5-1.

Table 5-1: Basic facts concerning eastern, central and western regions (2000)

Index / Region	Square		Population		GDP		Per capita GDP	
	Total (10000 square kilometer)	Share %	Total (10000)	Share %	Total RMB 100 million	Share %	Total RMB	Take East as 100
East	129.89	13.5	53595	42.3	57527	64.3	10734	100
Central	285.35	29.7	43482	34.4	26250	29.4	6037	56.2
West	544.84	56.8	29506	23.3	13091	14.6	4437	41.3

Sources: National Bureau of Statistics of China (2002). *China Statistical Abstracts 2001* (Beijing: China Statistics Press).

2. Gap among the Eastern, Central and Western Regions: The Tendency of Expansion

Twenty years ago the gap among the eastern, central and western regions was relatively narrow, but it has been growing steadily in the recent 20 years, as is shown in Table 5-2 and 5-3.

Table 5-2: Shares of eastern, central and western regions in the GDP

Year	East	Central	West
1978	52.5	29.7	17.8
1992	56.6	28.6	14.8
1995	59.0	26.5	14.5
1998	56.0	29.1	14.6
2000	64.3	29.4	14.6

Sources: *China Statistical Yearbook* of relevant years and *China Statistical Abstracts 2001*. The sum of the shares of these three regions is larger than 100% for the year of 2000, which is a result of our calculation based on the statistics provided in the *China Statistical Abstracts 2001*.

Table 5-3: Absolute difference and relative difference in per-capita GDP among the eastern, central and western regions

(Unit: RMB)

Year	1981	1985	1988	1991	1993	1994	1995	1998	2000
East	1602	2502	3262	3788	5235	6043	6823	9480	10734
Central and West	1099	1627	1986	2238	2782	3097	3405	4220	5390
Absolute Gap in per capita income	503	875	1276	1550	2453	2946	3417	5260	5344
Central and West as a percentage of East in per capita income %	68.6	65.0	60.1	59.1	53.1	51.2	49.9	44.5	49.8

Source: ibid.

The growing gap in the level of economic development among the eastern, central and western regions is a result of differences in the speed of economic growth. From 1979 to 1995, China's GDP's annual growth averaged 9.8%, and it was 12.8%, 9.7% and 8.7% respectively for these three regions. In 1999, the GDP grew by 8.1% in the eastern region, 7.4% in the central region and 6.2% in the western region – the tendency of the eastern region growing faster than the central and western regions continuously.

5-2: Geographical Distribution of FDI Inflow

The regional differences in economic development in the past twenty years can, to a large extent, be interpreted by the differences in the degree of openness towards the outside world. Since China adopted the policy of economic restructuring and opening up to the outside world towards the end of the 1970s, FDI inflow has been gravitated in the eastern region, with a little amount of it reaching the central and western regions. The uneven distribution of foreign investment has resulted in tremendous differences in the foreign-invested enterprises (FIEs)' contribution to the output value and exports of different regions.

1. High Concentration of FDI in Eastern Coastal Region

Most of the lion's share of FDI inflows has been distributed in the eastern coastal region in the last 20 years or so. In the 1980s, over 90% of the FDI found its way to the coastal region. In the 1990s the situation remained largely the same despite of a slight improvement. Towards the end of 2001, 86% of the realized FDI in China was made in the coastal region, and only 14% of it found its way to the central and western regions. Table 5-4 sheds some light on the geographical distribution of FDI in China. For statistics concerning various provinces, autonomous regions and municipalities, see Annex Table 5-1 of this chapter.

Table 5-4: Regional distribution of aggregates of foreign investment in China (towards the end of 2001)

(Unit: US$ 100 million, %)

Region	Number of Project	Share %	Contractual FDI value	Share %	Realized FDI value	Share %
Total	390025	100.00	7452.91	100.00	3952.23	100.00
East	315053	80.87	6439.23	86.46	3397.26	85.96
Central	46713	11.98	565.21	7.58	346.93	8.78
West	28259	7.24	448.47	6.02	208.04	5.26

Source: Department of Foreign Investment of the Ministry of Foreign Trade and Economic Cooperation (2002). *Statistics on FDI in China 2002*, not for sale.

2. Marked Changes in the Distribution of Foreign Capital in the Coastal Region

Since the 1990s, foreign investment has been concentrated in the coastal region, but marked changes have taken place in the distribution of foreign investment within the coastal region. For a look at such changes we have divided the eastern coastal region into northern, central and southern coastal areas. The northern coastal area includes Liaoning, Hebei, Beijing, Tianjin and Shandong; the central coastal area includes Shanghai, Jiangsu and Zhejiang; and the southern coastal area encompasses Fujian, Guangdong, Guangxi and Hainan. See Figure 5-2.

Figure 5-2: Northern, central and southern coastal areas

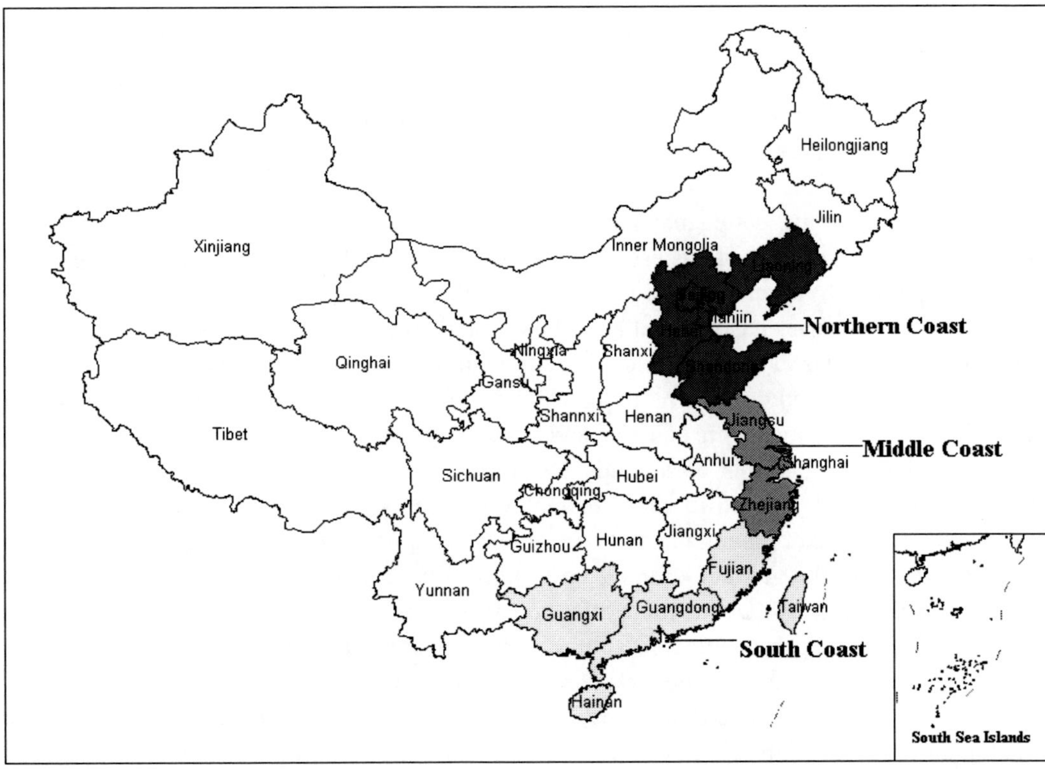

Table 5-5 indicates that since the 1990s, the foreign investment in the coast region has been gradually shifting from the southern area to the central and northern areas. The share of foreign investment in the southern area was 56.06% during the period 1983-1990, 42.74% during the period 1991-1999, and 38.09% in 2001; the central coastal area's share of foreign investment was 13.28% during the period 1983-1990, 24.17% during the period 1991-1999, and 27.77% in 2001; the northern coastal area's share was 20.76%, 20.81% and 21.97% respectively.

Table 5-5: Changes in the distribution of realized FDI in coastal areas (%)

Year	1983-1990	1991-1999	2000	2001
National Total	100	100	88.07	87.83
The Northern Coastal Area's Share	20.76	20.81	20.47	21.97
The Central Coastal Area's Share	13.28	24.17	26.63	27.77
The Southern Coastal Area's Share	56.06	42.74	40.97	38.09

Note: The northern coastal area includes Liaoning, Hebei, Beijing, Tianjin and Shandong; the central coastal area encompasses Shanghai, Jiangsu and Zhejiang; and the southern coastal area consists of Fujian, Guangdong, Guangxi and Hainan.

Sources: Department of Trading Materials of the National Bureau of Statistics of China (ed.) (1992). *Complete Statistics concerning China's Foreign Economics 1979-1991,* provided by the China Statistical Information Consulting and Service Centre; the National Bureau of Statistics of China. *China Statistical Yearbook* of relevant years, China Statistics Press; Wei Houkai. *Regional Changes in Foreign Investment after China's WTO Accession*, a working thesis of the Institute of Industrial Economics of the Chinese Academy of Social Sciences.

The gravitation of foreign investors' choice towards the central coastal area is associated with their intention to take advantage of this area's fine investment environment, its close ties with the domestic market, and its better scientific, technological and industrial conditions.

First of all, with the steady increase in the technological level of foreign investment in China, FIEs need to hire better managerial and technical personnel, and are becoming more demanding in their choice of accessory suppliers. The southern coastal area is losing its advantage granted by preferential government policies, and the congregation of foreign investment and industries has boosted land, labour and other production costs and strained the supply of professionals in various fields. By contrast, the central coastal area with Shanghai in the centre provides good conditions in such fields as financial service, modern logistics, the availability of professionals in science and technology, and good harbours. The Yangtze River Delta surrounding this area holds the appeal for foreign investment with its well-established industrial, scientific and technological foundation, better-educated residents, tremendous local market potentials, and convenient transportation.

Moreover, with the gradual opening up of the Chinese market, foreign investors' market goals are changing as well, and their attention is shifting from the overseas market to the Chinese market. Compared with the southern coastal area, the central coastal area is even more extensively and closely associated with the rest of the domestic market of China.

In addition, the central coastal area, Shanghai and vicinities in particular, are a most livable place with its relatively developed living conditions. Among the overseas investors in the central coastal area, particular mention should be made of those from Taiwan. With the deterioration of the political and economic situation in Taiwan, many Taiwan residents are considering not only investing in the mainland but also immigrating to the mainland or becoming permanent residents there. For historical reasons, many Taiwan industrialists and entrepreneurs came from Jiangsu and Zhejiang provinces, and because of this they are fascinated culturally and historically by Eastern China. Thanks to sustained the high-speed development, Shanghai's production and living conditions are approaching those of Taipei and have even surpassed it in some aspects. For those Taiwan investors with a desire for immigration, the central coastal area in general and Shanghai and the Yangtze River Delta in particular have become their favorites.

5-3: IMPACT OF FOREIGN INVESTMENT ON THE ECONOMIC GROWTH AND EXPORTS OF DIFFERENT REGIONS

Foreign-invested enterprises have carved out an important niche in the Chinese economy, and hold a vital position in the national industrial output value and exports. The regional differences in attracting foreign investment have resulted in glaring differences in the role of foreign-invested enterprises in promoting local economic development.

1. Contribution of Foreign-invested Enterprises to the Industrial Output Value

The high concentration of foreign investment enables the foreign-invested enterprises in the eastern region to contribute much more to the local industrial output value than in the central and western regions. In 2000, foreign-invested enterprises accounted for 23.98% of the national total value-added industrial outputs – 35.09% in the eastern region, and a meager 8.33% and 6.47% respectively in the central and western regions. In coastal provinces such as Fujian and Guangdong, the share of these enterprises in the local value-added industrial outputs has already exceeded 50%. See Table 5-6. For statistics concerning various provinces and autonomous regions, see Annex Table 5-2 of this chapter.

Table 5-6: Percentage of foreign-invested enterprises in the value-added industrial outputs of various areas (2000)

Region	Value-added Industrial Outputs	Value-added Industrial Outputs by FIEs	FIEs as a percentage of national total value-added industrial outputs
National	25394.80	6090.35	23.98
East	15440.52	5418.09	35.09
Central	5850.82	487.43	8.33
West	2855.42	184.86	6.47

Sources: Calculations are made according to the statistics provided in Tables 13-12 and 13-15 in National Bureau of Statistics of China (2002). *China Statistical Yearbook 2001* (Beijing: China Statistics Press).

2. Contribution of Foreign-invested Enterprises to Exports

Foreign-invested enterprises have already made up a high percentage in China's total exports, but there is a glaring difference in their contribution to local exports. The percentage of exports by foreign-invested enterprises in the gross industrial output value is markedly lower in the central and western regions than in the eastern region. In 2000, the exports by these enterprises made up 42% of their nationwide output value, but the figures were 13% and 12% respectively in the central and western regions. See Table 5-7. For detailed statistics of the various provinces and autonomous regions, see Annex Table 5-3 of this chapter.

Table 5-7: Percentages of exports by foreign-invested enterprises in their total output value in various regions (2000)

Region	Gross Industrial Output value by FIEs-RMB 100 million	Exports by FIEs		Exports as a percentage of Gross Industrial Output
		US$ 100 million	RMB 100 million	
National Total	23464.55	1194.41	9913.60	42
East	21332.37	1162.51	9648.83	45
Central	1557.81	24.33	201.94	13
West	574.37	8.47	70.30	12

Sources: Tables 13-15 and 17-12 in National Bureau of Statistics of China (2002). *China Statistical Yearbook 2001* (Beijing: China Statistics Press).

Foreign-invested enterprises in the central and western regions have a much lower rate of contribution to local exports than their counterparts in the eastern region as a result of their low percentages of exports. In 2000 all the foreign-invested enterprises in China made up 47.93% of the national total exports; in the eastern region these enterprises accounted for 50.99% of the local exports whereas the figures were 16.51% and 10.02% for the central and western regions. See Table 5-8. For the statistics concerning various provinces and autonomous regions, see Annex Table 5-4 of this chapter.

Figure 5-3 provides a comparison of foreign-invested enterprises' contributions to the industrial output value and exports of different regions.

Table 5-8: Rate of contribution of foreign-invested enterprises to the exports of various regions (2000)

Region	Total Exports US$ 100 million	Exports by FIEs US$ 100 million	The contribution rate of FIEs to Exports
National Total	2492.03	1194.41	47.93
East	2285.24	1165.18	50.99
Central	131.18	21.66	16.51
West	75.60	7.58	10.02

Sources: Calculations are based on the figures provided by Tables 17-11 and 17-12 in National Bureau of Statistics of China (2002). *China Statistical Yearbook 2001* (Beijing: China Statistics Press).

5-4: Quantitative Analysis: FDI Inflows and Regional Economic Growth

To be more accurate in our analysis of the relevance between the amount of FDI and the growth speed of regional economy, we have made a correlation analysis of the relationship between the realized FDI in various provinces and autonomous regions and the volume of exports.

Take realized FDI as independent variable and exports as dependent variable, regress the realized FDI and exports by province and municipality with the minimum square method, we can derive: Y=7.29E—05 X — 1.1206, the correlation coefficient is 0.993279, standard deviation is 54.08745. The results of correlation analysis indicate a highly correlation between realized FDI and exports (0.8< r <1 indicate a high correlation, with r representing correlation coefficient.).

Table 5-9: Sequence of provinces, autonomous regions and municipalities according to volumes of exports (2000)

Unit: US$ 100 Million

Rank	Province, Autonomous Region, Municipality	Exports	Realized FDI
	National Total	2492.03	3483.4552
1	Guangdong	934.28	981.9210
2	Jiangsu	263.77	437.3047
3	Shanghai	246.40	283.3979
4	Zhejiang	204.82	111.8759
5	Shandong	160.93	211.0910
6	Fujian	136.23	335.1038
7	Liaoning	105.90	148.4450
8	Tianjin	76.75	132.7461
9	Beijing	76.67	143.9843
10	Hebei	32.78	67.6948
11	Heilongjiang	24.24	36.6392
12	Anhui	21.19	30.3430
13	Shanxi	20.91	15.2585
14	Hubei	19.00	64.2956
15	Guangxi	16.41	69.4350
16	Hunan	16.32	52.4340
17	Henan	15.87	43.1743
18	Jilin	14.87	29.2167
19	Chongqing	14.34	22.4886
20	Shaanxi	13.27	30.4595
21	Jiangxi	11.89	27.1287
22	Xinjiang	11.47	3.6967
23	Inner Mongolia	11.14	6.4089
24	Yunnan	10.93	9.6978
25	Sichuan	10.61	31.7858
26	Hainan	6.09	62.2978
27	Guizhou	4.82	4.2238
28	Gansu	4.21	4.5616
29	Ningxia	3.55	1.2856
30	Qinghai	1.34	0.1968
31	Tibet	1.10	0.0003

Sources: National Bureau of Statistics of China (2002). *China Statistical Yearbook 2001* (Beijing: China Statistics Press).

The high relevance between the two is obvious by intuition. Tables 5-9 and 5-10 features the sequence of various provinces, autonomous regions and municipalities directly under the central government according to their 2000 volumes of exports and the realized FDI. It is obvious that the two different sequences do not show any change in the order of these administrative divisions. Where there is a higher realized FDI – such as Guangdong, Jiangsu and Shanghai -- there is a higher volume of exports, whereas where there is a low realized

FDI – such as Tibet, Hingham and Ningxia – there is a lower volume of exports. Xinjiang and Zhejiang, however, are two exceptions, as they rank higher in exports than in the realized FDI, but the changes are only marginal. In all, there is a high degree of positive relevance between the realized FDI and the volume of exports.

Table 5-10: Sequence of provinces, autonomous regions and municipalities according to realized FDI (2000)

Unit: US$ 100 Million

Rank	Province-Autonomous Region-Municipality	Realized FDI	Exports
	National Total	3483.4552	2492.026
1	Guangdong	981.9210	934.2792
2	Jiangsu	437.3047	263.7694
3	Fujian	335.1038	136.2282
4	Shanghai	283.3979	246.3961
5	Shandong	211.0910	160.9267
6	Liaoning	148.4450	105.8947
7	Beijing	143.9843	76.6723
8	Tianjin	132.7461	76.7427
9	Zhejiang	111.8759	204.8214
10	Guangxi	69.4350	16.4048
11	Hebei	67.6948	32.7814
12	Hubei	64.2956	18.9977
13	Hainan	62.2978	6.0853
14	Hunan	52.4340	16.319
15	Henan	43.1743	15.8683
16	Heilongjiang	36.6392	24.2393
17	Sichuan	31.7858	10.6048
18	Shaanxi	30.4595	13.2693
19	Anhui	30.3430	21.1942
20	Jilin	29.2167	14.8693
21	Jiangxi	27.1287	11.8837
22	Chongqing	22.4886	14.336
23	Shanxi	15.2585	20.9094
24	Yunnan	9.6978	10.9271
25	Inner Mongolia	6.4089	11.14
26	Gansu	4.5616	4.2079
27	Guizhou	4.2238	4.8166
28	Xinjiang	3.6967	11.4724
29	Ningxia	1.2856	3.5426
30	Qinghai	0.1968	1.3355
31	Tibet	0.0003	1.0902

Sources: Ibid.

5-5: Reasons for FDI Shortage in Central and Western Regions

The central and western regions lag behind the eastern region in attracting foreign investment for the following reasons.

1. Pushing the Open Policy Progressively from One Region to Another

The policy of opening up to the outside world is being carried out progressively from one region to another. Since 1979 a variety of economic zones, such as special economic zones, economic development zones, economic and technological development zones, economic cooperative border zones and bonded zones, have been set up one after another. In the 1980s and the early 1990s, these economic zones were mostly situated in the eastern coastal areas. With a good investment environment and a package of preferential policies, these zones were first choices for prospective foreign investors.

2. Geological Locations

In the past 20 or so years, many foreign-invested enterprises in China were engaged in the processing of export products. With their superb geological locations, the coastal areas are ideal for export-oriented foreign-invested enterprises. Dongguan in Guangdong, for instance, is 90 km from Hong Kong by land and 47 nautical miles from it by water, 48 nautical miles from Macao, and Huangtian Airport of Shenzhen and Baiyun Airport of Guangzhou are less than 50 km away. This means that a foreign investor can have imported goods which arrive at Hong Kong at noon hauled to his factory in Dongguan by night at the latest. Of all the geological advantages of Dongguan, Hong Kong is obviously the most precious factor. The highly efficient cargo harbours of Hong Kong can effectively guarantee the promptness of delivery of information and electronic products. As an international trading centre, Hong Kong also operates numerous oceangoing lines and airlines bound for various parts of the world.

3. Natural Conditions

Central and west of China compares unfavorably with the eastern coastal region in terms of natural conditions. Development of west of China, in particular, is seriously hampered because uninhabitable plateaus, deserts and snow-covered mountains and unarable land take up a large part of its land and make it much more difficult to develop transportation, telecommunications and other infrastructure facilities than in the eastern region. Development in central and west of China has all along been trailing behind east of China in the last century and more, except the 30 early post-liberation years when abundant central government investment fueled fast economic growth in central and west of China.

4. The Investment of Central Government and the Investment Environment of the Central and Western Regions

Since the adoption of the policy of reform and opening up to the outside world, China has pursued a strategy of giving priority to the development of the eastern coastal region. During the 6th Five-Year Plan period (1980-1985), the government placed large numbers of key projects in the coastal areas, and as a result, 47% of the total investment was gravitated in these areas. That figure further increased in the next five years to 51.7%, whereas the portion of the national total investment in central and west of China dropped to 40.2%. This trend continued in the 1990s. In 2000, the figure was 57.8% for the eastern region and 38.7% for the central and western regions. See Table 5-11.

This difference in central government investment has resulted in different investment environments in east, central and west of China. East of China appeals strongly to foreign investors with a relatively complete array of infrastructure facilities and a high level of urbanization. Central and west of China is far less appealing due to its inconvenient transportation, outdated telecommunications facilities and poor urban environment.

Table 5-11: Percentages of investment in capital construction in east and central regions in different five-year plan periods (%)

Plan Period	East	Central-West	Central	West
1953-1957 "1st Five Year Plan Period"	36.9	46.8	28.8	18.0
1963-1965 Adjustment Period	34.9	58.2	32.7	25.6
1966-1970 "3rd Five Year Plan Period"	26.9	64.7	29.8	34.9
1971-1975 "4th Five Year Plan Period"	35.5	54.4	29.9	24.5
1976-1980 "5th Five Year Plan Period"	42.2	50.0	30.1	19.9
1981-1985 "6th Five Year Plan Period"	47.7	46.5	29.3	17.2
1986-1990 "7th Five Year Plan Period"	51.7	40.2	24.4	15.8
1991-1995 "8th Five Year Plan Period"	54.2	38.2	23.5	14.7
1997	53.3	39.3		
2000	57.8	38.7	22.4	16.3

Sources: The statistics prior to 1997 are quoted from Wei Houkai (ed.) (2000). *The Strategy for Industrial Development in Central and West of China in the 21st Century* (Zhengzhou: Henan People's Publishing House). The statistics for 2000 are compiled by the author.

Note: The investment percentages of east, central and west of China do not add up to 100% because the statistics on certain investment projects, such as means of transportation, are not counted geographically.

5. Industrial Structure and the Composition of Enterprises

Because the economic development, industry in particular, of central and west of China depends to a large extent on large mining and heavy and chemical industrial projects invested by the government in the 1950s through the 1970s. For this reason, the mining of natural resources and the heavy and chemical industries take up a high percentage in the industrial setup of both regions.

Of the 40 industries of central and west of China, the ten with the highest output values are raw chemical materials and chemical products, nonmetal mineral products, food processing, transportation equipment manufacturing, smelting and pressing of ferrous metals, electric power, steam and hot water production and supply, textile industry, petroleum and natural gas extraction, coal mining and processing, and tobacco processing industries. In 1998, these ten industries yielded a total output value of 3771.79 billion RMB, or 57.7% of the total industrial output value of the central and western industries with independent accounting systems.

With the exception of the transportation equipment manufacturing and electronic and telecommunications industries, most of the above mentioned industries – the mining and raw materials industries in particular -- are traditional ones characterized by slow growth and low processing level. By contrast, some of the rising industries, such as garments and other fiber products, leather furs, down and related products, cultural, educational and sporting articles, chemical fibres, electric equipment and machinery, and instruments, meters, cultural and official machinery, make up a small portion of the gross industrial output value of the central and western regions, less than 20% of the output value of the same industries of the country, and far below the average level of 35% for various industries in the central and western regions. Even the electronic and telecommunications industry, in which the western region holds a relative advantage, makes up only 9.3% of the national total output value.

In the past 20 years, particularly prior to the mid-1990s, the FDI in China came mostly from medium-sized and small investors from Hong Kong and Taiwan, and most of such investment was made in the light processing industry. Central and west of China lacks the appeals for foreign investors and receives less foreign investment than east of China for the main reason that its industrial structure is predicated on resource-dependent industries, heavy and chemical industries and large enterprises.

5-6: The Strategy of Go to West and the Preferential Policy for Attracting Foreign Investment to Central and Western Regions

In 1999, the central government adopted the strategy of Go To West. The idea is to speed up western development and prevent the gap between regional economies from further widening. To open the western region wider to the outside world and attract more investment, technology and talents from other parts of the world are main steps in this strategic arrangement. Since 1999 the central government has formulated a series of preferential policies to encourage foreign investment in the western region.

1. Preferential Taxation

Foreign-invested enterprises in the western region pay their corporate income tax at a reduced 15% rate for ten years if they are of the types encouraged by the state. Transportation, power generating and water conservancy enterprises newly opened by foreign investors in the western region are exempt from enterprise income tax for two years and pay half of the tax in the next three years. The advanced technological equipment imported by a foreign-invested enterprise within its total investment and for its own use, is exempt from customs duties and import value-added tax if it belongs to one of the government-encouraged industries in this region or if it is a foreign investment project in an advantageous industry. These policies also apply to domestic-invested projects in the western region.

2. Expanding the Fields for Foreign Investment in the Western Region

Foreign investors are encouraged to invest in agriculture, forestry, water conservancy, transportation, energy development, urban utilities, environmental protection and other infrastructure facilities, the development of mineral resources and tourism, and the establishment of centres for technological research and development. Experiments with foreign investment in banking, retailing sales and foreign trade will be expanded to the central cities of the western region. Foreign-invested banks can deal in Renminbi business with authorization. Foreign investors may also go to west of China to invest in insurance, tourism, Certified Public Accountants, Law Firm, as well as equity joint ventures and contractual joint ventures in the building industry or providing related designing, engineering and other services. They may also run urban planning service enterprises and railway and highway transportation joint ventures.

3. Widening up the Channels for Foreign Investment in Western Region

Foreign-invested enterprises in China are encouraged to reinvest in the western region. A foreign investor whose investment exceeds 25% of the investment in a reinvestment project in the western region enjoys preferential treatment accorded to foreign-invested enterprises. As to such western Chinese projects as thermal power plants, hydroelectric power stations, high-grade highways, independent bridges and tunnels, local railways, urban water supply sources and water purification plants, and waste water or garbage disposal plants, experiments with the BOT method for attracting foreign investment will be expanded, and TOT and project financing methods will be used on a trial basis in order to solicit foreign investment. Other methods will also be explored to attract foreign investment, including listing enterprises on the capital market, management power transfer, sale of shares, mergers and acquisitions, industrial foundations, and venture investment funds.

4. Liberalizing the Conditions for the Western Region to Utilize Foreign Investment

Limitations on the percentage of shares to be held by foreign investors in infrastructure facilities and superior industrial projects may be loosened up. If they are building or managing pipelines for transmitting natural gas from west to east or urban natural gas supply networks, they are treated preferentially regarding terms of business and registered capital. If they are investing in infrastructure facilities or advantageous industries in the western region, the domestic banks may grant them with a higher portion of Renminbi loan grants for investment in fixed assets. Foreign-invested projects are allowed to engage in financing in Renminbi, among other currencies.

5. Carrying out Preferential Policies to Encourage Foreign Investment in the Development of Mineral Resources

Foreign investors in prospecting and tapping mineral resources other than petroleum and natural gas may, in addition to preferential policies granted by the state, also be exempt from prospecting and mining fees for one year and pay half of such fees for two more years. Those engaged in tapping those mineral resources other than oil and natural gas that are listed in the *Catalogue for the Guidance of Foreign Investment Industries* are exempt from the mineral resource compensation fee for five years.

6. Encouraging the Western Region to Open Wider to Peripheral Countries

Southwest and northwest China shares long borderlines with South Asia, central Asia and Russia. The Chinese government encourages the western region to expand its trade and economic relations with the neighbouring countries so as to promote local economic development.

There is tremendous room for the development of trade between China and South Asian countries. The major countries in South Asia will maintain sustained and stable growth, and some of them – India, Pakistan, Sri Lanka and Bangladesh – are likely to maintain a growth rate of 4-5% or even higher in the first decade of the 21st century. This region, with a huge population and vast market potentials, has a robust demand for Chinese products, consumer goods in particular, a fact that is beneficial for west of China to expand its trade and investment relations with these countries.

Despite of their small scale, the trade and economic exchanges among China and Russia and central Asian countries are characterized by a strong mutual-supplementary nature. Farm produce, textiles, manufactured goods and light mechanical and electrical products in general and consumer machinery and electrical products in particular are major Chinese exports to Russia and the three central Asian countries; and energy products, minerals, metals and metal products, chemicals, means of transportation, aircraft, ships and transportation equipment are major imports from these countries to China. The trade relations between both sides are obviously mutually supplementary, and the situation will continue for a long period of time to come for the benefit of expanding bilateral trade and economic relations and promoting the economic development of both sides.

As things stand now, the central government policy to guide more foreign investment to hinterland China is yet to play its full role. Because of this, and also because of the fact that the eastern region holds the advantage in attracting foreign investment, the coastal areas of east of China will remain the first choices for foreign investors and they will still hold 80% of the total volume of foreign investment in China.

However, major changes have taken place in central and west of China. Firstly, following large-scale investment and construction since 1998, the infrastructure of these regions have improved markedly, so much so that in urban areas, the roads, telecommunications services, power supply and other conditions are largely of the same standards as the eastern coastal areas. Secondly, some of the large cities in central and west of China have already possessed fine industrial and technological conditions, and, by continuously improving their investment environments, have become highly attractive to foreign investors. Xi'an, Chengdu and

Chongqing, the three central cities in west of China rank among the top ten Chinese cities that lead the nation in the number of institutions of higher education and research institutes, and all of them have a good industrial foundation. Foreign investment in them is growing conspicuously in the last few years. For instance, some of the world's top 500 companies have established 76 enterprises in Chengdu, 24 in Xi'an and 31 in Chongqing. Thirdly, dense foreign investment over the last few years has lead to saturation of industrial capacities in some coastal areas, and investment costs in these areas have shown a tendency of increase, while central and west of China is becoming more attractive to foreign investors with cheap labor and other low costs. Improvement in local conditions will enhance the appeal of central and west of China to foreign investors and it is likely that the scale of foreign investment in the central and western regions will expand tremendously, and both regions will take up a higher share of foreign investment in China. Such a transition will take place gradually in the next few years and will proceed progressively from the central region to the western region.

ANNEX TABLES

Annex Table 5-1: FDI Distribution by Province and Municipality (as of 2000)

Unit: US$ 10000

Province/ Municipality	Number of Projects	Share (%)	Contractual Value	Share (%)	Realized Value	Share (%)
National Total	363885	100	67609693	100	34834552	100
Beijing	14725	4.36	30775567	4.55	1439843	4.13
Tianjin	13029	3.75	2764503	4.09	1327461	3.81
Heber	9619	2.64	1412797	2.09	676948	1.95
Shanxi	2106	0.58	359755	0.53	152585	0.44
Inner Mongolia	1512	0.42	170361	0.25	64089	0.18
Liaoning	21218	5.83	3766505	5.57	1484450	4.26
Jilin	5964	1.64	562778	0.83	292167	0.84
Heilongjiang	6198	1.70	590977	0.87	366392	1.05
Shanghai	22032	6.05	6473959	9.58	2833979	8.14
Jiangsu	40569	11.15	8528740	12.61	4373047	12.55
Zhejiang	18369	5.05	2422142	3.58	1118759	3.21
Anhui	4677	1.29	551384	0.82	303430	0.87
Fujian	27766	7.63	6408271	9.48	3351038	9.62
Jiangxi	5236	1.44	467767	0.69	271287	0.78
Shandong	29046	7.98	4161716	6.16	2110910	6.06
Henan	6325	1.74	829036	1.23	431743	1.24
Hubei	8157	2.24	979907	1.45	642956	1.85
Hunan	5721	1.57	737737	1.09	524340	1.51
Guangdong	84237	23.15	17184960	25.42	9819210	28.19
Guangxi	7003	1.92	1338747	1.98	694350	1.99
Hainan	8894	2.44	1189665	1.76	622978	1.79
Sichuan	5404	1.49	779433	1.15	317858	0.91
Chongqing	2898	0.80	404758	0.60	224886	0.65
Guizhou	1423	0.39	162236	0.24	42238	0.12
Yunnan	1959	0.54	282019	0.42	96978	0.28
Tibet	20	0.01	1263	0.00	3	0.00
Shaanxi	3197	0.88	585219	0.87	304595	0.87
Gansu	1379	0.38	105908	0.16	45616	0.13
Qinghai	242	0.07	36876	0.05	1968	0.01
Ningxia	587	0.16	47215	0.07	12856	0.04
Xinjiang	1002	0.28	105834	0.16	36967	0.11
Central Ministries & Commissions	1601	0.44	1119669	1.66	845870	2.43

Source: Department of Foreign Investment of Ministry of Foreign Trade and Economic Cooperation. *Statistics on FDI in China 2001,* not for sale.

Annex Table 5-2: FIEs as a percentage of National Total Value-added Industrial Output by Province and Municipality in 2000

Unit: RMB 100 Million

Province-Region-Municipality	Value-added Industrial Output	Value-added Industrial Output by FIEs	FIEs' share in Total Value-added Industrial Output
National Total	25394.80	6090.35	23.98
Beijing	722.65	285.77	39.54
Tianjin	630.09	265.49	42.14
Heber	1132.66	101.05	8.92
Shanxi	428.71	18.68	4.36
Inner Mongolia	279.54	15.16	5.42
Liaoning	1194.03	239.87	20.09
Jilin	496.19	83.88	16.90
Heilongjiang	1213.05	41.33	3.41
Shanghai	1687.18	838.88	49.72
Jiangsu	2604.37	709.80	27.25
Zhejiang	1506.11	279.78	18.58
Anhui	507.38	55.81	11.00
Fujian	797.12	462.12	57.97
Jiangxi	269.73	22.79	8.45
Shandong	2549.35	324.89	12.74
Henan	1116.39	113.73	10.19
Hubei	1011.77	105.50	10.43
Hunan	528.06	30.55	5.79
Guangdong	3423.86	1866.98	54.53
Guangxi	323.88	33.37	10.30
Hainan	63.25	10.05	15.89
Sichuan	283.73	39.23	13.83
Chongqing	662.44	55.03	8.31
Guizhou	216.99	5.01	2.31
Yunnan	531.47	20.01	3.77
Tibet	9.25	0.03	0.32
Shaanxi	411.17	46.25	11.25
Gansu	244.73	6.33	2.59
Qinghai	65.34	2.60	3.98
Ningxia	73.68	6.83	9.27
Xinjiang	356.62	3.54	0.99

Source: ibid.

Annex Table 5-3: Exports by FIEs as a percentage of Total Industrial Outputs by them by Province and Municipality in 2000

Province/ Region/ Municipality	Gross Industrial Output Value by FIEs in RMB 100 mil.	FIEs Export		Export as a percentage of Gross Industrial Output Value
		in US$ 100 mil.	in RMB 100 mil.	
National Total	23464.55	1194.41	9913.60	42
Beijing	1150.32	28.71	238.29	20
Tianjin	1195.71	63.79	529.46	44
Heber	372.67	10.12	84.00	23
Shanxi	60.77	1.52	12.62	21
Inner Mongolia	54.56	1.38	11.45	21
Liaoning	845.71	62.45	518.34	61
Jilin	312.15	3.92	32.54	10
Heilongjiang	129.17	2.67	22.16	17
Shanghai	3431.20	142.61	1183.66	34
Jiangsu	2896.95	144.53	1199.60	41
Zhejiang	1232.40	53.49	443.97	36
Anhui	213.23	4.00	33.20	16
Fujian	1605.23	75.97	630.55	39
Jiangxi	96.86	1.63	13.53	14
Shandong	1173.34	79.82	662.51	56
Henan	257.71	3.09	25.65	10
Hubei	336.31	4.30	35.69	11
Hunan	97.05	1.82	15.11	16
Guangdong	7274.35	495.10	4109.33	56
Guangxi	114.53	3.41	28.30	25
Hainan	39.96	3.05	25.32	68
Sichuan	129.02	0.90	7.47	6
Chongqing	167.09	3.42	28.39	17
Guizhou	18.55	0.40	3.32	18
Yunnan	60.25	0.81	6.72	11
Tibet	0.06	0.04	0.33	--
Shaanxi	132.92	1.16	9.63	7
Gansu	29.91	0.38	3.15	11
Qinghai	4.83	0.02	0.17	4
Ningxia	18.05	0.43	3.57	20
Xinjiang	13.69	0.91	7.55	55

Source: calculations are made on the basis of figures of Table 13-15, 17-12 in National Bureau of Statistics of China (2002). *China Statistical Yearbook 2001* (Beijing: China Statistics Press).

Annex Table 5-4: Contribution Rate of Exports by FIEs to Local Exports by Province and Municipality in 2000

Unit: US$ 100 Million

Region	Total Export	FIEs Export	FIEs Export as a percentage of Total Export
National Total	2492.0255	1194.41	47.93
Beijing	76.6723	28.71	37.45
Tianjin	76.7427	63.79	83.13
Heber	32.7814	10.12	30.88
Shanxi	20.9094	1.52	7.27
Inner Mongolia	11.1400	1.38	12.39
Liaoning	105.8947	62.45	58.97
Jilin	14.8693	3.92	26.36
Heilongjiang	24.2393	2.67	11.01
Shanghai	246.3961	142.61	57.88
Jiangsu	263.7694	144.53	54.80
Zhejiang	204.8214	53.49	26.11
Anhui	21.1942	4.00	18.87
Fujian	136.2282	75.97	55.77
Jiangxi	11.8837	1.63	13.71
Shandong	160.9267	79.28	49.26
Henan	15.8683	3.09	19.47
Hubei	18.9977	4.30	22.61
Hunan	16.3190	1.83	11.18
Guangdong	934.2792	495.10	52.99
Guangxi	16.4048	3.41	20.79
Hainan	6.0853	3.05	50.06
Sichuan	10.6048	0.97	9.11
Chongqing	14.3360	2.46	17.10
Guizhou	4.8166	0.40	8.33
Yunnan	10.9271	0.81	7.42
Tibet	1.0902	0.04	3.57
Shaanxi	13.2693	1.16	8.75
Gansu	4.2079	0.38	9.11
Qinghai	1.3355	0.02	1.51
Ningxia	3.5426	0.43	12.12
Xinjiang	11.4724	0.91	7.95

Source: calculations are made on the basis of figures of Table 17-11 and 17-12 in National Bureau of Statistics of China (2002). *China Statistical Yearbook 2001* (Beijing: China Statistics Press).

Chapter 6

Foreign-invested Enterprises on the Capital Market

Investment is by far the principal behavior of foreign-invested enterprises (FIEs) on the Chinese market. However, a few of them are also financing on the Chinese capital market. Individual cases of M&As have taken place as well. Since 2001, foreign-invested enterprises have been paying more attention to the Chinese capital market that has shown bright prospects for more openness.

6-1: Entry of Foreign-invested Enterprises Into the Chinese Capital Market in Retrospective

Because the A-stock market of the Chinese capital market is not opened directly to foreign-invested enterprises, the mergers and acquisitions by these enterprises on the A-stock market are conducted indirectly by their parent companies and affiliates that have invested in listed companies. It is mainly through the B-stock market that foreign-invested enterprises pursue financing and M&As.

The involvement of foreign-invested enterprises in the Chinese stock market began in the early 1990s. By the first half of 2001, a total of 71 listed companies had acquired foreign-invested legal person shares. Direct listing and M&As are the two main channels by which foreign-invested enterprises enter the Chinese stock market. See Table 6-1.

Table 6-1: Channels by which foreign-invested enterprises enter the domestic securities market (by the end of June 2001)

Channel		Number of enterprises	Cases in point
Direct listing		66	Tsann Kuen (China) Enterprise Co., Ltd., Shanghai Dajiang (group) Stock Co., Ltd., Linca Industry (Fujian) Group Co., Ltd. etc
M&As	Contractual transfer of stocks	2	Beijing Aerospace Chengfeng Co., Ltd., Shenzhen Seg Samsung Glass Co., Ltd.
	Oriented additional issue of B stocks	2	Jiangling Motors Co., Ltd., Huaxin Cement Co., Ltd.
	Joint venture	1	Shanghai Tyre & Rubber Co., Ltd.

Sources: Li Xunlei and Hong Xiaobin (2001). "New Mileage into the Capital Market", *Securities Post*, November 21, 2001.

1. Direct Listing

Direct listing on the stock market by foreign-invested enterprises in the capacity of founders of shareholding company is the most important way for foreign investment to enter the B-stock market to raise funds from the stock market. Directly listed enterprises remain by far the mainstay of foreign-invested enterprises on the Chinese securities market. There are two ways for direct listing. The first and most important way for direct listing is for foreign-invested enterprises to participate in the transformation and listing of domestic enterprises as founders. The second way, similar to that of Tsann Kuen (China) Enterprise Co., Ltd., involves direct listing in the capacity of wholly foreign-owned enterprises. All but two of the 66 foreign-invested enterprises directly listed on the stock market are joint ventures with Chinese and foreign capital. The other two are Tsann Kuen (China) Enterprise Co., Ltd. and Shenzhen Capstone Industrial Co., Ltd. Among most of these enterprises, foreign investors hold 20-30% of the stocks. It is difficult for a foreign-invested enterprise controlled by the foreign partner to get directly listed.

2. Listing by M&As

Cases of foreign-invested enterprises getting indirectly listed on the stock market by M&As began to appear after 1995. By the first half of 2000, five such enterprises entered the Chinese stock market this way. Foreign-invested enterprises may acquire listed Chinese enterprises directly or indirectly. In a direct acquisition, a foreign-invested enterprise directly joins or controls a listed company by such means as the secondary market, oriented issuance of more stocks, and contractual acquisition. In an indirect acquisition, a foreign-invested enterprise joins or controls a listed company by other means, such as acquiring a listed company by establishing a wholly owned or joint-venture enterprise, and acquiring stocks from the parent company or the major stockholders of a listed company to gain the control of it.

1) Acquiring Legal Person Shares by Contracts on the A-stock Market

The stocks on the Chinese securities market have been artificially divided into negotiable A- and B-shares as well as nonnegotiable stocks. As nonnegotiable stocks make up 60% of the market, acquiring from the secondary market is inadequate for a foreign-invested enterprise hoping to realize its developmental strategy by gaining control of the stocks of a company, and nonnegotiable stocks have to be acquired as well. Nonnegotiable stocks are by far acquired mainly by contractual means. Foreign-invested enterprises began to acquire nonnegotiable stocks in 1995. On July 5, 1995, Isuzu and Itochu jointly acquired, in the form of a contract, the non-state legal person shares of Beijing Aerospace Chengfeng Co., Ltd. that comprised 25% of the total stocks of the parent company, thereby setting a precedent for foreign investors directly acquiring the legal person shares of listed companies in China. To prevent a drain of state-owned assets, in September that year the State Council General Office issued a circular of the China Securities Regulatory Commission on the "Proposals on Suspending Transfer of the State-owned shares and Legal person shares of Listed Companies to Foreign Investors", and as a result an end was put to this form of acquisition. This ban has not been lifted since, but there are still foreign-invested enterprises that have acquired stocks of listed companies through this form of acquisition. For instance, Samsung contractually received Shenzhen Seg Samsung Glass Co., Ltd.'s shares from Shum Yip Group to become Shenzhen Seg Samsung Glass Co., Ltd.'s second largest shareholder.

2) Oriented Additional Issuance of Stocks on the B-Stock Market

Two foreign-invested enterprises have used this method to enter the Chinese stock market.

In August 1995, Ford reached agreement with Jiangling Motors Co., Ltd. and bought 80% of the B-shares newly issued by Jiangling Motors Co., Ltd. for 40 million US dollars. The purchase turned Ford into Jiangling Motors Co., Ltd.'s second largest shareholder in the possession of 20% of its shares. In 1999 Huaxin Cement Co., Ltd. issued 77 million additional B-shares to Swedish cement manufacturing firm and turned it into Huaxin Cement Co., Ltd.'s second largest shareholder with 23.45% of the shares. Compared with contractual transfer of stocks, oriented issuance of stocks is more in accord with the principle of "Equity, Publicity, Impartiality", facilitates supervision, entails few legal obstacles and is therefore easy to operate. However, the relatively high prices of the B-stock market have discouraged some foreign-invested enterprises that wanted to buy stocks through this channel.

3) Running a Joint Venture with a Listed Company

In March 2001, Shanghai Tyre & Rubber Co., Ltd., the leading firm in the tyre-manufacturing industry of China, established a joint venture with Michelin, the world's top tyre manufacturer. For 320 million US dollars, the joint venture acquired the major business and assets of Shanghai Tyre & Rubber Co., Ltd. and put the control power into the hands of Michelin, and the shares of the joint venture are divided 70% and 30% between the two partners. Shanghai Tyre & Rubber Co., Ltd. today is actually controlled by a foreign company. Michelin keeps essential control of Shanghai Tyre & Rubber Co., Ltd., thereby indirectly entering the Chinese securities market.

3. M&As Behaviors of Foreign-invested Enterprises Listed on the Chinese Stock Market

Some foreign-invested enterprises that have directly entered the Chinese stock market are still engaged in M&As on the capital market not to get involved in financing on the Chinese capital market but to attain certain strategic goals, such as gaining control of a certain enterprise or superiority assets or achieving expansion quickly. The M&As behaviors of listed foreign-invested enterprises take place mainly in two ways.

1) Acquiring from the Secondary Market

The B-stock market of China open to foreign investors, who can acquire the shares they needed by acquiring negotiable stocks from the secondary market. Shanghai Yaohua Pilkington Glass Co., Ltd. is a typical case in this regard. As one of the earliest joint ventures to be listed on the stock market, Shanghai Yaohua Pilkington Glass Co., Ltd. has four major stockholders that have been in the possession of more or less the same amount of shares for a long time. However, the company's 2000 annual report indicated that the position of Pilkington of Britain as a shareholder had become the company's leading shareholder with 18.98% of all the shares.

Gaining indirect control of a domestic listed company by acquiring shares from its original foreign shareholder

In January 1996, Saint-Gobain of France, the world's leading glass manufacturing firm, gained control of the Wanda Industrial Co. Ltd., which is the largest company of the Fuyao Glass Industry Group Co., Ltd., by accepting 51% of its shares. In March that year, the French glass manufacturer acquired Fuyao Glass Industry Group Co., Ltd.'s two foreign-invested companies – Hongqiao and Sanyi from Hong Kong – and became its leading shareholder in control of 42% of its shares.

6-2: From Investing to Financing: A New Trend for Foreign-invested Enterprises in China

With China's accession to WTO, the prospects of a more open Chinese capital market are brightening increasingly. This has attracted the attention of many foreign-invested enterprises. According to incomplete statistics, by the end of February 2002, more than 100 such enterprises had indicated their intention to engage in financing on the Chinese capital market. These enterprises fall into two categories.

1. Famous Transnational Corporations

Some famous transnational corporations have made it clear that they want to seek financing from the Chinese capital market. Jeff Fraser, president of the Asian section of Unilever N.V., ranked 54th among the 2000 Fortune list of Top 500, said that no matter how difficult it is, his company will strive to be the first to be listed on the Chinese A-stock market. The move is not just designed for fund-raising purposes. As a corporation with a high degree of globalization that has issued stocks in many countries, Unilever N.V. also wants to become a localized transnational firm. Its appearance on the Chinese capital market has unified these two goals.

2. FIEs from Hong Kong and Taiwan

Some Hong Kong- and Taiwan-invested enterprises are expanding their businesses on the mainland fairly quickly, but their capital-accumulation and low-cost financing abilities are low. Taiwan's Wantwant Group, for instance, has had 33 affiliates on the mainland, but finds it impossible to accumulate enough capital by itself to expand its businesses and occupy the market for a series of products by preempting its competitors. Because of this Wantwant Group has begun to seek opportunities to get into the mainland securities market. The demand for colossal amounts of funds has driven many other Hong Kong-, Macao- and Taiwan-invested enterprises with large market shares and wanting to expand their businesses on the mainland onto the road of seeking financing from the Chinese capital market. Tinghsin, Giant, Microtek, Goodbaby, CPTF Optronics Co., Ltd. and many other Taiwan-invested enterprises have appeared on a list of foreign-invested enterprises wanting to be listed on the Chinese stock market. Quite a few Hong Kong-invested enterprises that have strong ties with the mainland and are doing a lot of businesses there, including China Resources (Holding) Co., Ltd. and Cheung Kong (Holdings) Limited, are also seeking to enter this market.

6-3: New Trends of Foreign-invested Enterprises' M&As on the Capital Market

While some foreign-invested enterprises seek opportunities to directly enter the Chinese capital market, many others are planning or pursuing direct or indirect M&As to enter the Chinese capital market. Many domestic enterprises have shown a willingness to cooperate with foreign investors through M&As on the capital market. Since the latter half of 2001, the numbers of foreign investors entering the Chinese capital market through M&As have been quickly increasing, and many have revealed plans for unprecedented deals in this regard.

1. Listed Companies Cooperates with Foreign Investors Directly

Some large domestic enterprises that have been listed on the Chinese capital market are looking for foreign cooperators in order to gain technological and financial support. Among the typical cases in point in 2001: In May, SVA Electron Co., Ltd. announced a plan for a cooperative project with IBM; in June, the Samsung (Shanghai) Vacuum Electronic Accessory Company was established as a joint venture between SVA Electron Co., Ltd. and Samsung (Hongkong) Co., Ltd.; in October, Northeast Electrical Development Company Limited and Alstom of France set up a joint venture for the manufacturing of mutual inductors; in October, Beijing Capital Co., Ltd. and Vivendi Universal of France signed an agreement on strategic cooperation; in October, a new emporium was established with joint investment from Beijing Xidan Market Company Limited and Hong Kong's Netvigator Company; in November, Henan Pinggao Electric Co., ltd. announced a foundry project to be undertaken in cooperation with foreign investors; Shenzhen Seg Samsung Glass Co., Ltd., Markor Furniture International Co., Ltd., Inner Mongolia North Hauler Joint Stock Company, BOE Technology Group Co., Ltd., Sinotrans Air Transportation Development Co., Ltd., , CITIC Offshore Helicopter Co., Ltd., , Beiya Industrial (Group) Co., Ltd., Tianjin Port (Group) Co., Ltd., Eastern Communications Co., Ltd., Shanghai Automotive Co., Ltd., Fujian Furi Electronics Co., Ltd., changan automobile liability co ltd., Dalian Bingshan Group Co., Ltd., Shenyang Jinbei Auto Motive Company Limited, Datang Telecom Technology Co., Ltd., XJ Electronic Co., Ltd., Shenzhan Yan Tian Port Holdings Co., Ltd., Shanghai Electrical Apparatus Co., Ltd. and Liaoning Chengda Co., Ltd. also fostered new cooperative relations with foreign investors.

2. Listed Companies' Parent Companies and Subsidiaries Speed Up Cooperation with Foreign Investors.

The parent companies of some listed companies in China have speeded up the process of setting up new joint ventures and cooperative projects with foreign investors since 2001. Typical cases in point: the strategic regrouping of China Qingqi Group Co., Ltd., the parent companies of Jinan Qingqi Motorcycle Co., Ltd. and Hainan Sundiro Motorcycle Co., Ltd. with Hans from Indonesia. One affiliate of Shanghai Maling Aquarius Co., Ltd. , Shanghai Aquarius Co., Ltd. was converted into a joint venture with Chinese and foreign capital in June; the parent company of Shan Dong Xiaoya Electrical Appliance Co., Ltd. fostered a strategic alliance with Toshiba; the Northeast Pharmaceutical Group, which is the parent company of Northeast Pharmaceutical Group Co., Ltd. cooperates with a South Korean firm in the production of anti-AIDS drugs; TCL International, an affiliate of TCL Communication Equipment Co., Ltd., set up a new company jointly with Hong Kong's Yanguang; Beijing New Distribution Hardware Co., Ltd., an affiliate to the Beijing New Building Material Public Limited Company, has planned to build the B&Q (Shenzhen) Decoration and Building Materials Company, a joint venture with the British B&Q Co., Ltd.

Around the end of 2001, large transnational corporations took a series of major influential actions. A typical case in this regard was the Shenzhen Energy Investment Co., Ltd.'s intent for a joint venture. On January 10, 2002, nine foreign companies including Electricite de France and Asian Industrial signed a letter of intent with the Shenzhen Energy Investment Co., Ltd. on a plan to convert the group into a joint venture by reducing State-owned shares and increasing investment to expand the shares. The Chinese side will control 51% of the joint venture's registered capital of 7 billion RMB, and the foreign side will control 49% of it.

3. Foreign-invested Enterprises Acquire the Parent Company of a Listed Company, or Large Shareholder Taking Control of a Listed Company

In October 2001, Shanghai Bell Co., Ltd. announced a decision to officially convert itself into a foreign-invested company with limited liability, in which Alcatel's shares were increased from 31.65% to 50% plus one share, while the Chinese partner held 50% minus one of the shares. Shanghai Bell Co., Ltd. was thus officially renamed Alcatel Shanghai Bell Co. Ltd. This turned Alcatel into Shanghai Bell Co., Ltd.'s leading shareholder and the second largest shareholder of Shanghai Belling Co., Ltd. of which Shanghai Bell is the second largest shareholder. This brilliant move of capital operation was the first of its kind on the Chinese securities market, and set a precedent for a foreign investor taking control of a Chinese telecommunications company.

6-4: Major Motive Force Behind Foreign-invested Enterprises' Entry Into the Chinese Capital Market

Foreign-invested enterprises enter the Chinese capital market for the following purposes:

1. Raising Funds from the Capital Market to Expand their Capital and Meet their Financial Need for Expanding their Businesses

Because the Chinese securities market is too small to meet the financing demand of large projects invested in China by large transnational corporations, most of the listed foreign-invested enterprises that are basically for financing purposes are of small or medium sizes. Among the companies listed on the A-stock market, 30 or so are the ones in which foreign investors directly come into possession of shares or stocks through such channels as legal person shares and B-shares, and about two thirds of them, such as Winsan (Shanghai) Industrial Corporation Ltd. and Far East Industrial Stock Co., Ltd. are the ones in which Hong Kong-based Chinese companies as well as Hong Kong and Taiwan companies of medium or small sizes serve as foreign shareholders. Most of the foreign shareholders of this kind of listed company are medium-sized or small enterprises with Hong Kong capital, and some of them have a Chinese capital background. Financing is the primary or first goal for most of these investors, but a few of them are also operating the capital market, that is to say, within the framework of government policies, and under the precondition of getting remarkable returns from their investment, some Hong Kong shareholders may transfer the A-shares of their listed companies to transnational corporations in the same field of endeavor.

2. Speeding Up Expansion on the Chinese Market

In the early days of reform and opening up to the outside world, many products were in short supply in China and domestic enterprises were weak, which provided considerable room for development for foreign investors who entered the Chinese market by establishing new enterprises. After the mid-1990s, however, the Chinese market became a buyer's market, and competition was intensifying with the rise of a group of highly competitive enterprises in China. Under these circumstances a foreign investor may find it difficult to enter the Chinese market by establishing new enterprises. M&As on the capital market thus becomes a speedy and efficient way of entering the Chinese market.

When a retailing sales system is opened to FDI, the distribution network becomes as important as local clients for foreign-invested enterprises, but such distribution networks cannot be brought into China from the parent companies as conveniently as technology, nor can they be developed in a short period of time. For this reason, to acquire enterprises with available distribution networks and a long list of clients is better than establishing new distribution networks or organizations in a locality. Those transnational corporations that are latecomers on the Chinese market and have thus failed to win considerable market shares and competitiveness are inclined towards this method so as to gain quick access to the Chinese market. Those foreign companies that use this method are often famous transnational corporations, and their targets are often the leading enterprises in Chinese industries. Examples are Shanghai Automotive Co., Ltd., targeted by General Motors; Shanghai Bell Co., Ltd., targeted by Alcatel; and Shanghai Brilliance Holdings Co., Ltd., targeted by BMW of Germany.

Some joint ventures that have become shareholders of listed companies are also seeking control in enterprises through operations on the capital market. Most of these shareholders gain control in a shareholding structure by a variety of means, such as making strategic investment through issuing additional B-shares and signing contracts to gain nonnegotiable shares. The last couple of years, however, have also witnessed certain Stock-A companies using various ways and means to woo cross-border strategic investors. The French Alcatel took indirect control of Shanghai Belling Co., Ltd. by taking control of Shanghai Bell Co., Ltd.; Greencool Co., Ltd. gained control of Guangdong Kelon Electrical Holding Co., Ltd. by signing an agreement to accept 20.6% of its shares from the Ronggui Town Government of Shunde, Guangdong Province. Both of them were major M&As that took place on the Chinese A-stock market in 2001.

3. Formulating Effective Corporate Governance Structures to Safeguard the Interests of Partners

Seeking opportunities to be listed is a major approach by which Chinese enterprises transform themselves to formulate effective corporate governance structures, Foreign-invested enterprises are doing the same. When a foreign-invested enterprise finds that its governance structure is not effective enough, it may make the feasible choice of readjusting its share structure by seeking opportunities to be listed or by M&As on the capital market. Of the 112 B-stock companies that had been established by the end of 2001, nine had overseas strategic investors that are basically transnational corporations with a strong industrial background. In three of these nine companies, overseas strategic investors are the biggest shareholders; and the overseas strategic investors of six of these companies are second largest shareholders in control of relatively the same amounts of shares as the Chinese leading shareholders, thereby forming an effective check-and-balance share structure. In these nine companies, overseas strategic investors have representatives on the directorate to take active part in corporate governance; in four of them, representatives of overseas investors have entered the management echelon to take direct part in day-to-day operations.

Of these nine B-stock companies, Jiangling Motors Co., Ltd. is a typical case in point. When this company was issuing B-shares, it adopted a plan to bring in strategic investors by selling its shares according to a strategy for long-term development. As a result, Ford came into possession of 20% of the shares and became the second largest shareholder while Jiangling Motors Group Company owned 50.95% of the shares and was the leading shareholder. After it became an owner, Ford appointed three representatives on the directorate of Jiangling Motors Co., Ltd., and another representative as the company's executive Vice

President. Today, five of the 11 members of the Jiangling Motors Co., Ltd.'s directorate and an executive VP are appointed by Ford. By the end of June 2001, Ford had gained control of 29.96% of the shares, while Jiangling Motors Group Company had 41.03%. By holding and expanding its shares from a strategic and long-term perspective, Ford effectively overcame the phenomenon in which the state was the dominant shareholder and helped formulate a relatively reasonable share structure in which the two leading shareholders are in an effective balance-and-check relationship, thereby protecting the interests of all the shareholders.

4. Taking Entry Into the Chinese Securities Market as Part of a Localization Strategy

Foreign companies began investing in China by localizing their market, which means to produce their products and sell them in China. With improvement in the level of the domestic manufacturing industry and the emergence of local professional talents, the foreign-invested enterprises are localizing the production of component parts and tapping local human resources. In the days to come, a number of these enterprises will speed up their pace of localizing capital, that is, financing on the local capital market. Localization of capital will bring about tremendous changes in the image and nature of transnational companies, narrow their gap with local enterprises, enhance the host country's sense of identity with foreign-invested enterprises, raise their prestige and improve their images.

5. Taking the Opportunity of Listing to Realize Shares Incentives for Local High-Echelon Managers and Strengthen Cohesive Relationship among Employees

It is the hope of some foreign-invested enterprises to provide, in the process of becoming listed companies to meet their financing goals, incentives in the form of shares and options for high-echelon managers and key researchers and technicians, so as to enhance their enterprises' appeals and rallying the efforts of the employees. For example, Unilever N.V. announced that one of their purposes of becoming a listed company is to woo more outstanding professionals by offering their employees attractive stock and options plans.

Generally speaking, by the end of 2001, the number of foreign-invested enterprises engaged in financing and M&As on the Chinese capital market was few and far between. With the Chinese capital market being further opened to the outside world, and with the importance of regrouping domestic enterprises being increasingly driven home to government policymakers, foreign-invested enterprises will be more deeply and widely involved in the Chinese capital market, and China will be ushered into a new stage in which foreign investment is introduced for simultaneous promotion of investment, financing and M&As. One important aspect in this regard, however, is to promote the reform of state-owned enterprises through foreign investment in M&As. Chapter Ten will make an exclusive analysis of the significance of the cross-border M&As for promoting reform of state-owned enterprises.

Chapter 7

Transnational Investment, Market Structure and Changes of Competitive Behaviors of Foreign-Invested Enterprises

The probability of transnational corporations monopolizing the market of a host country and their important positions in certain industries in China have prompted people in many fields to ask: Will transnational corporations monopolize the Chinese market by means of abundant resources and high competitiveness? If the Chinese market becomes the monopoly of these transnational giants, domestic investment will be hampered, the entry of new investors blocked, high prices exacted from consumers to yield monopoly profits, and the interests of domestic producers and consumers jeopardized. If this situation really exists, it means that increased investment, technological progress, improved efficiency and other gains from attracting FDI are not benefiting Chinese producers and consumers in the form of more applicable products and lower prices but absorbed by transnational corporations in the form of high profits.

An analysis is made in this chapter of the changes in the market structure for the Chinese manufacturing industry and of the impact of these changes on the competitive behaviors of foreign-invested enterprises (FIEs). Development and introduction of technology, the speed of upgrading the products, and pricing are three major factors with which the behaviors of foreign-invested enterprises in competition are appraised.

7-1: The Leading Position of Transnational Corporations and the Probability of Monopoly

Since the mid-1990s, famous transnational corporations have been engaged in large-scale investment in China. Most of the *Fortune*'s Top 500 transnational corporations invested in China. A few of them could not do so because of government ban on the entry of FDI into certain industries.

These large transnational corporations come mainly from the United States, Europe and Japan. With large investment, high-grade products and high level of technology they have considerably improved the Chinese industrial structure and technological level. The presence of enterprises invested by large transnational corporations is keenly felt in some industries where large-scale operations yield conspicuous economic returns and where the tendency towards industrial globalization goes strong.

Generally speaking, the projects invested by large transnational corporations are larger than their Chinese counterparts to take the lead in terms of scale, and they account for a high percentage in total industrial output. For example, since the late 1990s, over two thirds of the 10 leading enterprises in the microelectronic, mobile telecommunications equipment, car, pharmaceutical, or engineering machinery-manufacturing industry have been foreign-invested. Foreign-invested enterprises have all along made up 90% of the cell phone market and two thirds of the cars made in this country.

By a theoretical inference, the leading position of transnational corporations on the Chinese market and their high market shares tend to lead to monopoly. It goes without saying that all commercial companies, domestic or transnational ones alike, are after maxim profits. If supervision of the market is weak, all companies, whether transnational or domestic, may resort to monopoly. However, with their multiple advantages in scale, brand and technology and their powerful influence on the market, their behaviors are of particular concern to people.

Analyses of the competitive behaviors of transnational corporations on overseas markets are an important aspect of theories on industrial organization and transnational investment. In its formative stage the theory on transnational investment already maintained that one of the purposes of transnational corporations investing in overseas markets is to control the enterprises in different countries, eliminate competition, put them in an advantageous position, and gain colossal profits. The overseas investment by transnational corporations is, in essence, an expansion of their superiority in monopoly as well as a distortion of the market that yields pernicious anti-competition results (Hymer, 1970, 1976). Some scholars believe that a transnational corporation has the intention for monopoly in both parent and host countries, but this intention tends to succeed more easily abroad than at home because on the overseas market there are fewer competitors and temptations are high for them to work in collusion. Through collusion they can keep prices at a relatively high level so as to gain high profits steadily (Caves, 1982). An opposite opinion, however, holds that overseas investment by transnational corporation serves to increase the number of enterprises on the market of a host country and reduce the degree of concentration of both production and market, thereby strengthening competition on that market instead of weakening it (Fishwick, 1981; Gorechi, 1976). Shortly afterwards, some scholars devoted their efforts to a study of interaction between transnational corporations and the enterprises of a host country. If a transnational corporation holds a monopolistic advantage in a host country while local enterprises are locked in competition, then in the early stage of the transnational corporation's entry into that market it tends to increase its monopoly. However, from a long-term point of view, technological spillover as an inevitable phenomenon is a potential cost of a transnational corporation's overseas investment, because local enterprises that benefit from this technological flow will sooner or later become strong enough to challenge transnational corporations. The result is that the competitiveness of the market of the host country is increased (Das, 1987).

Transnational investment has been growing fairly rapidly worldwide since the 1990s, which has greatly enriched researches in this field. The massive incorporation of FDI by developing countries and Central and Eastern European countries with economies in transition, in particular, have provided new materials for such researches, which have yielded many research results based on multiple national situations and large numbers of case studies. However, the conclusions from these researches are divergent. Some studies indicate that investment by large transnational corporations, especially investment in the form of M&As, is often used to wipe out competition (UNCTAD, 1997); other studies, however, show that the changes in the pattern of competition caused by transnational investment are only temporary because once the overseas investment behavior of one enterprise has upset the balance of a market, its competitors will inevitably react strongly to ensure their positions on the market. They will expand their investment, form alliances or seek M&As – all for the purpose of preventing competitors from controlling their market shares (Schenk, 1996). Conclusions from empirical researches, too, are conflicting. A study on India proves that transnational corporations have won control of the local market. For instance, Unilever N.V. is in control of 75% of the soap market and 30% of the detergent market in India (Mehta, 1999). A study on the degree of concentration of 87 manufacturing industries in the Czech Republic has proved otherwise. Although concentration of Czech manufacturing industries was intensifying simultaneously with a massive FDI inflow in the latter half of the 1990s, a statistical analysis shows that there is no correlation between transnational investment and the degree of market concentration (Zemplinerova and Jarolim, 2000).

Studies of the competitive behavior of transnational corporations in China have reached the basic conclusion that "transnational corporations have monopolized the Chinese market". However, it is necessary to point out that these studies are seriously flawed in that they countered transnational corporations as a whole group of interest when calculating their market shares. This concept is inappropriate, because foreign-invested enterprises belong to different transnational corporations and have independent interests, and because their relationship on the Chinese market is one of competition rather than one of stable collusion. For these reasons even though these foreign-invested enterprises have controlled a high share of the Chinese market as a whole, if this market share is divided between a number of transnational corporations, then this market should be regarded as a competitive market rather than a monopolistic one. In this chapter, individual foreign-invested enterprises are studied for an analysis of changes in the market structure of the Chinese manufacturing industry as well as the impact of such changes on the behaviors of foreign-invested enterprises in competition.

7-2: Competitive Behaviors of Enterprises Invested by Transnational Corporations in China

1. Monopolistic Intentions and Behaviors

The possibility of transnational corporations becoming monopolistic on the market of a host country, and their major position in certain industries in this country have prompted many people in China to ask: will these corporations form a monopolistic force on the Chinese market by relying on their powerful resources and competitiveness? If the answer is yes, then domestic investment will be restrained, new investors will be denied market access, and these corporations will exact high prices from consumers and gain monopolistic profits, thereby jeopardizing the interests of domestic manufacturers and consumers. If this situation exists, it means that the multiple interests resulting from increases in investment caused by capital inflow, technological progress, improvement in efficiency, etc., are not shifted to Chinese manufacturers and consumers in the form of more applicable profits and lower prices – rather, they are absorbed by transnational corporations in the form of high profits.

It is, therefore, of major significance theoretically and practically to judge the position of transnational corporations in certain major industries in China and their competitive behaviors. As we see it, monopoly is not a serious problem in transnational corporations' investment in China. The behaviors of transnational corporations in China as a whole have experienced a changing process. In the early days they attempted at monopoly; now their major attention has been shifted to competition. A major reason behind this change lies in the fact that the domestic market structure has changed from one in which a few transnational corporations were in a superiority position to one of intense competition.

When many transnational corporations had just entered the Chinese market, they had the intention for monopolistic profit and worked to seek it as well. When they began entering China on a large scale, there were possibly only one or two powerful transnational corporations in a local industry that was highly monopolistic on the market. In the Chinese auto motives, mobile telecommunications equipment and engineering machinery industries, a large chunk of the market was monopolized for a time by one or two famous transnational corporations, and prices were running high in these fields, with little being done to upgrade the products for a long time.

Take the car-manufacturing industry for instance. During the period from the mid-1980s to the mid-1990s, car production in this country was highly concentrated and there was no adequate competition on the market, with Shanghai Volkswagen Co., Ltd.—— a joint venture between Germany's Volkswagen and the Shanghai Automotive Co., Ltd. —— figuring prominently on the Chinese car market. In April 1983, the first Santana car rolled off the assembly line in Shanghai, and in March 1985 Shanghai Volkswagen Co., Ltd. was established which was to monopolize the Chinese car market for more than a decade. Santana almost occupied almost the entire market for cars of the same grade by the late 1980s, accounted for 90% of that market in the early 1990s, and had over 60% of it by the mid-1990s. By March 1998, Shanghai Volkswagen Co., Ltd. had produced 1 million Santanas, including a second-generation model – Santana 2000 – which rolled off the assembly line and went on sale in 1995.

For 16 years from 1983 to 1999, the first-generation Santana remained the leading product for Shanghai Volkswagen Co., Ltd., with little change made to it. Its parent company phased out the first-generation Santana on the global market in the mid-1980s, but Shanghai Volkswagen Co., Ltd. continued to produce it during that period without introducing any new models its parent company had introduced to the global market. The market price of Santana remained high -- nearly twice as high as what it was on the world market – until 1998 year-end.

This behavior of Shanghai Volkswagen Co., Ltd. was based on its market monopoly, and it was censured by public opinion and various quarters in China for a long time. Even the Shanghai Automotive Co., Ltd. was discontented with its German partner for its refusal to introduce advanced models. In 1998, the Shanghai Automotive Co., Ltd. established a joint venture with General Motors. A major reason for this was because General Motors agreed to produce its new models in China.

2. Changes in Market Structure and Formation of the Competitive Behavior

However, transnational corporations' tendency of monopoly of the Chinese industry and market is weakening with time. Three main factors are behind this quick change in their behavior.

1) Anticipation of competition from imported commodities after China's accession to WTO. For many years high import duties and excessive non-tariff barriers had obviously protected the domestic and foreign-invested enterprises in China. In those industries where foreign-invested enterprises figured prominently, these enterprises were major beneficiaries of trade barriers. Towards the end of the 1990s, China's accession to WTO had become a foregone conclusion, and the prospects of lowering government protection of the domestic industry were brightening. Under these circumstances, if transnational corporations continued to use or produce in China technology or products that were no longer competitive on the global market, consumers would choose to buy imported goods. This is a major reason why auto-manufacturers in China have repeatedly cut their prices since 1999.

2) Competition among transnational corporations. When one or two transnational corporations entered China and gained high economic returns, the others certainly would not turn a blind eye to this market with great potentials. Rather, they would follow suit. With their investment in China these transnational corporations are locked in a competition on the Chinese market.

3) Competition with domestic Chinese enterprises. The entry of enterprises invested by transnational corporations has brought the pressure of competition to bear on their Chinese counterparts. They have also set good examples, enabling Chinese enterprises to markedly improve their competitiveness and become foreign-invested enterprises' tough competitors. The intensifying competition between transnational corporations and between these corporations and their Chinese counterparts has cultivated a competitive market structure for most manufacturing industries in China.

Since the mid-1990s, the tremendous potentials of the Chinese market have come to be accepted by more and more transnational corporations. None of them can afford to neglect the potentials of that market and the strong competitiveness of the Chinese manufacturing industry and give it up to their rivals. With more and more transnational corporations arriving in China to invest, competition between them is escalating as well. Since the late 1990s, the Chinese government has considerably eased up on its long years of insistence on the distribution of three large and three small car-making factories across the land. The result was that by the end of 2001, all the nine major auto groups that have emerged through global mergers and acquisitions have made large-scale investment and established joint-venture automobile enterprises in China. General Motors alone are operating Shanghai GM, Jinbei GM Automotive Company Limited, Chongqing Changan Suzuki Automobile Co., Ltd, Jiangxi Changhe Suzuki Automobile Co., Ltd, Jiangling Motors Co., Ltd, Chongqing Changan Automobile Co., Ltd, Beijing Light Automobile, Beiling Special-purpose Automotive Co., Ltd, Nanya Company, Naveco Limited Company and Yunque Company. Volkswagen is an investor in joint ventures with the Faw Volkswagen Co., Ltd and the Shanghai Volkswagen Co., Ltd. Ford operates Jiangling Motors Co., Ltd, Changan-Ford and Mazda Co., Ltd. Toyota has Tianjin Toyota Motor Co., Ltd and Sichuan Toyota Motor Co., Ltd, Daimler-Chrysler has invested in Beijing Jeep Corporation, Ltd, Yaxing Benz Co., Ltd, Baotou North-Benz Heavyduty Truck Co., Ltd, Chang Feng Co. (Group) Ltd, Shenyang

Aircraft Corporation, Southeast Automotive Co., Ltd and Yuedakia Co., Ltd. Honda has invested in Guangzhou Honda Co., Ltd. Citroen-Peugeot is an owner of Dongfeng Peugeot Citroen Automobile Co., Ltd. Renault-Nissan have invested in Sanjiang-Renault, Zhengzhou Nissan Automobile Co., Ltd, Dongfeng Nissan Diesel Motor Co., Ltd and Fengshen Motor Co., Ltd. BMW is an investor in Shenyang Brilliance Jinbei Automobile Co., Ltd. The global major automanufacturers are locked in a fierce rivalry on the Chinese market. The formation of a competitive market structure has speeded up transnational corporations' use of the latest technology in China, vastly expedited the upgrading of the products, and resulted in a general reduction in product prices. By the late 1990s, the fact that Jetta and Citroen had increased their shares on the Chinese market, especially the Shanghai GM introduced Buick and Honda had begun producing Accord cars, Germany's Volkswagen changed its attitude and introduced its Passat model to Shanghai Volkswagen, thereby raising its production of the B2-class Santana by three grades to the B5-class Passat. In 2002 transnational corporations unveiled 11 new car models; in 2003, a total of 14 new models will roll off assembly lines.

The manufacturing of telecommunications equipment is another typical case in point[1]. In the 1990s, the telecommunications industry developed at a high speed in China. The number of telecommunications lines rose from 12 million in 1990 to 170 million in 2000. In the early 1990s when analogue cell phone held sway, the Chinese market was monopolized by a single transnational corporation – Motorola, and Chinese consumers were paying high prices to use the brick-like mobile phones produced by that company. The amazing economic returns of Motorola from the Chinese mobile telecommunications market attracted one transnational corporation after another into China. After a digital mobile telecommunications network was established in China in 1994, Nokia, Ericsson and some others quickly expanded their production in China, and the monopoly of Motorola began to shake. In 1996, Ericsson became the largest cell phone producer in China with a 37% share of the Chinese market, but two years later it was replaced by Nokia whose market share reached 36%. Since then the three transnational corporations have been locked in a cutthroat struggle on the Chinese market. The entry of so many transnational giants has intensified competition between them, and to expand their market shares, they are vying with one another to bring in the most advanced technology and products, and the prices of their products are sliding steadily. Within a short span of time, the Chinese consumers are able to buy cell phones that are as good and cheap as those on the world market. Beginning from 1999, the grades and prices of products on the Chinese cell phone market have already been changing in pace with those on the world market, and new cell phones are appearing at quarterly or monthly intervals. Almost all the cell phones will see their prices drop considerably two or three months after they appeared on the market. For instance, the price for Motorola V998 dropped from 9,000 RMB to 6,000 RMB two months after it appeared on the market.

Massive investment by transnational giants in the Chinese telecommunications equipment industry does not hold back the development of Chinese manufacturers. On the contrary, the manufacturing of telecommunications equipment has become one of the fastest growing industries in China. Take the program-controlled switchboard market for instance. In the late 1990s, the competitive behavior of domestic enterprises contributed impressively to technological progress and reductions in prices as a result of competition. Apart from competition between transnational corporations, the rise and growth of domestic enterprises

[1] The author derived her data and information for this section of the book from media coverage.

turned the competition between foreign-invested brands on the Chinese market for program-controlled switchboards into one between foreign-invested and domestic brands. Hot market competition and the ability of domestic enterprises to provide low-price products are reducing switchboard prices in a multiple way. For instance, the price of local-use program-controlled switchboard dropped from 300 US dollars per line in the early 1990s to 35 US dollars towards the end of that decade. The reduction of prices is accompanied by increases in the variety of services provided by various enterprises, and these include financing, installation and after service. The several successful Chinese telecommunications equipment enterprises owe their success to their ability to adopt their products to the minute differences between the demands on the market by relying on their own research and development efforts. In 2000, newly acquired domestic program-controlled switchboard production capacity made up upwards of 90% of the Chinese market, and the products with Chinese intellectual property rights accounted for over 60% of the total output.

The Chinese experience has vindicated a basic principle in the theory on industrial organization: In a monopolized market the speed at which enterprises develop new products and new technology is rather slow, and the prices will be kept at a high level in order to secure monopolistic profits, whereas a competitive market structure can lead enterprises to behave properly, speed up their development and introduction of new technology and new products, and constantly reduce their costs and prices so as to be winners in market competition. What is followed in this chapter is a case study of the detergent industry for an elaborate description of the relationship among transnational investment, market structures and enterprise behaviors.

7-3: Transnational Investment, Market Structures and Enterprise Behaviors: A Case Study on the Detergent Industry[2]

1. Crowded Entry of Transnational Giants and their Much-Criticized Market Behaviors

In the early and middle of the 1990s, the Chinese detergent industry was crowded with giant transnational corporations.

Proctor & Gamble Co. and Unilever N.V. were the two earliest transnational giants to begin investing in China, with the former entering this country in 1988 and the latter in 1986. The period 1992-1995 saw the large-scale entry of large transnational corporations into the Chinese detergent industry. While Proctor & Gamble Co. and Unilever N.V. continued their

[2] A considerable amount of information and statistics come from 1) the *China Light Industry Yearbook*, *Almanac of China's Economy*, *China Statistical Yearbook*, *China Electronic Industry Yearbook*, and *Almanac of China's Foreign Economic Relations and Trade* of the corresponding years, as well as reports from the Chinese press; 2) the author's 1996 and 2002 surveys, both of which included interviews with government administrative departments and enterprises and collections of market statistics, with the results of the 1996 study reflected in the "Investigation and Study of Foreign Investment in China's Detergent Industry" carried in the *Foreign Investment Study* issue No. 1, and the results of the2002 study reflected mainly in this article; and 3) statistics and information provided by websites of the enterprises covered in this article. Ms. Li Rui participated in the 2002 survey and the collection of some of the statistics concerned; she also took part in drafting part of this section.

large-scale investment in China, Henkel KGaA, which is one of the world's three detergent manufacturing giants, was also engaged in large-scale investment in China

Proctor & Gamble Co., Unilever N.V. and Henkel KGaA are all among the Fortune group of Top 500. In 1999, Unilever N.V. reported 28 billion US dollars worth of assets and 44 billion US dollars worth of total sales; Proctor & Gamble Co. registered 32.1 billion US dollars in total assets and 38.1 billion US dollars in total sales that include 18.4 billion US dollars garnered from overseas sales. By contrast, the 1999 total sales of China's detergent industry as a whole amounted to only 19.282 billion RMB, equivalent to 2.3 billion US dollars[3], and its total output value was one nineteenth that of Unilever N.V. and one seventeenth that of Proctor & Gamble Co.. This glaring difference led people to believe that under the onslaught of foreign investment, the Chinese detergent industry would suffer a serious concussion or even "complete collapse".

By the end of 1995, foreign-invested enterprises had seized an important position in the Chinese detergent industry. The leaders in this industry were basically joint ventures. Proctor & Gamble Co., Unilever N.V. and Henkel KGaA were major foreign investors, and they conducted strategic distribution of their outlets in China according to the characteristics of the production and sales of detergents.

By the end of 1995, in the Chinese detergent industry there were 15 large joint ventures. The 14 Chinese partners to these joint ventures (one Chinese enterprise owned partnership in two joint ventures) were among the 20 largest detergent factories in China. These 15 joint ventures accounted for 35-40% of China's total washing powder and soap output.

Proctor & Gamble Co. invested in five of these 15 joint ventures, Unilever N.V. invested in five of them and Henkel KGaA was a partner to three. The three giants had outlets in central south, east, northeast and southwest of China and their production and sales networks covered the entire country.

Of these joint ventures, only two were controlled by the Chinese partners. In most of the foreign-controlled joint ventures, the foreign partners own a high percentage of the shares – there were three of them in which foreign partners owned 80-98% of the shares, seven in which foreign partners owned 60-79% of the shares, and three in which foreign partners owned 50-59% of the shares. Generally speaking, the mainstay enterprises in the Chinese detergent industry were controlled by large transnational corporations. For information about these 15 joint ventures, see Table 7-1.

[3] The detergent industry mentioned here refers to the "soap and synthetic detergent industry" according to the Chinese way of industrial statistical classification. The statistics, which are provided by the National Bureau of Statistics of China, are derived from the "industrial enterprises as independent accounting units in the light industrial system of various regions" within the framework of the statistical work of the National Bureau of Statistics of China.

Table 7-1: Statistics about the joint investment in leading enterprises in the Chinese detergent industry (By the end of 1995)

Name of the joint venture	Chinese and foreign parts of the joint venture
Shanghai Lever Co., Ltd.	Shanghai Soap Plant Unilever Co., Ltd.
Shanghai Soap Co. Ltd.	Shanghai Soap Plant Unilever Co., Ltd.
Unilever China Limited.	Shanghai Synthetic Detergent plant Shanghai Daily Chemical Group Inc td. Unilever N.V..
Shanghai Whitecat Co Ltd.	Shanghai Synthetic Detergent plant Sun Hung Kai & Co., Ltd.
Procter & Gamble Panda Deterge	Beijing No.2 Daily Chemical plant Procter & Gamble Co.
Procter & Gamble Chengdu Ltd.	Chengdu Synthetic Detergent Plant Procter & Gamble Co.
Procter & Gamble Lonkey Guangzhou Ltd.	Lonkey Industrial Co Ltd. Guangzhou Procter & Gamble Co.
Tianjin Henkel Detergents and Clean Products Co., Ltd.	Tianjin Synthetic Detergent Plant Henkel KgaA
Procter & Gamble, Guangzhou Ltd.	Guangzhou Soap Plant Procter & Gamble Co.
Unilever, Zhangjiakou Ltd.	Zhangjiakou Synthetic Detergent Plant Unilever N.V.
Guilin Henkel Detergents and Clean Products Co., Ltd.	Guilin Synthetic Detergent Plant Henkel KgaA
Procter & Gamble Manufacturing Tianjin Co., Ltd.	Tianjin soap plant Procter & Gamble Co.
Siping Henkel Detergents and Clean Products Co., Ltd.	Siping Petrochemical Plant Henkel KgaA
Hefei Lever Co., Ltd.	Hefei Daily Chemical Plant Unilever Co., Ltd.
Hubei Power-Benckiser Detergent and Cleaning Products Company., Limited	Hubei Power 28 Group Co., Ltd. Benckiser Germany Co., Ltd.

Source: collected and arranged according to the author's survey in 2002.

At the time, the government, the Chinese partners, and observers were dissatisfied with the behaviors of these joint ventures on the Chinese market. For instance, the prices of these joint ventures' products with foreign brands were considerably higher than those of similar products by domestic enterprises; in advertising and publicity campaigns they often give prominence to foreign brands to neglect Chinese brands, so much so that for a time the market was overflowing with advertisement for foreign brands. A study of 35 large and medium-sized cities reveals that during the period 1997-1999, the advertisement spending of Proctor & Gamble Co., Unilever N.V. and Henkel KGaA on the products using their own brands were all along the highest among all the products in the Chinese detergent industry.

Therefore, they were actually using the sales revenues of the Chinese partners to promote their products. In one of the joint ventures, 95% of its 1995 sales revenue came from the products using the brands of the Chinese partner, but the enterprise spent a whopping 50 million RMB to advertise its foreign brand, and the advertisement cost for the Chinese brand accounted for a meager one twentieth of the total.

According to these joint ventures' expansion and development plans, the administrative department estimated that by 2000 the joint ventures would occupy a rather high share of the Chinese detergent market. For instance, they would have amounted to over 60% of the Chinese washing power market, in which the share of foreign brands would have been vastly increased. The administrative department also maintained that once these joint ventures had gained a firm foothold, they would acquire well-founded Chinese counterparts through joint ventures, cooperation, M&As, and further expand their shares of the Chinese market. For this reason, it was likely the Chinese detergent market would end up to a large degree under the control of the world's three leading detergent manufacturing transnational corporations, the prices would remain high, and these corporations would obtain high profits from China.

2. Market Competition and Changes in Enterprise Behaviors

Competition on the Chinese detergent market intensified towards the latter half of the 1990s, and the behaviors of foreign-invested enterprises changed accordingly. According to the estimates of professionals, in the mid-1990s, among the products of largely the same quality, foreign brands would carry price tags that were 50% higher than Chinese brands. The original market strategy of foreign investors was to replace ordinary washing powders with what was popular abroad, i.e., condensed washing powders containing a high percentage of high-activity substances. For this purposes they invested in massive advertisement campaigns. However, due to Chinese consuming level and habits, Chinese brands continued to lead the home detergent market, and joint ventures had to rely mainly on Chinese brands in production and sales. Chinese brands made up over two thirds of their sales, surpassing 90% in some cases.

After some of the leading Chinese detergent enterprises became joint ventures, little was done to promote the brands of the Chinese partners and as a result their influence on the market went down while vigorous efforts were made to promote foreign brands. However, due to their high prices, their shares of the Chinese market rose slowly. This situation offered opportunities for second-echelon domestic detergent enterprises to expand their production and sales. A number of listed companies, joint stock enterprises, and collective and private firms seized the opportunities and grew robustly. Table 7-2, the 1992 group of top ten washing powder producing enterprises is very much different from the 2000 top ten group. Among the four leading washing powder-producing enterprises in 2000, the first, third and fourth were China NaFine Group International Co., Ltd. (state-controlled listed company), Quanli Group Company (collective enterprise), and Zhejiang Nice Chemical Industry Co., Ltd. (joint-stock enterprise).

Transnational corporations showed no remarkable increases in both market share and ranking. Among the four leading washing powder producers, only one was a transnational corporation, Henkel KGaA, which ranked second. Among the top ten, Unilever N.V. and Proctor & Gamble Co. ranked sixth and eighth respectively. The results of market competition show that large transnational corporation failed to achieve obvious advantage on the Chinese market.

Table 7-2: Top ten washing powder producing enterprises (1992 and 2000)

Rank	The top 10 washing powder producing enterprises in 1992	The top 10 washing powder producing enterprises in 2000
1	Lonkey Industrial Co., Ltd. Guangzhou	China NaFine Group International Co., Ltd.
2	Tianjin Henkel Co., Ltd.	Henkel KGaA
3	Shanghai Synthetic Detergent Plant	Quanli Group Company
4	Xuzhou Synthetic Detergent Plant	Zhejiang Nice Chemical Industry Co., Ltd.
5	Nanjing Benzene Alkyl Plant	Whitecat Co., Ltd.
6	Beijing No.2 Daily Chemical Plant	Unilever Co., Ltd.
7	Chengdu Synthetic Detergent Plant	Hubei Power-Benckiser Detergent and Cleaning Co., Ltd.
8	Weifang Synthetic Detergent Plant	Procter & Gamble Co.
9	Jining Synthetic Detergent Plant	Hangzhou Wanli Co., Ltd.
10	Wuhan Petrochemical Plant	Kaifeng Maodun Group Co., Ltd.

Source: the author's two surveys in 1996 and 2002.

Although the composition of the top ten enterprises changed obviously, there was no obvious change in the degree of concentration of production. In 1992, the four leading enterprises accounted for 27.6% (C_N4=27.6) of the total washing powder output, while the top ten made up 52.9% (C_N10=52.9) of the total; in 2000, the four leading enterprises accounted for 37.5% (C_N4=37.5) of the total washing powder output, while the top ten made up 59.0% (C_N10=59.0) of the total. The monopoly of the detergent industry by a few transnational giants, a prospect feared by many people, did not appear.

Counted on an individual basis, among the industry's leading enterprises, the position of joint ventures was sliding. Counted according to factory acts, among the top ten washing powder manufacturing enterprises, there were four joint ventures, which accounted for 18.6% of the national output, in 1997; three joint ventures, accounting for 11.4% of the total output, in 1999; and four joint ventures, accounting for 15.2% of the total output, in 2000. The contribution of joint ventures that ranked among the top ten washing powder enterprises to the total washing powder output was 3.4% lower in 2000 than in 1997.

By the end of 2001 there were six wholly foreign-owned enterprises and five joint ventures among the washing powder enterprises in China. The six wholly foreign-owned enterprises were Procter & Gamble (Guangzhou) Ltd, Procter & Gamble (Chengdu) Ltd, Procter & Gamble Panda Deterge, Siping Henkel Detergents and Clean Products Co., Ltd, Hefei Lever Co., Ltd and Tianjin Henkel Co., Ltd; the five joint ventures: Unilever (China) Limited, Xuzhou Henkel Co., Ltd, Guilin Henkel Co., Ltd, Power 28 and Lonkey Industrial Co., Ltd. Guangzhou.

Because of the hot competition on the washing powder market, the business of some famous transnational corporations did not go as smoothly in China as they thought, and they were forced to continuously redirect their investment and readjust the shareholding structures of their enterprises. Unilever N.V., for instance, began producing soap when it arrived in China in 1986. In the mid-1990s, Hefei Lever Co., Ltd., Unilever (China) Limited and

Unilever (Zhangjiakou) Ltd. went into washing powder production one after another, but they found it hard to keep expanding their market shares, so much so that in 1998, Unilever N.V. withdrew all its shares from these companies, causing a drastic reduction in the washing powder output. In 1999, Unilever N.V. regrouped its four joint ventures in Shanghai into Shanghai into Unilever (China) Limited, which closed its production of washing powder in the same year. By 2000, only Hefei Lever Co., Ltd. was producing washing powder, and its ranking in the washing powder industry dropped from fifth in 1997 to sixth in 2000. In 1998 and 1999 Unilever N.V. failed to become one of the top ten washing powder producers in China. The washing powder produced by Hefei Lever Co., Ltd. comes under two brands, OMO and Fangcao, the latter being originally owned by the Hefei Daily Chemical Plant.

Table 7-3 features the rankings of foreign-invested enterprises and the brands of foreign partners in these enterprises in China's total washing powder output. It indicates that after a robust growth in the first half of the 1990s, the market shares of these foreign-invested enterprises went down considerably in the latter half of that decade. However, the market shares of the brands owned by the foreign partners rose slightly, and so did their percentage in the total output of joint ventures.

Table 7-3: Percentages of FDI in the output of the Chinese washing powder producing industry

Year	FIEs as a percentage of National Total Output	Joint Ventures Enterprises with dominating shares from foreign partners as a percentage of National Total Output	Foreign Brand Product by Joint Ventures Enterprises as a percentage of National Total Output	Foreign Brand Product as a percentage of Total Output by Joint Ventures Enterprises
1996	35%	25%	8%	22.86%
1997	35%	26%	7%	20.00%
1998	28%	19%	4%	14.29%
1999	22%	17%	7.73%	34.60%
2000	22%	19%	9.50%	42.81%

The rise in the percentage of foreign brands in the washing powder output certainly had something to do with the intensive advertisement campaigns of joint ventures as well as the relatively higher quality of their products. Another major fact behind this is that hot market competition forced these foreign brands to cut down their prices by large margins. Take Ariel, a brand under Proctor & Gamble Co., for instance. The price of 400-gram package of "Ariel Super-effective" (second generation) averaged 7.99 RMB in 1998, 6.14 RMB in 1999, and 5.16 RMB by the end of 2000. During that three-year span the price of this foreign brand dropped by 35%, whereas home-brand washing powder of the same quality reduced by less than 8%. By the end of 2001, the price of "Ariel Piaozi", Proctor & Gamble Co.'s so called the third-generation washing powder on sale, was cut to 4.98 RMB, which was more or less the same as the prices of Chinese brands.

Case studies of the detergent industry and many other industries indicate that even transnational corporations find it hard to monopolize the Chinese market and gain long-term profits from such monopoly. The domestic market of China has a huge capacity, domestic enterprises have strong abilities of seeking survival and development, and market competition always put those enterprises that provide high-quality, low-price products at an advantage. In industries similar to the detergent industry, the technology of the leading products on the Chinese markets is mature, technical barriers are not high, the Chinese enterprises are at an advantage with their low costs and domesticated brands, and therefore they are able to coexist and develop with transnational corporations in market competition. The idea that domestic enterprises will collapse against the colossal transnational corporations does not tally with the ground rules of the market economy and the practice of opening the Chinese market to FDI.

7-4: The International Experience: The Mammoth Scale of Transnational Corporations and the Competitive Global Market

There is nothing special about the behaviors of transnational giants in the Chinese detergent industry. The international experience over the last one or two decades shows that cases of large transnational corporations monopolizing a host country's market for a long time are few and far between. The following is an analysis by taking the transnational corporations in the world's petroleum industry as an example.

1. The Colossal Scales of the World's Major Petroleum Corporations

Giant petroleum transnational corporations originated in America. Senior Rockefeller established the Mobil Oil Company as early as the 1950s, which quickly became a monopolistic petroleum company in the United States and even the entire world. In 1913, Mobil Oil Company was forced to disband into 38 companies, three of which quickly grew in strength. They were Exxon, MOBIL and SOCAL. Standing shoulder to shoulder with the trio at the time were Gulf and Texaco.

In 1906, the Royal Dutch Petroleum (NL) and the Shell (UK) merged to become a giant petroleum corporation, the Royal Dutch/Shell Group. In 1908, Britain established BP with the government holding 51% of the shares.

Since then these seven large petroleum firms – five American companies, a British company and a British-Dutch company – have emerged as the main force of the global petroleum industry and determined the basic pattern of petroleum enterprises the world over.

After World War II, with the discovery and exploration of oil resources in the Middle East, these seven petroleum giants gained robust growth and basically monopolized the exploring, extraction, transportation, trade, processing and refining and sales of most of the petroleum resources in the world. In 1950, they occupied 98.3% of the world petroleum market. For this they were nicknamed "Petroleum Crocodiles" or "Seven Petroleum Sisters".

The positions of these petroleum giants on the global oil market went down considerably as a result of the struggle between petroleum exporting countries and transnational oil corporations in the 1970s and the 1980s. But they continued to occupy high shares of the global oil market. So far no other companies can replace them as the global leading oil companies. On the 1998 *Fortune* list of the global Top 500, these seven companies were among the top 20, with Shell, Exxon, and BP Amoco ranking third, sixth and eighth respectively.

These transnational oil giants remain as the global largest organizations, owning their own fleet, oil transmission pipelines, refineries and chain gas stations. Their immense worldwide interests run the gamut from petroleum to petrochemical industry and substitute energy sources from coal to nuclear energy. Their annual profits are gargantuan.

Despite their unrivalled strength, these transnational corporations are still seeking to expand their scales. As a result, cases of mergers between giant enterprises have been frequent in recent years, as they seek to further sharpen their competitiveness through mergers and acquisitions. Among the most typical cases are the merger of BP and Amoco and Exxon's acquisition of Mobil.

Exxon is the world's largest petroleum exploration company, while Mobil is the world's fourth largest petroleum company. They are united for the main purpose of making up for each other's deficiencies, coordinating their development efforts, and further consolidating their leading positions geographically in their business scale and market shares. Geographically, these two companies operate development and production in regions that are seldom overlapped, and the merger enables them to vastly expand the coverage of their prospecting and development efforts. In oil refining and sales, they are also mutually supplementary in various regions. Take lubricant oil for instance. Exxon is one of the world's largest lubricant base oil producers, while Mobil leads the world in lubricant sales, and because of this their union will help further strengthen their position on the world lubricant oil market.

The merger of BP and Amoco is also designed to seek superiority. This is indicative in four aspects: first, BP's international business strength and Amoco's business in the United States are mutually supplementary; second, BP's powerful petroleum business and Amoco's natural gas business are mutually supplementary and the participation of Amoco serves to better balance oil and gas production of the joint venture; third, BP's European sales network and Amoco's American sales network are mutually supplementary; and fourth, BP's low prospecting costs and Amoco's low development costs are mutually supplementary.

Table 7-4: Major M&As in the global petroleum and petrochemical industries 1998-1999

Pattern	Company	Home Country	Note
M&As	Exxon-Mobil	United States-United States	The largest merger in the world whether on the side of assets, business revenue, reserves of petroleum and gas or ability of refining. The transaction value amounted to US$ 77 billion.
	BP-Amoco	United Kingdom-United States	The third largest merger in the world on the side of both reserves of petroleum and gas and ability of refining. The transaction value amounted to US$ 48 billion.
	Total-Fina	France-Belgium	The sixth largest merge in the world on the side of assets. The transaction value amounted to US$ 13 billion.

Pattern	Company	Home Country	Note
	Baker Hughes/ Western Atlas	United States-United States	The third largest oil field server in USA. The transaction value amounted to US$ 5.5 billion.
	Nippon Oil-Mitsubishi Oil	Japan-Japan	Assets amounted to US $21.8 billion, sales revenue per year US$ 30.2 billion, gas station 147000.
Complete Consolidation	Hoechst AG.-Rhone Poulenc	Germany-France	R&D expenditures were reinforced after the merger.
	Monsanto Co.-AHP	United States-United States	The largest merger in life sciences industry with sales revenue amounted to US$ 23 billion and market value approximately US$ 100 billion.
	Royal Dutch/Shell Group-Mobil	United Kingdom/ Netherlands-United States	The downstream business in Australia was consolidated. Ability of refining amounted to 20 million tons per year.
Consolidation of regional business	Royal Dutch/Shell Group-Texaco	United Kingdom/ Netherlands-United Kingdom	A new joint venture enterprise named Equilon was created with business covering refining and marketing in both western and central western part of USA.
	Royal Dutch/Shell Group-Texaco-ARAMCO	United Kingdom/ Netherlands-United States-Saudi Arabia	A new joint venture enterprise named Moting was created with business covering refining and marketing in both western part of USA and Mexico Gulf.
	Royal Dutch/Shell Group-Chevron	United Kingdom/ Netherlands-United States	Engaging in reconnoitering and conveying petroleum in Caspian Sea
Strategic Alliance	Royal Dutch/Shell Group-Fina	United Kingdom/ Netherlands-Belgium	Royal Dutch/Shell Group exchanged gas station in Netherlands with Fina's downstream assets in Norway.
Replacement of Assets	Arco-Mobil	United States-United States	Arco exchanged part of its assets in California with Mobil's shares in Mexico Gulf.
	Royal Dutch/Shell Group - Statoil ASA	United Kingdom/ Netherlands-Norway	Exchange of shares.
Other Exchange of Shares			

Source: cleared up according to concerned data.

2. Competition Remains Tense on the Global Oil Market

The mammoth scales of transnational corporations and their trend for further expansion have given rise to concern that if the Chinese market is opened, the global petroleum giants will be too much for domestic enterprise to handle and that these giants are likely to monopolize the Chinese market. China National Petroleum Corporation and Sinopec Corp. were established for the main purpose of putting Chinese oil and petrochemical industries in a better position to compete with these transnational giants after China's accession to WTO.

The following analysis will prove that, despite the powerful strength of giant petroleum corporations, the petroleum industry remains as an industry with a high degree of globalization against the background of a global market. Large transnational petroleum corporations are still faced with a competitive market structure, and despite their tremendous scales, the largest oil companies' shares of the global oil market are still limited.

Table 7-5 indicates that in the early 2001, global top four leading petroleum companies combine to occupy a meager 19% of the global oil processing capacity, and the world's ten leading oil companies made up only 34.4% of the global crude oil processing capacity.

Table 7-5: Shares of the world's ten largest companies in the global crude oil processing capacity (January 2001)

Rank	Company	Ability of processing crude oil ten thousands barrel/day	Share in Global Total Output
	Global Total	8130.0	100.00
1	Exxon Mobil	543.2	6.68
2	Royal Dutch/Shell Group	399.9	4.92
3	BP	318.6	3.92
4	Sinopec Corp.	288.0	3.54
5	PDVSA	263.4	3.24
6	TotalFinaElf	250.3	3.08
7	ARAMCO	197.0	2.42
8	China National Petroleum Corporation	192.0	2.36
9	Petrobras	179.2	2.20
10	Pemex	166.2	2.04
	Total of above 10 companies	2797.8	34.4

Source: Calculated according to figures in Sun Yan (2001). "A Roundup of the World's Oil Refining Capacity in 2000", *International Petroleum economics*, No. 5.

Of the companies listed in the table, Sinopec Corp., PDVSA, China National Petroleum Corporation, Petrobras and Pemex are state-controlled oil companies. If large non-state transnational corporations are counted alone, their degree of market concentration is even lower. Table 7-6 features the percentages of the world's six largest non-state petroleum transnational corporations in the global oil processing capacity.

Table 7-6: Percentages of the world's six largest transnational corporations in the global oil processing capacity (January 2000)

Rank	Company	Ability of processing crude oil ten thousands barrel/day	Share in global total output %
	Global Total	8130.0	100.00
1	Exxon Mobil	543.2	6.68
2	Royal Dutch/Shell Group	399.9	4.92
3	BP	318.6	3.92
4	TotalFinaElf	250.3	3.08
5	Chevron	142.0	17.5
6	Texaco	130.7	16.0
	Total of above 6 companies	1784.7	21.95

Source: same as Table 7-5.

The global oil market is a competitive market, and so are the domestic markets of various major oil consuming countries. Even in the United States, a major parent country for the world's largest oil companies, oil production is subjected to a competitive market structure. The ten enterprises with the largest crude oil processing capacities each process an average of 1.015 million barrels a day. BP Amoco, the largest of them all, processes 1.9 million barrels a day, or 18.7% of the total of these ten companies. The Valero, the smallest of them all, processes 570,000 barrels a day, or 5.6% of the total of the ten companies. Obviously, none of them hold a monopolistic position on the market. See Table 7-7.

Table 7-7: Market shares of the ten leading oil companies in the United States (2000)

Rank	Company	Ability of processing crude oil ten thousands barrel/day	Share in total output of 10 companies %
1	BPAmoco	190	18.7
2	Exxon Mobil	182	17.9
3	Chevron	105	10.3
4	USX	94	9.3
5	Tosco	91	9.0
6	Equilon	83	8.2
7	Motiva	83	8.2
8	Sunoco	69	6.8
9	Citgo	61	6.0
10	Valero	57	5.6
	Total of above 10 companies	1015	100.0

Source: same as Table 7-5.

The foregoing analysis shows that mammoth enterprises do exist on the global market and are still expanding themselves. However, with the continuous deepening of economic globalization, market is growing as well, and the boundary of the market is pushing forward continuously too. Compared with the isolation of many countries in the early days, the coordination of an open home market with the global market has considerably reduced the possibility of a few giant enterprises controlling the market and making monopolistic profits. With its mammoth capacity, the domestic market of China is even more unlikely to be monopolized by a few transnational companies. For this reason, so long as China opens its market to many transnational corporations while cultivating an environment and formulating government policies for the benefit of domestic enterprises, it can build up competition-oriented market structures in the overwhelming majority of the industries.

Chapter 8

Two Controversial Issues in Utilizing FDI: Foreign-invested Enterprises' Contributions to Tax Revenue and Net Exports

Controversial issues have arisen from the utilization of FDI in China. Here are two major ones. First, do China's preferential policies for foreign-invested enterprise lead to unequal competition between foreign-invested and domestic enterprises, and are these policies major causes for the strong competitiveness of foreign-invested enterprises (FIEs)? Second, the performance of foreign-invested enterprises in net exports and their contributions to national total net exports. These two issues are analyzed in the first two sections of this chapter. The third section deals with the influence of foreign capital inflow on the changes in the Chinese foreign exchange administrative system from the perspective of a typical case resulting from the formation of a new system under the impetus of the open policy.

8-1: Preferential Tax Policy for Foreign-invested Enterprises: Scope and Degree

The contributions of foreign-invested enterprises to the tax revenue and their tax burden have all along been a rather controversial issue. One viewpoint holds that the tax rate for foreign-invested enterprises is far lower than that for domestic enterprises and this is a major reason why foreign investment flows into China and why domestic enterprises are at a disadvantage in competition with foreign-invested enterprises. The following is a discussion of this issue.

1. General Contributions of Foreign-invested Enterprises to Tax Revenue

Throughout the 1980s, the bulk of FDI in China, or, to be exact, 75% of the total volume of FDI, came from medium-sized and small investors from Hong Kong, Macao and Taiwan. Most of the foreign-invested enterprises were set up in coastal regions and engaged in processing trade. Even investors from the United States, Japan and EC countries and regions, too, were engaged in an explorative way in medium-sized and small projects of processing work. These enterprises got a low percentage of accessories from domestic enterprises, their processing work was handicapped by a low ratio of incremental value, and a considerable number of them did not have a long-term strategy for development in China. These enterprises were mainly attracted by the preferential tax treatment accorded to them in China. The degree of favorable treatment was a main factor in their choice of products, location of investment and partners.

Since the 1990s, considerable changes have taken place in the composition of foreign-invested enterprises. The number of large investment projects by large transnational corporations from the United States, Europe, Japan and the Republic of Korea is increasing quickly, and some of the foreign-invested enterprises that have long established themselves in China are also expanding their scales and upgrading their products and technology, and investing and developing in China has become their long-term strategies. When choosing products, investment location and partners, they set their eyes on long-term development. The preferential tax policy remains an important factor, but it is no longer the only or decisive factor.

China's foreign-related tax revenues, predicated on tax revenues from foreign-invested enterprises, have been on the rise on an annual basis since the 1990s. In 2001, it reached 288.278 billion RMB, or 19.01% of national total tax revenue from industry and commerce as opposed to 4.25% in 1992. See Table 8-1.

Table 8-1: Total tax revenue from foreign-invested enterprises[1]

(Unit: RMB 100 million)

Year	National Total Tax Revenues from Industry and Commerce	Total Tax Revenues from Foreign-invested Enterprises	Foreign-related Tax Revenues' share (%)
1990	2344.96	52.10	2.22
1991	2563.99	81.26	3.17
1992	2876.10	122.26	4.25
1993	3970.52	226.56	5.71
1994	4728.74	402.64	8.51
1995	5515.51	604.46	10.96
1996	6436.02	764.06	11.87
1997	7548.00	993.00	13.16
1998	8551.74	1203.00	14.38
1999	10311.89	1648.86	15.99
2000	12665.00	2217.00	17.50
2001	15165.28	2882.72	19.01

Source: Department of Foreign Investment of the Ministry of Foreign Trade and Economic Cooperation (2002), *Statistics On FDI In China 2001*, not for sale. Data of 2001 were provided by Department of Foreign Investment of the Ministry of Foreign Trade and Economic Cooperation.

Of the total tax revenue, foreign-invested enterprises' contributions to the value-added tax revenue are the greatest, accounting for 25.91% of national total value-added tax revenue. Their contributions to the enterprise income tax revenue come second, making up 19.48% of

[1] Excluding customs duties and land fees.

national total. Their contributions to the personal income tax revenue come third, accounting for 16.16% of national total. See Table 8-2.

Table 8-2: Composition of tax revenue from foreign-invested enterprises (2001)

Taxes	National Total	Tax Revenues from Foreign-invested Enterprises	Share %
Value-added Tax	7091	1837	25.91
Consumption tax	946	103	10.89
Operation Tax	2085	223	10.70
Corporate Income Tax	2634	513	19.48
Personal Income Tax	996	161	16.16
Other	1413	46	3.26
Total Tax Revenues	15165	2883	19.01

Source: the same as Table 8-1.

2. A Comparison between the Contributions of Foreign-invested Enterprises to Value-Added Industrial Outputs and to Value-Added Tax

In 2000 the value-added tax payable by foreign-invested industrial enterprises totaled 73.888 billion RMB, 20.05% of the total value-added tax payable by industry as a whole. The amounts due by foreign-invested enterprises are the highest in those industries where these enterprises hold a high percentage.

For the Chinese industry as a whole, or for most of the industrial branches, the contributions of foreign-invested enterprises to the value-added tax are only marginally lower than their contributions to value-added industrial outputs. Take the industry as a whole, in 2000 these enterprises accounted for 23.98% of total value-added industrial outputs, and 20.05% of total value-added tax payable. See Table 8-3. In the electronic and telecommunications and food manufacturing industries, foreign-invested enterprises accounted for more than half of the total value-added tax payable. These enterprises accounted for more than 40% of value-added tax payable in food manufacturing, furniture manufacturing, leather, furs, down and related products, chemical fibers, garments and other fiber products industries. There are eight industries in which foreign-invested enterprises accounted for over 30% of value-added tax payable. For a look at the industries in which foreign-invested enterprises accounted for a high portion of the value-added tax payable, see Table 8-4. For detailed statistics concerning value-added tax payable by foreign-invested enterprises and their ratios to total value-added tax payable by all the industries, see Annex Table 8-1 of this chapter.

Table 8-3: Ratios of foreign-invested enterprises to value-added industrial outputs and value-added tax (2000)

	Total Industry	FIEs	Share
Value-added Industrial Outputs	25394.80	6090.35	23.98
Value-added Tax Payable	3685.20	738.88	20.05

Source: calculated according to Table 13-5 and Table 13-13 in National Bureau of Statistics of China (2002). *China Statistical Yearbook 2001* (Beijing: China Statistics Press).

Table 8-4: Industries in which foreign-invested enterprises accounted for a high percentage of total value-added tax (2000)

Industry	FIEs as a percentage in national total value-added tax payable	FIEs as a percentage in national total value-added industrial outputs %
National Total	20.05	23.98
Electronic and Telecommunications	57.49	65.39
Food Manufacturing	50.11	4.19
Furniture Manufacturing	46.00	43.88
Leather, Furs, Down and Related Products	45.38	54.62
Chemical Fibers	41.91	39.28
Garments and Other Fiber Products	40.88	48.83
Plastic Products	39.93	44.32
Transportation Equipment Manufacturing	38.74	30.84
Instruments, Meters, Cultural and Official Machinery	37.76	49.39
Timber Processing, Bamboo, Cane, Palm Fiber and Straw Products	35.57	27.99
Cultural, Educational and Sports Articles	35.25	59.46
Rubber Products	33.67	35.58
Beverage Manufacturing	31.40	27.86
Metal Products	31.36	34.82

Source: calculated according to Table 13-5 and Table 13-13 in National Bureau of Statistics of China (2002), *China Statistical Yearbook 2001* (Beijing: China Statistics Press).

According to a comparative study on the tax burdens of 100 foreign-invested and domestic enterprises in 21 industries on the basis of statistics for four consecutive years (Yang Zhigang etc., 2000), the differences between foreign-invested and domestic enterprises are not big in terms of burdens of value-added tax and indirect tax. With regard to value-added tax, the burdens for foreign-invested enterprises are slightly higher than that for domestic enterprises; as to indirect tax, domestic enterprises have heavier burdens than their foreign-invested counterparts. Generally speaking, no conclusive evidence is available that domestic enterprises have obviously higher value-added tax and indirect tax burdens than foreign-invested enterprises. See Tables 8-5 and 8-6.

Table 8-5: A comparison of value-added tax burdens between domestic and foreign-invested enterprises[2] (Value-added tax/sales revenue)

Industry	Basic Industry	Materials Manufac-turing	Mining and Quarry-ing	Chemical	Food/ Beverage	Textile and Gar-ment	Equip-ment Manufac-turing	Average *
1Domestic Enterprises	7.79	5.63	5.47	5.35	4.47	3.87	2.68	5.04
2 Foreign-invested Enterprises	10.92	6.74	5.15	5.1	4.38	4.05	1.58	5.42
1 2	-3.13	-1.11	0.32	0.24	0.09	-0.18	1.10	-0.40

Source: Yang Zhigang et al (2000). "A Pragmatic Study on the Value-added Tax and Income Tax Burdens of Enterprises", *Economic Research Journal,* No.12. Data with "*" were calculated by the author according to original figures in text.

Table 8-6: A comparison of indirect tax burdens between domestic and foreign-invested enterprises (Indirect tax/sales revenue)

Industry	Basic Industry	Materials Manufac-turing	Mining and Quar-rying	Chemical	Food/ Beverage	Textile and Gar-ment	Equip-ment Manufac-turing	Average *
1 Domestic Enterprises	8.44	6.44	8.23	8.25	9.52	4.60	3.26	6.68
2 Foreign-invested Enterprises	10.96	5.41	7.05	7.37	5.02	4.25	5.73	5.54
1 2	-2.52	1.03	1.18	0.88	4.50	0.35	-2.47	0.14

Source: same as Table 8-5.

The year 2001 marked a turning point in the contributions of foreign-invested enterprises to national tax revenue, as their ratio to national total value-added tax revenue outstripping their ratio to national total value-added industrial outputs. In that year, national value-added industrial outputs totaled 2695 billion RMB, 662.2 billion RMB or 24.57% of which were contributed by foreign-invested enterprises; national total industrial value-added tax was 709.1 billion RMB, 183.7 billion RMB or 25.91% of which was contributed by foreign-invested enterprises, or 1.34 percentage points higher than their contributions to national total value-added industrial outputs.[3]

3. Foreign-invested Enterprises' Contribution to Income Tax

Income tax reduction and exemption are one of the most preferential policies China has accorded to foreign-invested enterprises. Many studies indicate that the income tax burden is

[2] The tax burdens in this book refer to the actual tax rates – note from the original text.

[3] The statistics were provided by the Department of Foreign Investment of the Ministry of Foreign Trade and Economic Cooperation.

much lighter on foreign-invested enterprises than on domestic enterprises. The aforementioned study of Yang Zhigang and others exactly includes a comparison of the income tax burdens on foreign-invested and domestic enterprises. Researches of seven major business trades show that domestic enterprises are paying higher income tax than their foreign-invested counterparts, with the actual income tax rate for domestic enterprises being 5.96 times more than that for foreign-invested enterprises. Our studies have also revealed the fact that this gap is widening with each passing year. Domestic enterprises' income tax burden was 8.65% higher than that of foreign-invested enterprises' in 1996, 17.17% in 1997, 18.75% in 1998, and as high as 31.71% in 1999. See Table 8-7.

Table 8-7: A comparison of the income tax burdens between domestic and foreign-invested enterprises

Industry		**Basic Industry**	**Materials Manufacturing**	**Mining and Quarrying**	**Chemical**	**Food/ Beverage**	**Textile and Garment**	**Equipment Manufacturing**	**Average**
Domestic Enterprises	Direct Tax Profits	15.84	23.56	9.78	32.25	16.54	39.95	25.16	23.30
FIEs	Direct Tax Profits	0	4.13	0	7.47	7.76	7.38	5.99	4.68
Times (Domestic Enterprises / FIEs)									4.96 *

Source: simplified from Yang Zhigang et al (2000). "A Pragmatic Study on the Value-added Tax and Income Tax Burdens of Enterprises", *Economic Research Journal*, No.12. Data with "*" were calculated by the author according to original figures in text.

However, national statistics indicate that foreign-invested enterprises' contributions to the nation's income tax revenue are on the rise, and the increases in the last few years are particularly impressive. The portion of foreign-invested enterprises in the total volume of enterprise income tax rose from less than 1% in 1992 to 21.58% in 1999. However, in comparison with the fact that these enterprises accounted for 29% of the national total industrial profits of the same year, their percentage in the income tax revenue is too low – evidently they are still enjoying remarkable preferential treatment in income tax. See Table 8-7.

Table 8-8: Composition of enterprise income tax during the period 1992-1999 (%)

Year	State-Owned Enterprises	Collective-Owned Enterprises	Private Enterprises	Foreign Investment Enterprises
1992	—	14.25	0.13	0.67
1993	—	15.08	0.21	4.13
1994	76.3	18.32	0.35	6.80
1995	—	20.55	0.73	9.10
1996	68.09	22.64	1.39	12.86
1997	62.88	22.10	1.81	15.36
1998	54.75	24.78	2.72	21.31
1999	54.35	17.14	3.31	21.58

Sources: State Administration of Taxation of China (1999-2000). *Tax Year Book of China* (Beijing: China Taxation Press).

All the analyses made in the foregoing from different perspectives have attested to the fact that foreign-invested enterprises are enjoying preferential treatment in taxation. Such preferential treatment, however, is only marginal, and it is diminishing on a yearly basis. Foreign-invested enterprises have begun to make more contributions to the value-added tax than to their own value-added industrial outputs.

8-2: Net Exports by Foreign-invested Enterprises: Contributions and Trends

1. Exports and Net Exports by Foreign-invested Enterprises

Foreign-invested enterprises have large exports, but their imports are large too. Therefore, their contributions to China's net exports are smaller than their contributions to total exports. As a matter of fact, their contributions to the net exports of China had all along been negative before 1997, which gave rise to doubts about the wisdom of utilizing FDI in China. The net exports by foreign-invested enterprises began to be positive from 1997. Though the amounts were not big, they have been growing in a sustained way for six years. In 2002 the figure showed an impressive growth from 2001. See Table 8-9.

Table 8-9: Net exports by foreign-invested enterprises

(Unit: US $ 100 million)

Year	Imports by FIEs	Exports by FIEs	Net Exports by FIEs
1991	169.08	120.47	-48.61
1992	263.87	173.60	-90.27
1993	418.33	252.37	-165.96
1994	529.34	347.13	-182.21
1995	629.43	468.76	-160.67
1996	756.04	615.06	-140.98
1997	777.20	749.00	28.20
1998	767.17	809.62	42.45
1999	858.84	886.28	27.44
2000	1172.23	1194.41	22.18
2001	1258.63	1332.35	73.72
2002	1602.72	1699.36	96.64

Source: calculated according to Table 4-1 of this book.

2. Reasons for the Growth of Net Exports by Foreign-invested Enterprises

The advent and growth of net exports by foreign-invested enterprises are under the influence of three major factors: equipment and materials imported as investment by foreign-invested enterprises, the rate of domestic value-added of the export commodities of the foreign-invested enterprises and the ratio of exports by these enterprises to national total exports. The former two factors determine the amount of imports by the foreign-invested enterprises, and the third factor determines the amount of their exports.

1) Imports of Equipment by Foreign-invested Enterprises

In the early and middle 1990s, FDI increased quickly in China. Generally speaking, no input and output nor export take place the year a foreign investor makes his investment; but instead large amounts of equipment and materials are imported, thereby bringing a negative impact on the net exports by the foreign-invested enterprise. Since 1997, realized FDI has maintained a large scale in China but foreign-invested enterprises' imports of equipment have decreased somewhat, which is a major reason why the net exports by foreign-invested enterprises have turned positive since 1997. See Table 8-10. The phenomenon that foreign investment maintains a large scale while the imports by foreign-invested enterprises are on a decline may be attributed to increased purchases of equipment and materials in China by foreign-invested enterprises and increased foreign investment in non-manufacturing industries.

Table 8-10: Equipment and materials imported by foreign-invested enterprises as part of their investment

(Unit: US$ 100 million)

Year	Imports by FIEs	Equipment and materials imported by FIEs as investment	Investment Equipment and Materials as a percentage of Imports by FIEs (%)
1991	123.02	7.68	4.5
1992	263.87	80.2	30.4
1993	418.33	166.7	40.0
1994	529.34	202.8	38.3
1995	629.43	187.4	29.8
1996	756.04	248.5	32.9
1997	777.20	179.3	23.1
1998	767.17	145.0	18.9
1999	858.84	110.7	12.9
2000	1172.23	130.9	11.2
2001	1258.63	145.2	11.5
2002	1602.72	171.4	10.7

Source: Customs General Administration People's Republic of China (1993-2000). *Customs Statistical Almanac of the People's Republic of China* (Beijing: *Customs Statistics* Editorial Department of Customs General Administration People's Republic of China). The statistics about 2001 were provided by Customs General Administration People's Republic of China.

2) Increase of the Rate of Local Content of Exports by Foreign-Invested Enterprises

In the early days, the commodities exported by foreign-invested enterprises were marked by a low value-added rate, indicating that these export commodities had a high content of imports. The main reasons behind this situation are, first, the low ability of domestic enterprise to provide accessories for foreign-invested enterprises, and second, few of foreign-invested enterprises' overseas accessory factories had entered China during those days. In recent years, domestic enterprises have steadily increased their ability to provide accessories for foreign-invested enterprises, more and more overseas accessory factories have arrived to invest, and as a result foreign-invested enterprises' domestic value-added rate has shown an obvious increase.

Take processing trade for instance. Foreign-invested enterprises' value-added rate in this field increased from 1.13 in 1995 to 1.43 in 2002, and the figure for 2001 was 1.52. This indicates remarkable growth of export commodities of foreign-invested enterprises in a short span of seven years. See Table 8-11.

Table 8-11: Imports and exports by foreign-invested enterprises in processing trade

Year	Imports by FIEs in processing trade (US$ 100 million)	Exports by FIEs in processing trade (US$ 100 million)	The rate of local content of processing trade by FIEs
1995	370.7	420.7	1.13
1996	415.1	530.9	1.28
1997	476.9	638.5	1.34
1998	483.3	691.8	1.43
1999	527.6	745.6	1.41
2000	687.4	972.3	1.41
2001	703.0	1066.0	1.52
2002	941.5	1346.1	1.43

Sources: Customs General Administration People's Republic of China (1993-2000). *Customs Statistical Almanac of the People's Republic of China* (Beijing: *Customs Statistics* Editorial Department of Customs General Administration People's Republic of China). The statistics about 2001 were provided by the Ministry of Foreign Trade and Economic Cooperation.

3) Ratio of Exports by Foreign-invested Enterprises to their Outputs

The ratio of the exports by a foreign-invested enterprise to its outputs has a marked impact on its net exports. When other conditions remain unchanged, the higher the ratio of exports, the bigger the enterprise's contribution to net exports. In the latter half of the 1990s, foreign-invested enterprises showed a strong tendency towards exports, and two fifths of their total outputs was exported. See Table 8-12.

Table 8-12: Ratio of exports by foreign-invested enterprises to their outputs

Year	Gross Industrial Output Value (RMB 100 million)	Exports (Converted to RMB 100 million)	Exports as a percentage of Gross Industrial Output Value %
1996	12117	5105.33	42.13
1997	14399	6216.70	43.17
1998	17750	6719.68	37.86
1999	20078	7356.29	36.64
2000	23464	9913.52	42.25
2001	26524	11058.51	41.69

Source: calculated according to related data in National Bureau of Statistics of China (1997-2002). *China Statistics Yearbook* (Beijing, China Statistics Press). Data of 2002 were provided by National Bureau of Statistics of China. The exchange rate between RMB and US$ was 8.3:1.

3. Reflective Comparative Advantage of Exports by Foreign-invested Enterprises: A Comprehensive Index

In the following let us analyze the reflective comparative advantage (RCA) of the exports by foreign-invested enterprises.

$$(\text{RCA}) = \frac{\text{Exports by foreign - invested enterprises/National total exports}}{\text{Imports by foreign - invested enterprises/National total imports}}$$

RCA is an index used to compare the relative advantage of a certain commodity in a certain aggregate. Here, it is used to indicate the relative positions of the exports and imports by foreign-invested enterprises in national total exports and import. The calculation methodology is as follows:

The connotation of this index is to compare the ratio of exports by foreign-invested enterprises to national total exports with the ratio of imports by these enterprises to national total imports, and is therefore more meaningful than merely calculating the net exports by these enterprises. If RCA>1, which shows the exports by foreign-invested enterprises have a higher ratio to national total exports than their imports to national total imports, this indicates that these enterprises are not only contributing to net exports but also making more contributions in this regard than domestic enterprises. On the contrary, if RCA<1, that is, exports by foreign-invested enterprises have a lower ratio to national total exports than their imports to national total imports, this indicates that although these enterprises have contributed to net exports, such contributions are smaller than those made by domestic enterprises.

The changes in the RCA of foreign-invested enterprises featured in Table 8-13 show that: 1) the RCA of these enterprises was always smaller than 1, meaning that they always had a higher ratio to national total imports than to national total exports and, as a result, they contributed less to national net exports than their domestic counterparts; and 2) in the last few years of the 1990s, the RCA of these enterprises rose considerably to 0.96 in 2001 as compared with 0.63 in 1991, meaning that their ratio to national total exports was nearly as high as their ratio to national total imports and that they were making more or less the same contributions to national net exports as domestic enterprises. A foreseeable trend is that the RCA of foreign-invested enterprises will soon exceed 1, indicating that they will contribute more to China's net exports than domestic enterprises.

Table 8-13: RCA of exports by foreign-invested enterprises

Year	Exports by FIEs as a percentage of National Total Exports(%) (A)	Imports by FIEs as a percentage of National Total Imports(%)(B)	A/B (RCA)
1991	16.75	26.51	0.63
1992	20.44	32.74	0.62
1993	27.51	40.24	0.60
1994	28.69	45.78	0.63
1995	31.51	47.66	0.66
1996	40.71	54.45	0.75
1997	41.00	54.59	0.75
1998	44.06	54.73	0.81
1999	45.47	51.83	0.88
2000	47.93	52.10	0.92
2001	50.10	51.67	0.96
2002	52.20	54.29	0.96

Source: calculated according to Table 4-1 of this book.

8-3: ATTRACTING FDI AND THE PROGRESSIVE ECONOMIC REFORM OF CHINA

1. The Policy to Attract Foreign Investment and the Progressive Economic Reform

Apart from preferential tax policies, China has also carried out a series of other favorable or convenient policies. In the short run, because these policies applied only to foreign-invested enterprises, they caused inequity between domestic and foreign-invested enterprises. In the intermediary and long run, however, quite a lot of these policies will have promoted the progressive reform in China.

In the course of the progressive reform in China, the "new system elements" as increments consisting mainly of two parts: the non-state sector with rural industry as the mainstay, and the foreign-invested sector. Both sectors are playing an important role in increasing supplies and in promoting the formation of a competitive market structure, a market-oriented legal framework, a new macroeconomic management system, a new foreign trade system and a new foreign exchange administrative system.

The FDI inflow has promoted integrating the legal system of China with the market economy. After the adoption of the policy of reform and opening up to the outside world in the late 1970s, the earliest package of legislation made in an attempt to dovetail the Chinese legislation with the legal framework of the market economic were directly related to FDI. *Law of the People's Republic of China on Chinese-foreign Equity Joint Ventures* endorsed on July 1, 1979 at the 2nd Session of the 5th National People's Congress was the first legal document passed by the NPC after the open policy was adopted, and this was followed by a series of laws and regulations concerning foreign-invested enterprises that were promulgated earlier than new legislation governing domestic enterprises. These documents covered a wide range of fields – the establishment of enterprises, the use of land and labor force, imports and exports, accounting, taxation, investment, etc. A considerable part of these laws concerning the utilization of foreign capital has later become the basis for legislation that applies to both domestic and foreign-invested enterprises.

The investment of transnational corporations has participated and expedited the course of diversification of the Chinese property ownership structure. The growing weight of foreign-invested enterprises in the Chinese economy has promoted the formation of diverse economic sectors. By taking part in the transformation of state-owned enterprises through joint ventures and cooperative projects, foreign investment has become a major source of funds for diversifying the property ownership structure of state-owned enterprises. With their financial input, transnational corporations are transferring their concepts, technology, managerial expertise, and marketing networks to the recipients, catalyzing fundamental changes in the behaviors of state-owned enterprises. Large numbers of case studies show that without the entry of foreign investment changes in the behaviors of state-owned enterprises would be out of the question even if large sums of domestic funds were earmarked.

The FDI inflow has caused competition in some monopolistic industries. For a considerably long period of time it was difficult to form competitive market structures in some industries where huge investment scale and high technological level and entry barriers discouraged the entry of non-state enterprises. These included industries manufacturing cars, heavy-duty equipment and telecommunications equipment, where it was by relying to a large degree on the entry of foreign capital that the monopoly of a few state-owned enterprises was broken. The formation of competitive market structures has provided a great impetus for both foreign-invested and domestic enterprises to constantly improve their efficiency.

The growing weight of foreign-invested enterprises has also prompted the government to use administrative methods that accord with the laws of the market economy. Massive FDI inflow is a major motive force behind the transition of the entire economic system. For instance, the increased domestic supply results from massive FDI inflow and bars government price control and therefore promotes gradual liberalization of prices.

FDI inflow is also promoting the formation of a market-oriented macroeconomic administrative system in China. The advent of large sums of FDI has prompted the government's macroeconomic control and regulation to go from an introvert mode to an extrovert mode. Because this extrovert mode of macroeconomic administration calls for a sound domestic financial market and better monetary and financial policies, the central government feels compelled to quicken the pace of improving its macroeconomic control and regulation system. The activity of large numbers of foreign-invested enterprises on the Chinese market has also weakened direct government intervention in enterprises' managerial behaviors and quickened the change of the government's economic management philosophy. The massive FDI inflow and the massive imports and exports by foreign-invested enterprises have set new requirements for China's foreign trade system, exchange rate system and foreign exchange administrative system, promoted the continuous relaxation of control on foreign trade and the formation of a new exchange rate system and a new foreign exchange administrative system. The following is a description of the role of Chinese policies for the preferential treatment and convenience of foreign investment in promoting economic restructuring in China, with the changing Chinese foreign exchange administrative system as a case in point.

2. Case Study: Utilization of FDI and the Reform of Foreign Exchange Administrative System

During the period from the early 1950s to the eve of reform in 1979, China's foreign exchange administrative system was one of centralized administration by the state and unified operation by the Bank of China. In other words it was a system of unified state control over income and expenditure and fixed exchange rates. The adoption of the policy of reform and opening up to the outside world in 1979 unveiled the gradual reform of this system with a view to facilitate FDI inflow and the operations of foreign-invested enterprises in China. The entry of foreign investment set new requirements for the old Chinese foreign exchange administrative system and catalyzed the relaxation of foreign exchange control in this country.

When China commenced attracting FDI towards the end of the 1970s, the law required that foreign-invested enterprises balance their foreign exchange revenues and expenditures on their own. Under normal conditions the state would not provide these enterprises with foreign exchange.

However, the foreign-invested enterprises regarded this strict control as a serious problem that got way in their China business and on many occasions they expressed their desire to relax such control. Under the pressure the Chinese government formulated some foreign exchange administrative methods in favor of foreign-invested enterprises. Among other things, foreign-invested enterprises were allowed to freely receive foreign exchange incomes and pay foreign exchange expenses; they might open foreign exchange accounts at the Bank of China or any bank in Hong Kong, Macao or a foreign country for their foreign exchange stocks, loans and incomes from export; foreign investors had the freedom to remit their portion of tax-paid profit to foreign countries. As a result of these stipulations the nation's foreign exchange administration of foreign-invested enterprises was greatly different from the domestic foreign exchange administrative system where control over revenue and expenditure were centralized. However, generally speaking, during the period from the late 1970s to the early 1980s utilization of FDI was not a main issue because the amount involved was rather small, nor had the measures to relax control over foreign-invested enterprises had any overall impact on the reform of the entire foreign exchange administrative system.

By the mid-1980s, the accumulated FDI inflow had reached a sizeable scale, the number of foreign-invested enterprises was rising continuously, and the old foreign exchange administrative system was falling increasingly short of the demand. Foreign-invested enterprises' imbalance in foreign exchange revenue and expenditure was a major cause behind the sharpening contradiction. Especially in 1984 and 1985, when foreign-invested enterprises developed rapidly, imbalance between foreign exchange revenue and expenditure, with revenue not enough to cover expenditures, emerged as an outstanding problem. The government had tried to redress this problem without changing the old foreign exchange administrative framework. However, runaway inflation and an explosion in imports in China in and around 1985 resulted in acute shortages in foreign exchange and a serious drain of the state's foreign exchange reserve. As a result the government's foreign exchange supplying ability was held back, affecting foreign investors' confidence in investing in China and the normal operation of foreign-invested enterprises in China. Under these circumstances, reforming the foreign exchange administrative system and adapting it to the new situation in the utilization of FDI began to become the focus of attention in the reform of the foreign exchange administrative system. It was in this situation that foreign exchange regulation centers were established.

In November 1985, the nation's first foreign exchange regulation center was set up in Shenzhen. Two others were established in Shanghai and Beijing in 1986 and 1988 respectively. By the end of 1989, about 90 such centers had emerged across the country. A main purpose for establishing these centers was to provide foreign-invested enterprises with a place to trade in foreign exchange and regulate foreign exchange surpluses and shortages. In the beginning only foreign-invested enterprises were allowed to coordinate the supply of foreign exchange among them on the foreign exchange regulation market; later, green light was given to coordination of foreign exchange between foreign-invested and domestic enterprises. In the beginning the state imposed certain limitations on the regulatory prices of foreign exchange; after 1988, however, the limitations were basically lifted. The establishment of foreign exchange regulation centers marked the beginning of the transition of the Chinese foreign exchange administrative system from centralized state control of foreign exchange revenue and expenditure to foreign exchange trading on the market; it weakened to a great degree the negative influence of foreign exchange control and the overrating of Renminbi on the utilization of FDI, and was therefore a major step of great significance for the reform of the Chinese foreign exchange administrative system.

The prices on the foreign exchange regulation market are by and large the result of a process of free bid. However, whether the prices for foreign exchange regulation can be approximated to "market-oriented exchange rates" is determined not only by whether the prices can be freely decided but also by the trade volume. The larger the trade volume is, the closer the approximation becomes. After the establishment of foreign-exchange regulation centers, rapid growths were achieved in both the amount of foreign exchange involved and their ratio to total exports. By the eve of the initiation of a new foreign exchange administrative system in 1994, foreign exchange regulated amounted to one quarter of exports. Table 8-14 features the volumes of foreign exchange regulated and their ratios to exports.

Table 8-14: Market regulated foreign exchange and their ratios to exports

Year	Regulated Foreign Exchange (US$ 100 million)	Exports (US$ 100 million)	Regulated Foreign Exchange as a percentage of Exports %
1987	47	394.4	11.9
1988	62	475.2	13.0
1989	86	525.4	16.4
1990	125	620.9	20.1
1991	180	718.4	25.1
1992	250	849.4	29.4
1993	228	917.4	24.9

Source: data about regulated foreign exchange in 1987-1992 were quoted from Yang Yuchuan and Duan Wenbin (ed.)(1994) *Foreign Exchange Market and Business of Foreign Exchange* (Beijing: Economic and Management Publishing House). Data of 1993 were provided by State Administration of Foreign Exchange. Figures about exports in each year were quoted from Table 4-1 of this book.

A considerable part of the exports of China are exports in processing trade. As a result the rate of net foreign exchange revenue is rather low. If calculated according to net foreign exchange revenue from exports, foreign exchange regulated would have a much higher ratio to net foreign exchange revenue from exports. According to authorities of the Bank of China, in 1992 the volume of business on the foreign exchange regulation market amounted to one half of national total volume of foreign exchange used.[4] This high ratio is an ample reason why people were approximating the prices on the foreign exchange regulation market as the "market-oriented" exchange rates.

The Chinese foreign exchange administrative system underwent a major reform beginning from January 1, 1994, whereby a controlled floating exchange rate system on the basis of the market, and a unified and standardized foreign exchange market were established. The main contents of the reform were: different exchange rates were replaced by a unified, controlled floating exchange rate system; a system of settling accounts and conducting sales in foreign exchange was instituted; a inter-bank foreign exchange trading market was established; and compulsory plan for foreign exchange revenue and expenditure were abolished, so that economic and legal measures could be adopted to put foreign exchange and international revenue and expenditure under macroeconomic regulation and control. The foreign exchange regulation market and the regulatory exchange rates offered major mechanisms and references for the establishment of a new foreign exchange administrative system in China.

4 Zhou Xiaochuan: "Renminbi on Its Way to Convertibility", an essay submitted in 1994 to the High-level International Symposium on China's Strategy for Foreign Trade and Economic Cooperation in the 1990s.

ANNEX TABLE 8-1 FIES AS A PERCENTAGE OF NATIONAL TOTAL VALUE-ADDED TAX PAYABLE IN 2000

Unit: RMB 100 Million

Industry	Value-added Tax Payable of Total Industry	Value-added Tax Payable by FIEs	FIEs' share in Value-added Tax Payable of Total Industry
National Total	3685.20	738.88	20.05
Electronic and Telecommunication	179.69	103.30	57.49
Food Manufacturing	64.34	32.24	50.11
Furniture Manufacturing	9.89	4.55	46.00
Leather, Furs, Down and Related Products	26.40	11.98	45.38
Chemical Fibers	42.16	17.67	41.91
Garments and Other Fiber Products	55.11	22.53	40.88
Plastic Products	50.46	20.15	39.93
Transportation Equipment Manufacturing	202.50	78.45	38.74
Instruments, Meters, Cultural and Official Machinery	23.89	9.02	37.76
Timber Processing, Bamboo, Cane, Palm Fiber and Straw Products	20.83	7.41	35.57
Cultural, Educational and Sports Article	13.05	4.60	35.25
Rubber Products	26.97	9.08	33.67
Beverage Manufacturing	108.06	33.93	31.40
Metal Products	68.50	21.48	31.36
Papermaking and Paper Products	62.91	18.51	29.42
Printing and Record Pressing	31.02	9.23	29.75
Electric Equipment and Machinery	156.39	45.73	29.24
Medical and Pharmaceutical Products	115.43	30.13	26.10
Raw Chemical Materials and Chemical Products	213.78	54.02	25.27
Ordinary Machinery Manufacturing	122.96	26.07	21.20
Food Processing	70.25	14.52	20.67
Nonmetal Mineral Products	172.58	28.66	16.60
Textile Industry	158.41	25.85	16.32
Special Purpose Equipment Manufacturing	73.57	10.88	14.79
Electric Power, Steam and Hot Water Production and Supply	532.19	61.99	11.65
Gas Production and Supply	6.82	0.52	7.62
Smelting and Pressing of Nonferrous Metals	82.31	5.27	6.40
Petroleum Processing and Coking Products	118.37	6.13	5.18
Smelting and Pressing of Ferrous Metals	247.76	10.03	4.05
Nonmetal Minerals Mining and Processing	16.43	0.44	2.68
Tap Water Production and Supply	18.44	0.34	1.84
Nonferrous Metals Mining and Processing	12.90	0.10	0.78
Ferrous Metals Mining and Processing	7.09	0.04	0.56
Tobacco Processing	143.95	0.72	0.50
Coal Mining and Processing	98.11	0.24	0.24
Logging and Transport of Timber and Bamboo	2.61	--	--
Petroleum and Natural Gas Extracting	297.41	--	--

Source: calculated according to figures of Table 13-5, 13-13 in National Bureau of Statistics of China (2002). *China Statistical Yearbook 2001* (Beijing: China Statistics Press).

Chapter 9

ACCESSION TO WTO: IMPROVED INVESTMENT ENVIRONMENT AND ENHANCED APPEALS

After 16 years of hard work, China became an official WTO member in December 2001. This was one of the most important events since the adoption of the policy of reform and opening up to the outside world. China committed itself to major reductions of tariffs and the use of fewer non-tariff measures, further opening its service to foreign investors, and the adoption of an open and transparent trade policy. These changes indicate that the opening of China has extended from an open government policy to the adaptation of the entire Chinese system to the outside world and changed from being government-oriented to being market-oriented. The accession to WTO has laid a systematic foundation for the nation's open economy.

The commitments of China to opening up to FDI as a precondition for its accession to WTO mainly manifest themselves in the adaptation of its policies and laws to the various TWO principles and requirements as well as in access to service and trading markets. In 2001 and 2002, China amended a series of legislation concerning foreign investment. China is carrying out its commitments to its accession to WTO in real earnest and speeding up economic restructuring and the process of becoming part of the global economy. These changes will help further improve the investment environment and boost the confidence of foreign investors for long-term development in China.

This chapter sheds some light on the improvement of the investment environment and China's sustained appeals for FDI as a host economy, the new trends of the manufacturing industry in wooing FDI, and the role of FDI inflow in turning some industries in China into global manufacturing centers.

9-1: CHINA STRIVES TO IMPROVE ENVIRONMENT FOR FOREIGN INVESTMENT AFTER ACCEDING TO WTO

1. Revising Three Laws Governing Foreign Investment

There are three basic laws governing foreign investment, that is, *Law of the People's Republic of China on Chinese-foreign Equity Joint Ventures, Law of the People's Republic of*

China on Chinese-foreign Contractual Joint Ventures, Law of the People's Republic of China on Wholly Foreign-owned Enterprises. According to WTO rules and the commitments China made during negotiations with WTO, these three Chinese laws have specific provisions concerning the stipulation of the TRIMs Agreement, the most important WTO agreement concerning investment that bans demands on local contents and foreign exchange balance for enterprises established by foreign investors.

(1) On the Clause on Balance of Foreign Exchange

According to the WTO TRIMs Agreement provision that no country shall restrict these enterprises' import by imposing the demand for foreign exchange balance on them, the amendments made to the three Chinese laws abolished this demand. Will this have any negative impact on the balance of China's international revenue and expenditure? Foreign-invested enterprises (FIEs) have accounted for nearly 50% of the Chinese total imports and exports in recent years, and the situation in the foreign exchange balance of these enterprises will have major influence on the balance of the nation's balance of international revenue and expenditure. China's compulsory stipulations for foreign-invested enterprises have been weakened since 1986, all the foreign-invested enterprises have been engaged in foreign exchange settlement and sales on the foreign exchange market, and none of them have incurred glaring deficits in foreign exchange settlement and sales as they have generally maintained an annual foreign exchange balance with a surplus.

(2) On the Clause on "Local Content"

The WTO TRIMs Agreement stipulates that there shall be no demand on the local content of foreign-invested enterprises and requires that national treatment be accorded to all these enterprises. The original versions of the three Chinese laws demanded that foreign-invested enterprises first buy their input articles in China, the new amendments have deleted this demand. Foreign-invested enterprises enjoy the same freedom of purchase as that of domestic enterprises.

(3) On the Requirements for Performance in Exports

The WTO TRIMs Agreement specifically stipulates that member countries and regions shall not limit the quantity, value or percentages of products exported by enterprises. The original laws' demand that foreign enterprises should export part of their products falls into the category of "requirements for performance in exports" prohibited by the WTO rules, and it was naturally abolished in the amendments, so that foreign-invested enterprises and domestic enterprises equally share the right to make their own decisions on sales.

(4) On the Clause on Entering Enterprise Production Plans in the Records

The three original laws demanded that foreign-invested enterprise enter their production plans in the records of Chinese government departments concerned. This was a manifestation of central planning, but it was by no means discrimination against foreign-invested enterprises because it applied to domestic enterprises as well. It is normal for the amendments to abolish this requirement because various kinds of domestic enterprises are no longer asked to report their production plans, thereby rendering the old legal stipulation obsolete.

2. Grant National Treatment to Foreign-invested Enterprises

The principle of national treatment is a major WTO principle. Its basic meaning is that in investment activities foreign investors should not be treated differently from the enterprises and citizens of the host country. In recent years China has acted on WTO's national treatment rules by abolishing dual prices imposed on the train and boat tickets, entrance tickets to public parks and air tickets that enabled domestic enterprises and local citizens to pay lower prices than foreign-invested enterprises and foreign residents. In 2002, discrimination against foreign-invested enterprises was abolished in the distribution of import and export quotas.

3. Revising the *Catalogue for the Guidance of Foreign Investment Industries*

The State Council promulgated the newly amended *Provision on Guiding Foreign Investment Direction* on February 11, 2002 on the occasion of strategic adjustment of the structure of the national economy and the new situation arising from China's accession to WTO. On March 11 of the same year, the State Development Planning Commission, the State Economic & Trade Commission and the Ministry of Foreign Trade and Economic Cooperation announced the new *Catalogue for the Guidance of Foreign Investment Industries* with the approval of the State Council. Both documents, which came in force as of April 1, 2002, have continued to carry out the principle of utilizing foreign investment in active, rational and effective ways.

The New Catalogue features four categories on industries, in which foreign investment is encouraged, allowed, restricted or prohibited. It has vastly increased the country's openness to foreign investment: 1) the number of clauses on encouraging foreign investment has increased from 186 to 262, and the number of restriction clauses has reduced from 112 to 75; 2) restrictions on the percentage of foreign investment in stocks are relaxed, for example, the demand that the Chinese side control the majority shares of harbors for joint Chinese and foreign use has been abolished; 3) more areas where foreign investment was prohibited are now open to foreign investment, such as telecommunications, fuel gas, heating power, water supply and drainage, and other urban service networks; 4) banking, insurance, commerce, foreign trade, tourism, telecommunications, transportation, accounting, auditing, law and other service fields have been further opened; 5) foreign investment is encouraged in the western regions by granting foreign investors with higher shares and opening more industries to them; 6) in order to give full play to the role of market competition, general industrial products are put into the "permitted" category so as to promote the upgrade of the industrial structure and the product mix.

4. Opening Service Sector Wider to FDI

1) China Commits to Opening Its Service Sector to FDI

During its WTO membership negotiations China committed to opening most of its service sector to foreign investment. As a result the course of liberalization for these industries has been greatly expedited. Services in distribution, banking, insurance, securities, telecommunications and transportation, special-purpose services and travel agencies have begun to open or expand their openness to FDI.

In banking, for instance, China made the following commitments: A) geographical restriction: no geographical restriction is imposed on foreign exchange business as of the day of China's accession to WTO; geographical restrictions on domestic currency business shall be gradually abolished according to the following timetable – Shanghai, Shenzhen, Tianjin and Dalian as of the day of China's accession to WTO; Guangzhou, Zhuhai, Qingdao, Nanjing and Wuhan within one year after the country's accession to WTO; Jinan, Fuzhou, Chengdu and Chongqing within two years; Kunming, Beijing and Xiamen within three years; Shantou, Ningbo, Shenyang and Xi'an within four years; and all the geographical restrictions shall be lifted within five years; B) clients: in foreign exchange business, foreign financial organizations shall be allowed to provide services in China as of the day of the nation's accession to WTO and there will be no restrictions to clients whatsoever; in domestic currency business, foreign financial organizations shall be allowed to provide services for Chinese enterprises within two years after China's accession to WTO, and they will be allowed to provide services for all Chinese clients within five years. Any foreign financial organization that has been granted permission to deal in domestic currency business in a certain place might provide its services for clients in other places where such business has been opened to foreign investment.

Take distribution services for another example. China has made unequivocal commitments to commission services, wholesales, retailing sales, and franchise rights.

A) Commission services (excluding salt and tobacco) and wholesale service (excluding salt and tobacco)

Restrictions on market access in commerce: foreign services providers were allowed to establish joint ventures in commission and wholesales services for all imported and home-made products within one year after China's accession to WTO with the following exceptions: foreign service providers shall be allowed to deal in distribution of books, magazines, pharmaceuticals, insecticides and mulches for agricultural use within three years, and they shall be allowed to engage in distribution of chemical fertilizers, finished oil and crude oil within five years.

Foreign control of majority shares shall be allowed within two years after China's accession to WTO, with the quantitative and geographical restrictions lifted. Such restrictions shall be lifted within three years, but those imposed on chemical fertilizers, finished oil and crude oil shall be lifted within five years.

Other commitments: foreign-invested enterprises are allowed to distribute the China-made products listed in the categories and sub-categories and those in the market access column, and foreign service providers are allowed to provide all the associated services, after-sale services included, for the products they distribute as defined in *Related Statistics* of the book.

B) Retailing sales service (not including tobacco)

Restrictions on market access in commerce: Foreign Service providers are allowed in five special economic zones (Shenzhen, Zhuhai, Shantou, Xiamen and Hainan) and six cities (Beijing, Shanghai, Tianjin, Guangzhou, Dalian and Qingdao). In Beijing and Shanghai, no more than four joint retailing sales enterprises are allowed while in each of the other cities no more than two such joint ventures are allowed. Two of the four joint retailing sales enterprises to be established in Beijing shall be allowed to set up branches in the same city.

Zhengzhou and Wuhan were opened to joint retailing sales enterprises immediately after China acceded to WTO. In two years after China's accession to WTO, foreign investment was allowed to control joint retailing sales enterprises in all the provincial capital cities as well as Chongqing and Ningbo.

Foreign service providers shall be permitted to deal in retailing sales of all products with the exception of the following: retailing sales of books, newspapers and magazines within one year; retailing sales of pharmaceuticals, insecticides, farm-use mulches, and finished oil within three years, and chemical fertilizers within five years.

Restrictions shall be lifted within three years after China's accession to WTO, but the following products are exceptions: retailing sales of chemical fertilizers within five years; and as to those chain stores that operate more than 30 branches and deal in different kinds and brands of products from many suppliers, foreign investors are not allowed to hold majority shares if they sell one of the following products: automobiles (this restriction shall not be lifted until five years after China's accession to WTO) as well as the products listed in the 2A category of the Appendix to the Protocols on China's Accession to WTO. Managers of foreign chain stores shall be entitled to choose any partner established in China according to the Chinese law.

C) Franchise Rights

Restrictions on market access and national treatment shall be lifted within three years after China's accession to WTO.

2) A Series of Policies and Legislation Concerning Foreign-invested Services Were Promulgated and Improved

In 2001, the Ministry of Foreign Trade and Economic Cooperation, the Ministry of Science and Technology of the People's Republic of China, and the State Administration for Industry & Commerce jointly promulgated the *Provisions Concerning the Administration of Foreign-funded Business-starting Investment Enterprises*. By drawing on and referring to the venture investment mechanisms of various countries and established international practices, this document provides the norms for foreign investors who come to China to establish initial investment enterprises, invest in the shares of unlisted high-tech enterprises and provide services for their initial investment. These stipulations are being amended to further liberalize the conditions.

Circular on Printing and Distributing Some Opinions Relevant to Foreign Investment in Listed Companies promulgated jointly by the China Securities Regulatory Commission and the Ministry of Foreign Trade and Economic Cooperation in 2001 clarifies the conditions and procedures for the entry of foreign-invested enterprises into A- and B-stock markets in China, allows these enterprises to purchase non-negotiable shares of listed companies in China in compliance with the *Interim Provisions Concerning the Investment within China of Foreign-invested Enterprises* and permits the unlisted foreign shares of foreign-invested companies with limited liability to negotiate on the B-stock market.

Interim Provisions on Drawing Foreign Capital into the Asset Restructuring and Disposal by Financial Asset Management Companies promulgated in 2002 by the Ministry of Foreign Trade and Economic Cooperation, the Ministry of Finance People's Bank of China and the People's Bank of China gives the green light to the participation of foreign-invested enterprises in the regrouping and handling of the assets of financial asset management companies and provides legal norms for the scope, valuation and transfer procedure of financial assets to be transferred to foreign investors.

The Ministry of Foreign Trade and Economic Cooperation also promulgated the *Supplementary Provisions (2) of the Provisional Regulations on the Establishment of Investment Companies with Foreign Investment* in 2002, which further expanded the business scope of investment companies, and allows these companies to provide relevant technical training for domestic enterprise, initiate foreign-invested enterprises with limited liability, purchase commodities from at home and abroad and sell them on Chinese and foreign markets after systematically sorting them out, and sell, on a trial basis, small quantities of products that they have imported from their parent companies and that are identical with or similar to their own products if such products are not subjected to import quotas.

Circular on Relevant issues Concerning the Expansion of Import and Export Right of Enterprises with Foreign Investment promulgated by the Ministry of Foreign Trade and Economic Cooperation in 2002 allows foreign-invested productive enterprises with an annual export volume of more than 10 million US dollars to purchase products from other enterprises for export and permits foreign-invested R&D centers to import some high-tech products for market-testing purposes. The ministry also revised the *Provisions on the Merger and Division of Enterprises with Foreign Investment to further standardize mergers between foreign-invested and domestic enterprises.*

In 2002 the Ministry of Foreign Trade and Economic Cooperation issued a circular on experimentation with foreign-invested logistics enterprises, allowing them to engage in part of or the entirety of international logistics and third-party logistics businesses.

The other service sector-concerned Chinese laws promulgated in the last couple of years are *Regulation of the People's Republic of China on the Administration of Insurance Companies with Foreign Investment, Provisions of the Ministry of Justice on the Execution of the Regulations on the Administration of Foreign Law Firms' Representative Offices in China*, Interim *Measures on the Administration of Examination and Approval of Lease Companies with Foreign Investment, Provisional Stipulations on Sino-Foreign Joint and Cooperative Job Organizations, the amended Provisions on Travel Services, Provisions on the Administration of Telecommunications Enterprises with Foreign Investment, Provisions on the Administration of Road Transport Services with Foreign Investment, Provisions on the Administration of Enterprises with Foreign Investment Serving as Agents for International Cargo Transport, Provisional Stipulations on Foreign-Invested Cinemas, the Procedures on Sino-Foreign Cooperative Audiovisual Products Sales and Distribution Enterprises, the Provisional Stipulations on Sino-Foreign Joint and Cooperative Medical Organizations,* Rules for the Establishment of Foreign-shared Securities Companies, *Regulations on Foreign-invested Construction Design Enterprise, Regulations on Construction Enterprises with Foreign Investment, Provision on Foreign Investment in Civil Aviation, Interim Provisions on the Establishment of Printing Enterprises with Foreign Investment, Interim Provisions on Introducing Foreign Investment to Reorganize State-owned Enterprise, Interim Provisions on Mergers and Acquisitions of Domestic Enterprises by Foreign Investors Circular of the China Securities Regulatory Commission (CSRC), the Ministry of Finance (MOF) and the State Economy and Trade Commission (SETC) on Issues Related to Transferring State-owned Shares and Institutional Shares of Listed Corporations to Foreign*

Investors, and Issues Related to Improving the Administration of Enterprises with Foreign Investment in Terms of Examination and Approval, Registration, Foreign Exchange and Taxation.

5. Further Improving the Investment Environment and Simplifying Government Examination and Approval Procedures

China is speeding up the transition of government functions and style of work according to principles on rationality, effectiveness, openness and sense of responsibility. It is further simplifying and standardizing examination and approval procedures for foreign investment. Accordingly, the procedures for examination and approval of establishment of investment projects, feasibility study reports, contracts and corporate constitutions are being simplified by integrating and streamlining the work of different administrative departments and streamlining the procedures so that investors can go through all the formalities through one window. Emphasis is put on enhancing government functionaries' consciousness of the legal system so that they can become well-versed in law, be exemplary in abiding by law. They are asked to aboveboard, fair and transparent in law enforcement and guard against arbitrariness in this regard; only thus can they contribute to the building of a clean, diligent, pragmatic and efficient government, raise their law-enforcement level and foster a fine administrative environment for foreign investors.

9-2: Good Prospects of Sustainable Economic Growth: China's Appeal for Foreign Investors

After China's accession to WTO, transnational corporation's investment in this country has been on the increase. Apart from continuous improvement in the local environment in the wake of the nation's accession to WTO, China also holds the following appeals for foreign investors:

1. Appeals of China's Robust Economic Growth and Tremendous Market

Since 2001, China's exterior environment for attracting investment by transnational corporations has left much to be desired. Firstly, global investment by these corporations has been shrinking considerably. According to UNCTAD, the global investment by transnational corporations totaled 760 billion US dollars in 2001, which was 40% lower than what it was in 2000, and it continued to drop in 2002 to an estimated 540 billion US dollars. Secondly, the growth of the global economy slowed down obviously. The growth of the United States, European Union and Japan were at low ebb in 2002 and 2002. A series of major event that took place in the wake of the "9.11" terrorist attack, the US-Iraq War in particular, aggravated the stagnation of the global economy and adversely affected its resuscitation process. Forecasting authorities around the world are not optimistic about the trends of the global economy in 2003. Under the impact of widespread stagnation, many large transnational corporations find the going tough. Some of the famous ones are getting less profit or are losing money, prompting them to lay off workers and staff and reduce production capacities.

Despite the disadvantageous external environment, foreign investment in China keeps growing robustly, a growth that is in striking contrast with the reduction in global investment aggregates. In 2002, while total global investment continued to go down, FDI inflow in China continued to grow by big margins, so much so that China had replaced the United States to become the global largest recipient of foreign investment. The portion of global investment by transnational corporations has risen to 9.98%. This trend indicates that foreign investors are confident in the intermediary and long-term development of the Chinese economy.

In 2002, the 16th National Congress of the Chinese Communist Party raised the goal to quadruple the 2000 GDP by 2020. Around that time, many scholars at home and abroad made many studies of the potentials of China for economic growth. The following are the findings of some representative researchers about the nation's economic growth rates for the first 20 and 50 years of the 21st century.

Table 9-1: China's potentials for intermediary and long-term economic growth

Growth Rate of GDP (%)	Xu Xianchun 2002	Li Jingwen 1999	Wang Xiaolu 2001	Xie Sanming 2001	Pan Wenqing et al 2001
2001-2010	7.5	8.0	6.58	7.5	7.98
2011-2020	6.5	6.4	6.21	7.0	5.90
2021-2030	5.5	5.4			
2031-2040	4.5	4.9			
2041-2050	3.5	4.3			

Source: see the bibliography of this book.

According to the aforementioned growth rates, the Chinese economy will continue to expand in scale in the first half of the 21st century. According to Xu Xianchun who makes his prognostication on China's future position in the world under the condition that Renminbi's exchange rate on the US dollar rises 100% and 200% respectively, China's per-capita GDP will have reached 10,916 US dollars and caught up with the 2000 level of Portugal in 2050 if the exchange rate remains unchanged, and will have reached 32,748 US dollars and approach the 2000 level of the United States if the exchange rate rises to 200%. Xu believes it is more likely for the exchange rate to rise to 100%, and thus the per-capita Chinese GDP will have reached 20,000 US dollars by 2050, thereby reaching or approaching the 2000 level of Italy, Australia and Canada.

Not only is the economic aggregates growing, the Chinese industrial structure is also being continuously upgraded. With the steady rise in the income level of part of the Chinese population, China is becoming a major market for the technology and products of transnational corporations. Given the huge population in China, even if only some of the Chinese are getting high incomes, they can form a sizeable market for the commodities of transnational corporations with high incremental value and technological content.

Some scholars predict that if average per-capita income keeps growing at an annual rate of 6% in China in the years to come while the nation's income elasticity for automobiles is the same as the United States' 1919-1970 level of 2.6, then by 2015 the Chinese will buy 10 million automobiles every year, but the nation's present annual production capacity is a meager 1.5 million, which means the Chinese auto output will increase six fold in 15 years. Suppose China's average annual economic growth rate will remain at 6% until 2024 and if the income elasticity for automobiles remains unchanged, then the Chinese demand for automobiles will reach 45 million, equivalent to the current global volume of automobiles held and purchased. Therefore, despite the intensifying competition between auto-manufacturers on the Chinese market, new and large auto projects continue to be established. All the world's major auto-manufacturers have set up joint ventures in China, and more than half of the global 50 auto component suppliers have established joint ventures in China in order to seize this huge market.

Judging from the reality of China, this expectation is coming true. In 2002, the Chinese auto industry scored rapid growth, with the annual auto output reaching 3.2 million, up 39% from the previous year; of this, the car output reached 1.08 million, up 48%. In 2003 and the next few years, the auto industry, car making included, will maintain a high growth speed.

The reason why the global wafer makers arrived in China one after another to invest is because of the nation's immense market for this industry. Graig Barrett, executive president of Intel, the world's leading wafer manufacturer, said in Tokyo on March 1, 2003 that the market of the mainland of China is already growing robustly and such a growth will continue. According to him, the mainland is likely to surpass Japan in 2003 to become Intel's largest market in Asia.

General Electric has invested nearly 1.5 billion US dollars in China. The company has entered the Chinese market in many fields such as aircraft engines, household electrical appliances, industrial systems, medical systems and power systems, and is actively open up its purchases in China. After China's accession to WTO, General Electric has increased its investment in this country so that its Chinese affiliate will become a company with 4 billion-5 billion US dollars of investment. When explaining why General Electric is particularly concerned with its development in China, Sun Dali, chairman and CEO of General Electric (China) said that in the next 20-25 years, China as a huge market will command his company's attention at least in the following six aspects: 1) a tremendous consumer market; 2) the global second or third largest market; 3) the global largest air aviation market; 4) the emergence of a middle class will bring about a large market for medical and health industries; 5) the shift of industry from coastal regions to the hinterland will boost the demand for clean energy sources; and 6) a potentially large consumer's financing market. All this, according to him, means a lot of opportunities for General Electric's aircraft engine group, medical system, power system, financial service system and industrial system[1].

2. Foreign Investors are Confident in Intermediary and Long-Term Growth of Chinese Economy

The confidence shown by those foreign investors who are already doing business in China is most convincing. A remarkable feature of FDI increases over the last couple years is that the existing enterprises have been continuously increasing their investment. According to our surveys in Beijing, Shanghai, Guangzhou and Shenzhen, additional investment by

[1] Chen Hongwei: "GE Grows Together with China", *Foreign Investment in China*, issue No. 1, 2002, Beijing.

foreign-invested enterprises in 2001 accounted for about 30-50% of the realized FDI. In Pudong Area, Shanghai, additional investment by these enterprises amounted to 1 billion US dollars, which was about half of the FDI inflow there in the same year; in Guangzhou, a considerable portion of the 3.3 billion US dollars of realized FDI came from additional investment made by existing foreign-invested enterprises in 408 projects with a total contractual investment of 900 million US dollars or 46% of the total amount of foreign investment involved in the newly approved contracts; in Shenzhen, additional investment by foreign-invested enterprises made up about one third of the city's 2001 contractual FDI value.

The smooth operation of earlier investment projects is a major factor behind these enterprises' decision to increase their investment in China. Take Pudong Area, Shanghai, for instance, the first batch of projects undertaken by some transnational corporations that have long entered the area. Because these projects have been in operation for some years and quite a few of them are doing fine, this has motivated these corporations to invest more and expand their businesses. These transnational corporations are using the profits they have won in China or the funds of their overseas headquarters to expand their investment in this country to serve their goal of enhancing their global market competitiveness. Intel's first investment in Pudong was 95 million US dollars; this year its additional investment will amount to 300 million US dollars. Among the foreign-invested enterprises that have increased their investment in Pudong by big margins over the last couple of years are Philips Electronics (100 million US dollars), IBM (300 million US dollars), Shanghai Bell (75 million US dollars), Hewlett Packard (76 million US dollars), Kyocera Electronics (100 million US dollars) and Kodak Electronics (30 million US dollars). Several hundred other foreign-invested enterprises of medium and small sizes are also making additional investment or planning to do so. The additional investment made by most transnational corporations is no less than their initial investment. The projects with such additional investment are marked by a considerable improvement in technological content as compared with the early investment projects.

Another major manifestation of foreign investors' confidence in the long-term development of China is that they are investing in projects that call for immense amounts of investment and from which the investment will be recouped after a considerably long period of time. In 2001 and 2002, a total of 19 large projects each with an investment of more than 1 billion US dollars, such as an 900,000-ton-a-year ethylene project jointly constructed by Sinopec Corp, Sinopec Shanghai Petrochemical Company, Ltd. and BP in Shanghai for a total investment of 2.7 billion US dollars; a large petrochemical factory to be built in Guangdong Province for about 4 billion US dollars by Royal Dutch/Shell Group, as well a 800,000-ton-a-yea ethylene projects and a 2.3 million-ton-a-year petrochemical factory to be constructed in Huizhou Daya Bay Economic & Technological Development Zone, Guangdong Province, by the same company.

3. Strong Competitiveness of "Made-in-China" Products

By investing in China, transnational corporations not only gain access to the snowballing but also share the multiple competitive advantages of the Chinese manufacturing industry.

First, the costs for products made in China are low. A 2001 survey conducted by the Japanese Ministry of Economy and Industry revealed great differences in the prices paid by

Japanese enterprises for purchasing industrial goods and services at home and abroad. A comparison of prices for 152 industrial goods and 33 industrial services in seven countries and regions during the September-November period of 2000 indicated that the Japanese prices were 2.08 times higher than those in Germany and 2.29-3.83 times higher than the prices in the Republic of Korea and Singapore and Chinese Taiwan and Hong Kong. A comparison with the mainland of China indicated that the Japanese prices were 2.49 times higher for industrial goods and 8.44 times higher for industrial services – the differences are glaring. When describing the strengths of the Chinese market, LG believes that Chinese manufacturing industry holds a tremendous advantage in labor costs. For each dollar a Chinese worker makes in a Korean-invested enterprise in China, the cost for Korean worker is 8.5 dollars. China's competitiveness in cost makes it more difficult for transnational corporations to limit their manufacturing in their own countries, thereby speeding up the formation of a new division of labor.

Secondly, China is strongly able to provide accessories. The sound industrial foundation of China makes it convenient for transnational corporations to find qualified accessory suppliers in this country. With the sharpening of domestic enterprises' competitiveness and the increase in the number of foreign-invested accessory enterprises, transnational corporations are able to steadily increase their accessory rate in China, which helps them reduce costs, speed up production, and make timely adjustment in their product mix. Dongguan in Guangdong Province is so thickly clustered with computer manufacturers and component suppliers that computer manufacturers are able to obtain all the components needed except chips, thereby greatly raising their international competitiveness. In Suzhou, Jiangsu Province, production of notebook computers has also developed a huge group of accessory-supplying enterprises. In the manufacturing of cell phones, automobiles and office equipment, domestic accessory supplying capacities are also expanding impressively and attracting more assembling manufacturers to expand their production in this country.

4. Global Economic Stagnation Has Set Off the Appeals of the Chinese Market

Information from the parent countries of many transnational corporations indicates that to invest in China has become a major strategy for these corporations seeking survival and development as they cope with unfavorable environments in their mother countries and the world as well.

In Japan, a 2001 Ministry of Economy and Industry survey showed that high domestic costs have enfeebled Japanese enterprises in international competition. Since the 1990s, the international positions of Japanese products in such fields as computer hardware and software, office equipment and household electrical appliances have been sliding quickly. In the manufacturing of duplicating machines, cameras, videotape recorders and many other electronic products, Japan's market shares are plummeting. The world market share for Japanese duplicating machines, for instance, has diminished from over 70% during the peak period to about 40% today. High domestic production costs are a major reason for the reduction of Japanese enterprises' competitiveness. A major choice for Japanese enterprises to deliver themselves from this predicament is to invest in competitive places overseas. The Chinese market with its colossal size and low-cost manufacturing abilities is, without a doubt, very attractive. In August 2001, the Japanese press revealed the findings of a survey: half of the 1,143 Japanese enterprises listed in the Tokyo and New York stock exchanges indicated that they wanted to move their production bases out of Japan in three years; and 71% of those Japanese enterprises intending to move out choose China as their main destination, and Shanghai, Suzhou, Kunshan and Ningbo of the Yangtze River Delta, Shenzhen and Dongguan of the Pearl River Delta, and Chengdu and Xi'an of West of China were their first investment options.

To invest in China as a strategic option in coping with the difficult times has become a trend not only among Japanese enterprises but also among many large transnational corporations in America and Europe that are coping with local economic slowdowns and management difficulties.

When many transnational IT corporations are laying off workers and staff members and curtail productions worldwide to cope with a global depression in the IT industry, China has become a lone exception. Since 2000, Motorola has shut down some of its factories in Europe and America, with a total layoff of more than 30,000, but it has been expanding both its investment and payroll in China. In 2002, Motorola announced a plan to invest a total of 1.9 billion US dollars in the construction of a semi-conductor producing center and its Asian telecommunication product manufacturing base in Tianjin; in five years it will achieve a triple "10 billion US dollar" program – 10 billion US dollars in output value, aggregate investment and volume of local purchases respectively; in a bid to strengthen its R&D work in China, it has planned to increase its number of Chinese employees in R&D work to 5,000 by 2005. The last couple of years has witnessed Ericsson suffering global business losses and engaged in large-scale layoffs and production cutbacks in its parent country and other countries. However, it has announced a plan to more than double its investment in China before 2006 so that its total China investment will exceed 5 billion US dollars; increase its investment in R&D work and in developing human resources from 290 million US dollars to upwards of 570 million US dollars; expand its volume of purchases of export products from China from 1.49 billion US dollars to 4.5 billion US dollars and increase the number of new jobs created from 29,000 to 58,000. Alcatel, a telecommunications group of France, was losing money and cut its labor force by a total of 23,000 or 30% in 2000 and 2001 and an additional 2,500 in its American affiliate in 2002, but at the same time it was increasing its investment in China. In October 2001, Shanghai Bell announced to officially transform itself into a foreign-invested company with limited liability, in which Alcatel's shares increased from 31.65% to 50% plus one share whereas the Chinese side held 50% of the shares minus one. The new company was renamed Alcatel Shanghai Bell Co., Ltd. as a result, and Alcatel shifted all its businesses in China to the new company, thereby forming the largest foreign-invested enterprise in the Chinese telecommunications industry.

Although most of these investment projects are still in a planning stage and uncertain of their practicality, one thing is certain: at this time of global business stagnation, many transnational corporations have shifted the focus for their future development to the Chinese market. To invest in China and share the benefits from the sustained high-speed growth of this mammoth economic entity is not only a countermeasure adopted by many transnational corporations in coping with economic adversities – it will also become a major part of the intermediary and long-term global strategy for a considerable number of these corporations.

Chapter 10

INVESTMENT TREND AND NEW FEATURES OF FOREIGN CAPITAL IN THE MANUFACTURING INDUSTRY

After China acceded to WTO, foreign investment in this country has taken on new characteristics and shown new trends. Both its scale and scope continue to expand, and associated technology and structure are quickly being upgraded as well. These new characteristics and trends are manifestations of positive FDI responses to China's open policy which has become even more extrovert after its accession to WTO, as well as the confidence of foreign investors in intermediary and long-term development in this country.

10-1: FDI IN MANUFACTURING INDUSTRY: EXPANDING THE SCALE AND UPGRADING THE STRUCTURE AND TECHNOLOGY

After China's accession to WTO, the manufacturing industry has remained a key area for FDI. In 2002 the manufacturing industry accounted for 67% of the total volume of FDI in China. Wholly foreign-owned projects are increasing in scale. In 2002 alone, there were 27 such projects each with a contractual value upwards of 100 million US dollars. The technical level of foreign-invested enterprises (FIEs) continues to rise, as more and more transnational corporations use the most advanced technology and manufacture the most sophisticated products in China.

The global major notebook computer manufacturers have begun to build large and advanced production capacities. Among the major projects invested since 2002, ground has been broken for the construction of a Toshiba notebook producing centre in Hangzhou, Zhejiang Province, with an investment of 7 billion yen and an annual output of 2.4 million notebook computers; a Samsung notebook computer manufacturing centre came into operation in 2002 with an ambitious plan to emerge as one of the five top notebook computer producers on the market; the newly merged Hewlett Packard decided to build a notebook computer production line in China in 2003; an affiliate of Sharp in Changshu has begun producing notebook computers with a goal to seize 10% of the Chinese notebook computer market. Earlier, six major Taiwan notebook computer manufacturers including Acer and

Inventec had already set up shop in Suzhou with a total annual output of 10 million. China will undoubtedly become the global most advanced notebook computer manufacturing centre.

The world's major chip producers have also started large-scale investment in China. Semiconductor Manufacturing International (Shanghai) Corporation, a company with American and Taiwan investment, produced its first batch of chips in August 2002 to become the first semi-conductor manufacturer to produce 0.18-micron, 8-inch wafers in China. In December 2002, SMIC signed a DRAM process agreement with Infineon of Germany, according to which the latter transferred its 0.14-micron channel DRAM technology to the former, and the former would also consider shifting its 0.11-micron technology to the latter as well. In the beginning of 2003, SMIC signed a five-year chip processing agreement with Japan's Elpida, according to which Elpida agreed to entrust SMIC's 8-inch wafer factory in Shanghai with the production of 0.13-micron tiered DRAMs. These agreements will elevate chip processing in China to the world's most advanced level. Apart from SMIC, the global other major chip manufacturers have basically acquired large-scale processing capacities using advanced technology. According to estimates, seven newly built semi-conductor factories in China will have come up with a new generation of made-in-China chips by 2004, and turn the nation into the largest chip producing country second only to the United States.

Apart from the IT industry, transnational corporations in other industries are also active in shifting the most advanced products and technology to China. Matsushita will start producing more than 20 new products in China in the next few years while continuing its production of notebook computers in this country. In 2002 alone, it conducted three major investment projects in China: expanding its investment so that the Hualu-Matsushita in Dalian could become the world's leading videocamera and DVD manufacturer and supplier; putting into operation a project for the production of key components for back-projection television sets; and shutting down a cell-phone oscillating motor factory in southeast Asia and shifting the production of such motors to Zhuhai in Hainan Province. SVA Group of China and NEC of Japan invested 850 million US dollars in a joint venture with an annual output of 500,000 large TFT-LCD pieces.

In 2002 Du Pont invested a total of 150 million US dollars, equivalent to one quarter of what it had invested in China in the previous ten years, and established six wholly owned companies and joint ventures in food nutrition, engineering plastics, agriculture, textile and some other industries. Transnational corporations that started early and invested heavily in China and had high shares of Chinese market are also following up with large investment and introducing more advanced products to China. Volkswagen announced that it would speed up development in China in three fields by investing an additional 2.5 billion euros so that its total investment in this country could reach 5.5 billion euros in the next three to five years.

Many transnational corporations are transferring or planning to transfer to China manufacturing industries with higher incremental value and more technological content. Toshiba started its China business by producing television components with low technological contents; when it began assembling final products in China, the degree of localization of such products was rather low, and the components made in China were low in technology and incremental value. Only after Toshiba started to gradually raise the technological grades of its production in China that the degree of localization of its products started improving. Toshiba began producing ordinary television sets in China for the Japanese market in 1998, but today its products run the gamut from 21- to 34-inch television sets to large back projection television sets developed for the Chinese market. Beginning from April

2001, Dalian Toshiba began producing digital color television sets and wide-screen color television sets for export to Japan.

Toshiba not only upgrades its television set production in China but also introduces new technology and new products in many other fields. Hirata Nobumasa, Toshiba's chief representative in China, said that China is Toshiba's only overseas market on which it has conducted all-encompassing and diverse investment to the tune of more than 6 billion US dollars, and that its investment has shifted from household electrical appliances, machinery and electrical products, and energy sources to information technology and software. He promised that in the days to come Toshiba will expand its investment in the IT industry, and its investment in LCD and semi-conductor technology will exceed 2 billion US dollars. Toshiba has obviously regarded China, a WTO member, as a major part of its global strategy.

Hitachi has decided that during the period 2001-2005 the emphasis of its China investment strategy will be shifted to the IT industry so as to quadruple its production and sales in China. The key areas for Hitachi in China in the future are: information and telecommunications represented by solutions to storage problems, new-generation telecommunications network technology, applicable financial terminal technology and e-government and e-commerce; production of semi-conductors for cell phones and personal computers and production of computer monitors; household electrical products and digital products represented by air-conditioners, back-projection television sets and cell phones.

Investing in industries with high incremental value and high technological contents is not limited to a few companies from Japan – it has become a common trend. For instance, Sony is producing high-end notebook computers in Wuxi; Olympus and Sanyo are producing digital cameras in Guangdong; Hitachi has established a household electrical appliance development centre in Beijing; Sony will set up a department in Shanghai for the development of software for use on audiovisual machines; and Canon will develop medium-grade duplicating machines in Jiangsu Province. According to sources in Japan, the trend of Japanese enterprises transferring high- and medium-grade manufacturing capacities to China will continue into 2003 and 2004.

The same is true with American and European transnational corporations. The Huaxia Semiconductor Manufacturing Co., Ltd., a joint venture of Shougang Group and American AOS Semiconductor Company, will invest 10 billion US dollars in ten years for the construction of six to eight 8- and 12-inch chip production lines, two of which came under construction in 2000. Alcatel, after making additional investment and acquiring control of Shanghai Bell Co., Ltd., will fully open its globally advanced technology and products to its joint ventures in China and the Chinese market. Alcatel Shanghai Bell Co., Ltd. will acquire all the latest technology and products developed by Alcatel, which will also establish a most advanced development centre in Shanghai with 3,500 researchers and engineers in order to further develop creative and global nuclear technology oriented to the world and local markets. In an interview carried in the 2002 February issue of *Fortune* magazine, Ron Spithill, president of Alcatel Asia Pacific, when asked if there are certain products that cannot be produced in China, said, "No, nothing can I think of. In China Alcatel can produce any products we want to produce."

Kodak has transferred its global production of the Easyshare digital camera, reportedly a world-class product, to Shanghai's Dahai Camera Plant, a joint venture between Shanghai Seagull Camera Co., Ltd. and Kodak. Motorola has announced to spend an additional 16 billion RMB (1.9 billion US dollars) on the construction of a semi-conductor producing centre and Asian telecom products centre in Tianjin, thereby raising Motorola's total investment in China to 28.56 billion RMB and maintaining Motorola's position as the largest foreign-invested corporation in this country. The Xingwang Industrial Garden built by Nokia in Beijing has begun operation in the hope that it will become a centre for the manufacturing and development of telecommunications equipment in China and enable Nokia to produce all its major products in China. The staff of Nokia's China Research Centre has been increased ten folds within one year's time. The two enterprises run by Ericsson in China have reached the company's most advanced technological level and turned China into one of Ericsson's four major global suppliers in the world.

Of the global 25 leading pharmaceutical transnational corporations, 20 have invested in China. However, for so many years these corporations never introduced their latest drugs to China for fear of pirating. Their misgivings in this regard have been vastly assuaged thanks to the protection of intellectual property rights resulting from China's accession to WTO. Since 2000, they have begun to produce their latest products in China. In 2000, GlaxoSmithKline put China on its global marketing list of countries for its new drugs and established a raw materials factory in Tianjin. Bristol-Myers Squibb China has recently released five new drugs; Sanofi-Synthelabo of Hangzhou released a new anticoagulant in China; GlaxoSmithKline of Britain and Novo Nordisk of Norway have begun producing new drugs for the treatment of diabetes. These products have come under the protection of Chinese pharmaceutical administrative authorities. China has a population of 1.3 billion. It is not only a tremendous market; it is more likely to become a mammoth clinic research centre as well. In foreign countries patients have to be paid highly for the clinical experimentation of new drugs; in China the expenses in this regard are considerably low, prompting many pharmaceutical enterprises to consider the possibility of China to become a center for the development and clinical application of new drugs.

The strong competitiveness of the Chinese manufacturing industry is a major reason why transnational corporations speed up transfer their most sophisticated manufacturing capabilities to China. It has been driven home to many transnational corporations in the possession of advanced technology and strong R&D capacities that although the parent companies master central technology, they still lack competitiveness in the domestic manufacturing industry and that only by establishing large manufacturing capacities in China can their colossal R&D costs be rationed and their investment in R&D be recouped and yield a profit. Japan's Pioneer Group has since 2001 continuously and quickly shifted the production of its latest commodities to China in the knowledge that if it limited such production to Japan its prospects for profit would have been greatly dimmed. During the 2001-2002 fiscal year, Pioneer's patent revenue amounted to 17.6 billion yen and its profit totaled 15.3 billion yen. That is to say, without the patent revenue Pioneer would have been running a deficit. This reflected from one aspect the nature of Pioneer as a technology developmental enterprise, but it may also be interpreted that Pioneer is an enterprise unable to profit from manufacturing these patented products. Managers of Pioneer have come to see the necessity to get rid of its patent-dependent profit structure. This is because the terms of its major patents will expire one after another and the company's revenues from these patents will shrink considerably – in a couple of years there may have no earnings from these patents. Thus Pioneer made the important policy decision to build up the capacity to manufacture its own patented products so as to seek survival and development.

In August and September 2001, Pioneer established an affiliate in Dongguan and another one in Shanghai. Both Pioneer High Technology in Dongguan, which produces DVD recorders, and Pioneer High Technology in Shanghai, which produces vehicular acoustic equipment and DVD players, accounted for 12% of Pioneer Group's total business volume. More importantly, these affiliates have enabled the group's latest products to be manufactured simultaneously in China and Japan. The Dongguan affiliate began with producing a latest model of DVD recorder only five months after this product went into production in Pioneer's Towada affiliate in Japan. In autumn 2002 both Dongguan and Towada began manufacturing the same new products developed by Pioneer at the same time.

To manufacture products in China helps greatly weaken the competitiveness of imitators. The top policymakers of Pioneer believe that in the past Pioneer was the first to release quite a few new products but was often beaten shortly afterwards by imitators. The high manufacturing costs in Japan also put Pioneer at a disadvantage, a situation that could be remedied by investing in China. By manufacturing its products in China, Pioneer can achieve large-scale production of its new products during the early stage of the sales, and give its products prices that are competitive enough to deny opportunities for imitators.

Transnational corporations' effort to raise the level of their investment in China manifests itself not only in their products and equipment but also in their better services. In 2001, Hoffmann-La Roche Ltd., the world's leading pharmaceutical enterprise, worked together with Compaq to successfully set in motion the first CRM in the true sense of the term in the Chinese pharmaceutical industry. Roche hoped that the construction of CRM could enable it to thoroughly change its relationship with its clients in three to four years' time and raise its internal abilities. SK&F, wanting to be the leader of the OTC market of China, recently started its Apollo program with emphasis on increasing the number of sales agents in hospitals, raising the aptitudes of these sales agents and expanding its marketing personnel in rural markets. The efforts of Roche and SK&F show that foreign-invested enterprises have begun to expand their input from products and finance to management and services. Such broader and deeper investment will further raise the transnational corporations' investment level in China.

To sum up, as transnational corporations continue to invest massively in the Chinese manufacturing industry and raise the level of their technology and industrial structure, the position of China in the global manufacturing networks of these transnational corporations is changing from being a processing and assembling base with low technological contents and low incremental value to being a manufacturing centre with a complete array of products and technology.

10-2: The Number of Large Foreign-Invested Projects in Heavy Chemical Industry Is On the Increase

Since the beginning of the 21st century, the heavy chemical industry has emerged as a key area for transnational corporations seeking to invest in China. This situation is in a striking contrast with 20 years ago, when foreign investment was concentrated in medium-sized and small manufacturing industries. In 2001 and 2002 many such large projects were agreed upon or came under construction.

Sinopec Corp, Sinopec Shanghai Petrochemical Company Limited and BP jointly invested 2.7 billion US dollars in an ethylene installation with an annual output of 900,000 tons. When completed and commissioned in 2005, it will become the largest of its kind in the world and make up one quarter of China's current annual ethylene output. Shanghai Tianyuan Group, BASF and Huntsman have finished feasibility studies and signed a land contract on a 1 billion-dollar isocyanate joint venture. The seven projects with a 3.1 billion US dollar Bayer AG investment came under construction in Shanghai on November 2, 2001. In the Shanghai Chemical Industry Park, a number of projects totaling 3.8 billion US dollars of foreign investment have been approved. The construction of these large projects will enable the Shanghai Chemical Industrial Zone to complete the construction of China's largest isocyanate, polycarbonate and polyvinyl chloride producing centers and the nation's largest ethylene pyrolysis installation by 2005. The zone itself will emerge as the largest chemical centre in Asia and compare favorably with such world-class chemical zones as the Mexico Bay of the United States, Antwerp of Belgium and Ludwig of Germany. The other large transnational corporations, including Michelin, Emerson, Rockwell and IBM, have also invested in large projects in Shanghai. Emerson, for example, bought, for an additional 700 million US dollars, all the shares of the Shenzhen Ansheng Electrics Co., Ltd. under Huawei Technologies Co., Ltd..

The transnational corporations have also done impressively in the heavy chemical industry in some other cities. In Nanjing, for instance, there is the Yangtze Petrochemical-BASF, a world-class integrated high-tech petrochemical base built with the Sinopec Corp and the Germany company equally sharing a joint investment of 2.6 billion US dollars. This is by far the largest Sino-German joint venture. Royal Dutch/Shell Group will establish a large petrochemical factory in Guangdong Province with an investment of approximately 4 billion US dollars and another factory, with an annual output of 800,000 tons of ethylene and 2.3 million tons of other products, which will start operation by the end of 2005 in the Huizhou Daya Bay Economic & Technological Development Zone of Guangdong Province. BP's latest plan calls for at least 5 billion US dollars of investment in the next five years in order to expand its chemical, oil, natural gas and electricity businesses in China.

Moreover, transnational corporations are also investing in Chinese heavy chemical industry by purchasing the stocks of Chinese companies listed on overseas markets. Exxon Mobil, for instance, has bought 20% of the stocks worth 1 billion US dollars issued by the Sinopec Corp, and the two parties are also running a number of joint ventures in the Fujian Refining and Chemical Company – an oil refining installation with an annual capacity of 8 million tons, an ethylene installation with an annual capacity of 600,000 tons, and a polyethylene installation with an annual capacity of 450,00 tons, and a polypropylene installation with an annual capacity of 300,00 tons. They have also established joint ventures to sell petroleum products in Fujian and Guangdong provinces -- according to an agreement, they will run 150 gas stations in the first year, and the number will reach 500 in the third year.

Royal Dutch/ Shell Group acquired 14% of Sinopec Corp stocks worth 430 million US dollars. Apart from cooperating in exploring oil and gas resources in Tarim and Erdos basins, the two companies also invested 150 million US dollars on a fifty-fifty basis to use Royal Dutch/Shell Group's coal-gasifying technology to transform the Dongting Chemical Fertilizer Factory as well as chemical fertilizer plants in Hubei and Anhui provinces. They have also established a joint oil product distribution network in Jiangsu Province, with 150 gas stations built in the first year and a total of 500 by the end of the third year. Royal Dutch/Shell Group also planned to acquire 20% (worth 300 million US dollars) of the shares of China National Offshore Oil Corp. The Huizhou Petrochemical Project in Guangdong Province, by far the largest joint venture in China, has been undertaken by the China National Offshore Oil Corp and Royal Dutch/Shell Group sharing fifty-fifty a total investment of 4.05 billion US dollars. When completed in 2005, the project will produce 2.31 million tons of quality petrochemical products on an annual basis.

BP acquired 400 million US dollars of stocks of the Sinopec Corp, or 13.5% of the shares on sale, as well as 2 million US dollars of stocks of the China National Offshore Oil Corp. BP has also planned to build 1,200-1,500 gas stations in China. It will also join the Sinopec Corp and the Sinopec Shanghai Petrochemical Company Limited in building an ethylene installation with an annual capacity of 900,000 tons for a joint investment of 2.5-3.0 billion US dollars as well as a refined terephthalic acid installation with an annual capacity of 450,000 tons. So far BP has invested in 26 enterprises with a total investment of 4 billion US dollars. After it was merged with Amoco, BP has continued to expand its investment in China. In 2001, BP Amoco won a hotly contested bidding and was awarded the contract for the construction of China's first imported LNG terminal in Shenzhen, Guangdong Province, along with a gas transmission pipeline and other ancillary installation. The project with an investment of 800 million US dollars came under construction in the latter half of 2002, and when it is completed in 2005, it will be able to accept an annual import of 3 million tons of LNG. BP Amoco will work together with a Chinese consortium headed by the China National Offshore Oil Corp to carry out this project in which BP Amoco will have 30% of the shares while the Chinese partner will hold 70% of the shares.

10-3: Improving the R&D Level and Raising the Position of R&D Institutions

After China acceded to WTO, the R&D centers run by transnational corporations will not only increase rapidly in number but also improve the level of their R&D projects in China. More innovative projects will be conducted, and some of the technologies developed by these centers have reached world advanced levels.

1. Raising the Level of R&D Projects

In recent years some transnational corporations have begun high-level R&D projects in China. According to our survey of 19 foreign-invested R&D centers in Shanghai and Hangzhou by the end of 2002, sixteen were already engaged in important projects oriented to their parent companies' global businesses whereas in 1997 less than one tenth of them were doing this kind of work.

The optical transmission products developed by Alcatel Shanghai Bell Co., Ltd., 1642EM1662SMC and 169MSE, have been incorporated into Alcatel's global sales network. In October 2001, Alcatel announced that R&D of original technology for use in the Asian-Pacific region will be mainly conducted by Alcatel Shanghai Bell Co., Ltd., which is one of Alcatel's three global R&D centers (the other two being in Western Europe and North America). In three years' time, Alcatel Shanghai Bell Co., Ltd. will have 3,500 technicians in its R&D center. The R407C Environment-Friendly Compressor for air-conditioners developed by Hitachi (Shanghai) has upgraded Hitachi air-conditioners and laid the foundation for Hitachi to occupy the European market. Sun established an engineering research institute in China in 2001 to conduct global R&D work; many of the corporation's products for overseas markets were researched and developed mainly by its Chinese research institute, including those products to be sold in the Unite States. In October 2002, Nokia's R&D center was established in Hangzhou with emphasis on software and the technology for the platform of third-generation mobile telecommunication networks; all of this center's development results are used in Nokia's global 3G network.

Major Japanese semi-conductor manufacturing enterprises are also strengthening their designing and development systems in China. They want to establish centers for designing and developing semi-conductors for electronic meters and apparatuses as part of their systems of global division of labor. For this purpose these Japanese enterprises will speed up the transfer of their knowledge-intensive central designing and development departments to China. Toshiba has 500 people engaged in development work in Japan, and it has planned to expand its teams of designers and developers to 1,000 members in Japan and China respectively. Mitsubishi Electric has also planned to increase its Chinese team of designers and developers to 300 members in 2003. Fujitsu, NEC, Matsushita, Sony and other semiconductor enterprises have also planned to design and develop semi-conductors in China.

The R&D centers of transnational corporations in China are also using Chinese resources to research and develop technology at the world's advanced level. In October 2002, Novartis AG of Switzerland announced that a research project on the natural active substances in traditional Chinese medicinal herbs it had conducted with an investment of 4.5 million US dollars in cooperation with the Chinese Academy of Sciences Shanghai Institute of Materia Medica had yielded initial results. That is to say, 1,058 new chemical compounds were selected from the 1,562 compounds offered by the Shanghai Institute of Materia Medica in two catalogues, and 500 of them had entered Novartis AG' registration process.

In November 2001, BP and the Chinese Academy of Sciences signed a ten-year cooperative agreement that involved an investment of 10 million US dollars in the strategic research and technological development of clean energy sources. Accordingly a BP research centre would be established in the Dalian Institute of Chemical Physics, CAS. The agreement is by far the largest of its kind it has ever signed with any Western companies.

2. Raising the Position of R&D Centers in China

Improvement in the level of R&D projects conducted by transnational corporations in China has helped raise the position of the Chinese R&D centers in these corporations' global R&D networks. Some of these centers have become full-fledged global R&D centers for their parent corporations, some of them have become the only R&D centers or headquarters for these corporations, and a few of them have emerged as these corporations' only overseas R&D centers outside the parent countries.

In 1998, Microsoft Research China was established in Beijing. Because of Microsoft's leading position in software development, many Asian countries have promised many preferential policies for Microsoft if it decides to set up basic research institutes in their territories. The governments of some of the countries have gone so far as to agree to pay half of the investment over and above a series of favorable policies. Microsoft, however, has not been impressed. Instead, it elevated its Chinese research institute to Microsoft Research Asia in 2001.

In May 2002, Hewlett Packard established its fourth global software R&D center in Shanghai directly affiliated to its American headquarters. Nokia's R&D center in Hangzhou is its third global R&D center -- the other two being in Finland and the Silicon Valley of the United States respectively.

In July 2002, Dell set up its Chinese designing centre in the Changning District Multimedia Industrial Garden of Shanghai, which is Dell's first overseas R&D center whose task is to support Dell's global business in such fields as product designing, engineering and testing. The designing center began by recruiting 270 technical personnel and will increase its contingent of technicians to 1,000 in a few years' time.

Towards the end of 2002, Japan's Omron announced its decision to move its new product R&D center to Pudong District, Shanghai, so as to develop more electronic health products for the Chinese market and consumers. Prior to this the company had never established any overseas R&D institution – all its products were developed in Japan. The Chinese new product R&D center is the first of its kind overseas for this company.

By the end of 2002, LG started operating is R&D headquarters in China. Situated in Beijing's Wangjing Science and Technology Garden as LG's largest R&D center on the overseas market, this institution shall not only develop products for China but also research and develop new products for global sales. This institution is about the same size as LG's R&D headquarters in the Republic of Korea, and the relationship between the two is one of close coordination and cooperation. The staff of the R&D headquarters in Shanghai will expand from 200 in 2002 to 1,600 in 2005, and its R&D results shall be used and promoted both in China and all over the world.

Ericsson established its Chinese general R&D institute in Beijing in May 2002. Prior to this move Ericsson had set up six major research centers in China, with projects covering many fields such as 3G technology, networks, mobile telecom systems and mobile Internet. After the general institute was established it will engage in overall readjustment of all the existing R&D centers and research projects, strengthen the research of key projects, and boost the technological exchange and cooperation between various centers and between various research projects so as to fully mobilize the resources of different quarters. The Chinese general R&D institute will raise Ericsson's development level in China in an overall way and undertake more key global R&D tasks for the parent company.

10-4: Formation of Industrial Clusters of Foreign-invested Enterprises in China and the Raising of Industrial Competitiveness

The past few years have seen some regions in China attract so much foreign investment as to give rise to industrial clusters of foreign-invested enterprises. These industrial clusters are eschewing labor-intensive industries and upgrading themselves into capital- and technology-intensive industries. The table computer industrial cluster in Dongguan and the notebook computer industrial cluster in Suzhou are two typical cases in point.

1. FIEs Industrial Clusters in Dongguan's Electronic Industry

Dongguan, a small city in Guangdong Province, was where the earliest and most typical FIEs industrial clusters appeared on the Chinese mainland. With its close proximity to Hong Kong, the city is conveniently located for the processing industry. Investors coming from Hong Kong invariably set foot first on Shenzhen and then on Dongguan, where the land is vast and labor and other costs are low.

Since the adoption of the open policy, Dongguan has never stopped wooing large amounts of foreign investment, especially from Hong Kong and Taiwan.

In 2000 the city accounted for 4.1% of the total amount of foreign investment attracted to China, or 14.6% of the amount attracted to Guangdong Province.

In the early 1980s, enterprises in Dongguan were mainly engaged in the processing of apparels, shoes, hats, toys, etc. from Hong Kong, Macao and Taiwan. In recent years, however, more computer part dealers are arriving. Beginning from the mid-1990s in particular, investment from Taiwan computer enterprises has been gravitating towards Dongguan. By the end of June 2000, Taiwan enterprises in this city numbered 3,926, made up 29% of the city's total number of foreign-invested enterprises, and actually invested a total of 3.36 billion US dollars or 28% of the total amount of FDI that had been utilized in Dongguan. For every ten Taiwan-invested enterprises in China, one is found in Dongguan, and one third of the Taiwan-invested enterprises in Guangdong Province are in Dongguan. Dongguan thus made a name for itself for its largest cluster of Taiwan-invested enterprises.

Taiwan PCB manufacturers, for example, have shifted over two thirds of their total production capacity to the mainland. During its heyday, FCB manufacturing in Taiwan boasted several dozen factories, but a poor water and electricity supply environment, and rising labor costs, have driven the manufacturers collectively to south China, where Dongguan has become the major destination. In recent years they have set their eyes on east China. Judging from this trend, in a few years' time, Taiwan's PCB manufacturing will be entirely moved to China, leaving behind only its financial headquarters, and some of the IC carrier boards that are difficult to produce. In other words, the mainland of China has become the globe's PCB manufacturing center. Taiwan enterprises are also manufacturing more than half of their mouses, disc players, encasements, keyboards, UPS, scanners, adobes, and sound blasters in the mainland

With Taiwan enterprises taking the lead, electronic enterprises from Hong Kong and foreign countries have also found their way into Dongguan, turning the electronic industry into one with the close clusters of FIEs. The FIEs in the electronic industry account for 32.5% of all the foreign capital in Dongguan. See Table 10-1.

Table 10-1: Distribution of FDI industries in Dongguan as of 2000

Industry	Share in Dongguan's actual volume of foreign capital utilized (%)
Electronics	32.5
Machinery and equipment	14.3
Textiles and apparels	11.2
Rubber and plastic products	10.5

Source: Dongguan Municipal Statistical Bureau.

In the late 1990s, computer and information industry developed rapidly to turn Dongguan into China's leading desktop computer and computer parts manufacturing center. The industrial chain in Dongguan is so complete that the city is able to supply 95% of all the component parts needed to assemble a computer. The Dongguan phenomenon attracted worldwide attention, and Dongguan-produced information and computer products have carved an important niche in the world market. The city finds itself among the front ranks in the manufacturing of computer magnetic heads, mainboards, monitors, scanners, drivers, etc. and is the purchasing center for the world's top ten computer companies including IBM, Compaq, Hewlett Packard. Of the importance of Dongguan's IT manufacturing industry, an IBM vice-president said to the effect that a mere 15-minute jam on the Dongguan-Shenzhen expressway is enough to cause worldwide fluctuations in computer prices.

The establishment of so many Taiwan-invested enterprises has brought in its wake the settlement of a large contingent of Taiwan investors and their families. This gave rise to a sizeable Taiwan community in Dongguan. Investors from Taiwan pooled 7 million yuan and set up a school to recruit their own children. The school runs 40 young children's classes, 20 elementary classes and seven junior middle classes. The teachers come from Taiwan and their teaching methods are the same as those in Taiwan. This school has enabled Taiwan investors to do business without misgivings now that the education of their children is being properly taken care of.

The massive foreign investment influx has fueled sustained economic development and readjustment in Dongguan. During the 1979-2001 period, the city's GDP recorded an average annual growth rate of 22%. In 2001, its GDP amounted to 57.8 billion yuan, its tax revenue totaled 10.1 billion yuan, and its total volume of exports reached 18.99 billion US dollars, accounting for 19.9% of the total of Guangdong Province and 7.1% of the national total. For five years running Dongguan has ranked third among all the large and medium-sized cities in terms of volume of exports, and its trade surplus has reached an all-time high of 11.935 billion US dollars.

2. FIEs Clusters in Suzhou's Electronic Industry

Since the end of the 1990s, Suzhou has been attracting large amounts of FDI. As a result the foreign-invested economy figures importantly in the local economy. In 2001, the foreign-invested sector contributed 40% of the city's financial revenue, accounted for 50% of the total number of employees, and made up 80 percent of the city's total volume of exports.

Eighty-one of the world's top 500 transnational companies had opened shop in Suzhou by the end of July 2002. Sixty-three of such projects recorded more than 100 million US dollars in investment. The FIEs have enabled Suzhou to form its new and hi-tech industrial clusters predicated on electronic information, precision machinery, biological pharmaceutical, and new materials industries.

The FIEs in Suzhou are marked for two salient features. Firstly, Taiwan investors are concentrated in this municipality and their products are increasingly becoming more technology-intensive. So far there are more than 600 Taiwan-invested IT enterprises in the entire Suzhou Prefecture. None of the ten major laptop computer manufacturers of Taiwan have invested in Suzhou and their total annual output has exceeded 10 million laptops. Suzhou has indeed become a major repository of hi-tech investors from Taiwan. Secondly, massive amounts of foreign capital are concentrated in the electronic industry. The FIEs have formed an industrial cluster in this industry, with the electronic information industry accounting for 39.7% of the total contractual volume of foreign investment in the local industry.

As the manufacturing of laptop computers is gravitating towards east China, successful Taiwan electronic enterprises in Dongguan often arrange their new production capacity in Suzhou when they shift their production to laptop computers and component parts. With the concentration of laptop manufacturers in Suzhou and the rest of east China, factories for the production of component parts have arrived one after another in the Yangtze River Delta. As a result a complete laptop computer manufacture cluster has emerged in the vicinity of Shanghai.

Foreign investors in Chinese computer industry have chosen to build new industrial clusters in Suzhou and even the entire Yangtze River Delta rather than upgrade and expand what they have built in Dongguan for a series of reasons.

1) Higher Technological Level of FIEs in Suzhou

Since the beginning of the 1990s, the industrial structure on the Taiwan Island has been upgraded rapidly. Accordingly, the Taiwan enterprises shifting their production to the mainland since the end of the 1990s have markedly upgraded their technological level. The Taiwan-invested enterprises in Dongguan, including those in the electronic industry are basically of an intensive-intensive type. Dongguan is a medium-sized city that has emerged in the last two decades. The education level of the local residents is relatively low, and employees in the Taiwan-invested enterprises come mostly from the hinterland and their wages are low. There is not a single college in Dongguan, making it impossible for the city to supply well-educated professionals.

Towards the end of the 1990s, mainland investment from Taiwan and overseas were marked by a remarkable increase in the technology employed. In Taiwan, for example, computer production was shifted to the production of laptops, which falls into the same category as the production of cellulous phones and PDAs and closely interacts with the designing, production and packaging of transistors. Today, both industrial clusters have begun shifting to the mainland. Given its commercial and cultural environment and industrial foundation, Dongguan, or even the entire south China, is not in a position to meet the demand of these industrial clusters whose degrees of intensiveness of capital, technology and human resources of capital and technological intensity are higher than the production system based on desktop computer production. That is why mainstream information and electronic enterprises from Taiwan began large-scale investment in Shanghai and peripheral areas around 1999.

An investment report issued in early 2002 by the Taipei Commercial Association pointed out that an upsurge of Taiwan investment in the mainland occurred in 2001. Towards the end of 2000, 30.5% of Taiwan's electronics enterprises had invested in the mainland, but a year later, towards the end of 2001, the figure rose to 52.8%. Moreover, the Yangtze River Delta became the major repository of such Taiwan investment – the investment in Jiangsu Province alone made up more than half of the total sum of investment in the mainland by Taiwan electronics enterprises. Judging from the scale of projects under construction, it will not take long for the production capacity of Taiwan enterprises in the Yangtze River Delta to exceed the production capacity of all the electronics enterprises in Taiwan.

2) Suzhou's Good Location

As the production of laptop computers that calls for higher technology is being shifted towards the mainland, the FIEs call for managers and technicians of a higher technological level, and have higher requirements for supplementary industries. In the meantime, FIEs in China are changing their market goals as well. In the past they aimed at the world market; today, they hope to seize larger shares of China's home market. Thus they hope that the place they have invested in will have large market potentials. With their well-developed industrial foundation, the high education level of local residents, and a potentially vast market, Shanghai and the Yangtze River Delta surrounding it are undoubtedly richly endowed with such market potentials.

However, Shanghai is also handicapped by a disadvantage: high costs. To explore Shanghai's strengths and avoid its disadvantages, foreign investors naturally choose Suzhou and vicinity as their destination because the industry of the area is well founded, its costs are relatively low, and it has the strong backings of Shanghai.

Suzhou is located in the neighborhood of Shanghai. Transportation is convenient. Kunshan, a city under Suzhou Municipality, borders on Shanghai, and a 50-km bus ride from downtown Kunshan to downtown Shanghai takes less than one hour. Trains shuttling between the two places on an hourly basis have virtually turned Kunshan into a suburban town of Shanghai. Because of such convenience in transportation, some transnational companies have their headquarters, sales departments and hi-tech manufacturing sections in Shanghai while setting up manufacturing centers in Suzhou, so that they can benefit from the advantages of both places. In 2001 and the first six months of 2002, Suzhou attracted largely the same amounts of foreign capital as Shanghai.

3) Temptations of Good Living Conditions in the Yangtze River Delta

Since the beginning of 2000, the deteriorating political and economic situation of Taiwan has compelled quite a few Taiwan residents to consider both investing in the mainland and immigrating to it. For historical reasons, many Taiwan residents actually hailed from Jiangsu and Zhejiang provinces and east China as whole holds forth the fascination and appeal of culture to them. As a result of high-speed development over the last few years, the infrastructure of east China in general and Shanghai in particular has approached the level of Taipei. East China has become the common favorite choice for immigrants from Taiwan.

4) China's Huge Market Potentials, and the Demand of OEM Clients

In 2001, laptop computer sales on the Chinese market totaled 570,000, and the sales volume approached 9.8 billion RMB. Investigations indicate that both Europe and China will become the fastest growing laptop markets in the world in three years' time. As the base number of laptops in China is fairly small, the market gap to be filled in is huge.

Well-known brands of many large transnational companies enjoy large shares of this potentially large market, and one after another they have announced plans to manufacture their products in China. Laptop manufacturers such as Toshiba, Sharp, Sony, Dell, IBM, Dell, and Compaq have set up manufacturing centers in China, and they demand Taiwan's EMS-supplying enterprises to invest and establish factories in the mainland. The initial mainland investment plans of many Taiwan manufacturers were catered to the demand of their OEM clients.

10-5: Participation of Foreign Investment in Transformation and Regrouping of Large State-owned Enterprises

Incorporating foreign investment in regrouping large state-owned enterprises was a major breakthrough China scored in utilizing foreign capital in 2002.

The 4th Plenary Session of the 15th Party Central Committee held in 1999 brought large and medium-sized state enterprises within the scope of reform, pointing out that the state-owned assets in competitive fields can be allowed to flow, listed companies can reduce their state-owned shares, and non-listed companies can sell their state assets. However, the ability of non-state investors in China to serve as strategic investors in the reform and regrouping of large state-owned enterprises is limited. After China's accession to WTO it has gradually dawned on top policymakers to involve transnational corporations in transforming and regrouping large state-owned enterprises.

Since 2002, major breakthroughs have been made in the overall joint ventures and cooperation between large state-owned enterprises in China and the world's giant transnational corporations. There are three major cases in point in this regard: first, full-fledged cooperation between FAW and Toyota; second, full-fledged cooperation between the DongFeng Automobile Co., Ltd. and Nissan; and third, the Municipal Government of Shenzhen put the shares of five state-owned groups for international bidding and transfer. All these three cases of corporate regrouping each involved upwards of 10 billion RMB and were therefore landmark events in China's effort to reform its state-owned enterprises.

On August 29, 2002, FAW of China and Toyota of Japan held a ceremony in Beijing to sign a cooperative agreement. FAW is a mainstay enterprise in the Chinese auto industry, and its products cover six series – medium-, heavy- and light-load trucks, cars, buses and minibuses – and it had led the Chinese auto industry in both output and sales for ten years running. In 2001, it was cited as the most influential industrial enterprise group in China. Toyota is a world-renowned automaker as well as a globalised enterprise that holds advantages in both technology and management. Although what was signed was merely a framework agreement, both partners announced that they had reached agreement and signed contracts on three lines of production -- medium- and high-grade buses, minibuses, and medium- and high-grade SUVs. It is estimated that the joint venture's annual sales will reach 300,000-400,000 by 2010. All these three lines of products are FAW's weak points or blanks, whereas Toyota has adequate resources for each line of production. The joint venture between FAW and Toyota will become a major landmark event in the Chinese history of large state-owned enterprises utilizing foreign capital.

On September 19, DongFeng Automobile Co., Ltd. and Nissan announced a plan to fully cooperate with each other to build the largest joint venture in China for the production of full lines of cars, light-load commercial vehicles and passenger automobiles. According to the agreement, Nissan will directly invest 1.03 billion US dollars (equivalent to 8.55 billion RMB) in DongFeng Automobile Co., Ltd. so as to earn control of 50% of the joint venture while its Chinese partner will own the other half of the shares by investment in kind and assets. Both partners believe that the Dongfeng-Nissan joint venture is totally different from previous joint ventures in the auto industry -- rather, it represents a new mode of regrouping state-owned enterprises in China, for it is no longer cooperation on the basis of a single automobile model but involves the merger of two companies. According to the agreement, Nissan will provide the new company with its managerial expertise in such fields as product planning, purchases, factory productivity, logistics, quality control, brand management, marketing, sales network and financial service. In addition, the new company will, apart from strengthening DongFeng's old commercial vehicle R&D center, establish a new center for the R&D of passenger automobiles. The new DongFeng will include not only projects in cooperation with French PSA and Japanese Nissan but also other central businesses.

In August 2002, the Shenzhen Municipal Government announced to put up 25% to 70% of the shares of the city's energy, water supply, gas, metro service, and foodstuff groups for public international bidding. The bidding involved more than 20 billion RMB worth of the finest state-owned assets. Many global buyers were impressed by the future economic returns of these assets. This was the first time ever in China for the government to directly put large amounts of state-owned shares for international bidding.

Apart from these three cases in point, many local governments have formulated policies to attract foreign investors in M&As. Shanghai, for instance, announced in November 2002 that the city was formulating, in the light of its situations, policies to facilitate foreign investment in mergers and acquisitions of state-owned enterprises. Seven fields were slated for this purpose: first, M&As that involve the introduction of new products, technology and technological processes and the promotion of industrial restructuring and the readjustment of the product mix; second, M&As concerning new agricultural technology, comprehensive agricultural development, as well as such fields as energy, transportation and major materials; third, M&As concerning the use of high technology and the expansion of new industry fields; fourth, M&As for multipurpose utilization of resources and renewable resources as well as the prevention of environmental pollution; fifth, M&As conducive for upgrading products and technology and opening up the world market; sixth, M&As that help raise enterprises' management level and use available assets to improve enterprises' economic returns; and seventh, M&As favorable for the regrouping of state-owned enterprises. To promote this work, Shanghai established ad hoc departments in the Shanghai Property Rights Trading Centre and other organizations to offer information for buyers and sellers, handle applications for M&As and provide valuation and trading services.

10-6: Transnational Corporations Rectifying and Consolidating their Business in China

Since 2001 many transnational corporations have been regrouping their enterprises in China. A major reason for this is that the Chinese market was still in a process of continuous improvement due to limitations in investment scales, venues and modes of management and that the major changes taking place after China's accession to WTO have made it possible and necessary for transnational corporations to rectify and consolidate their business in China.

Those transnational corporations that entered China in an early stage often had a number of investment projects that were thinly scattered because the overwhelming majority of them were undertaken in a sporadic fashion. The Roche Taishan (Shanghai) Vitamin Company and the Roche 3V (Shanghai) Vitamin Company, for instance, were established at the same time in 1995 and both are situated in the Shanghai Spark Development Zone and separated by a tiny lawn. Both are controlled by the Roche Company, which owns 70% of the shares of Roche Taishan and 60% of the shares of Roche 3V. Roche also owns 60% of the shares of the Roche Xinya (Shanghai) Vitamin Company, a joint venture set up in 1996 with a local vitamin factory in Shanghai.

Roche's separate investment was a result of the environment. According to the Chinese policy towards foreign capital at the time, joint ventures exceeding 30 million US dollars in investment had to be approved and examined by the central authorities, and the investment in each of these three joint ventures of Roche was precisely kept below that 30 million US dollar mark. In the meantime, Roche had a complete array of production lines but at the time there was not a single Chinese enterprise in Shanghai that could be turned into a joint venture capable of producing Vitamin A, E and B6 simultaneously.

Of the three Roche joint ventures, Roche Taishan produced Vitamin A, Roche 3V produced Vitamin E, and Roche Xinya produced Vitamin B6. Because Roche Taishan made Vitamin A as both a raw material and pre-mixed materials, it had to buy certain amounts of raw materials from the other two Roche joint ventures. With the changed Chinese policies, and its improved ability handling the Chinese market, Roche felt it was time to regroup its business in China on a large scale. By the end of 2001, the three joint ventures were merged into one and began, as of March 1, 2002, to conduct business exchanges with the outside world under a simpler name – Roche (Shanghai) Vitamin Company. The managerial staff was cut as a result. In the past the three joint ventures each had a general manager from Hong Kong and a manager in charge of technology. Roche (Shanghai) Vitamin today has only one general manager and one technological manager. The Chinese staff, too, was cut to size.

From 2001 to 2002, the world's top tyre-maker, Michelin, also regrouped its business in China. Michelin established its first joint venture in China with the Shenyang General Tire Factory towards the end of 1995; later it set up three other joint ventures in this country. By the end of 2002, Michelin finished merging these four joint ventures in Shenyang. Toshiba had 23 affiliates in China each reported its work to the headquarters in Tokyo. Since 2002, the functions of Toshiba (China) Company were gradually upgraded to the extent that it could integrate all the businesses of Toshiba in China. Today, Toshiba affiliates in China not only report to their Tokyo headquarters but also make financial reports to Toshiba (China) Company. The most typical case of Toshiba teamwork in China was that the 23 Toshiba affiliates in China formed a single team to bid for construction projects for the 2008 Beijing

Olympic Games, with all the liaison work with the Beijing Municipal Government handled uniformly by Toshiba (China) Company, whose chairman is also responsible for coordinating projects among the affiliates.

With 49 joint ventures and 41 manufacturing factories in China, Matsushita was one of the transnational corporations having the largest production and business lines in China. For a long time these 49 joint ventures follow instructions from different departments of the Matsushita headquarters in Japan. In the beginning of 2002, the top management of Matsushita announced that it was to merge its 41 manufacturing factories in China. The sales organizations scattered in the joint ventures were the first to be combined into an independent and unified sales department. In 2003, various joint ventures are being readjusted, regrouped and merged, and a wholly owned company Matsushita (China) Company will be established.

On April 1, Hitachi merged its two Shanghai affiliates – Shanghai Hitachi Household Electrical Appliances (SHHA) and the washing machine-producing Shanghai Hitachi Electrical Appliance (SHEA) – and established the Shanghai Hitachi Household Electrical Appliance Company. The merger took place in an “absorption and merger” fashion. Shanghai Hitachi Household Electrical Appliances was established in 1994, with the Shanghai Electrical Apparatus Co., Ltd. holding 40% of the shares and Hitachi and its Investment Company holding 60% of the shares. Shanghai Hitachi Electrical Machines was established in 1995, but it had the same partners and investment ratio as Shanghai Hitachi Household Electrical Appliance. In fact the two joint ventures had the same people on their boards of trustees. The difference was that the former was doing fine in the first few years whereas the latter was losing money for consecutive years due to flawed management and became consolidated when the merger took place. The new company had a total investment of 75.8 million US dollars and a registered capital of 48.67 million US dollars, with the Chinese partner holding 40% of the shares and the Japanese partner holding 60% of the shares. The merger of its two Shanghai affiliates signified Hitachi’s effort to regroup its businesses in China.

Hitachi is also preparing to merge its household electrical appliance business in China. Its plan is to turn Shanghai and Wuhu into its bases for the production of “white” household electrical appliances, and turn Shenzhen and Fuzhou into its centers for the production of high-standard color television sets and displayors. In sales, Hitachi tries to readjust its household electrical appliance sales channels in China to as to raise its multipurpose utilization efficiency. Specifically, Shanghai Hitachi’s sales network includes three branch companies and 20 or so outlets whose main task is to sell the company’s own air-conditioners and washing machines. After the Wuhu factory goes into production, products will be marketed by Hitachi (Shanghia). Hitachi’s logistics department has also entered China, where joined hands with Shanghai Airlines Co., Ltd. and Zhengda Shipping Company to establish a joint venture, the Dahang International Cargo Shipping Company, with Hitachi Logistics owning 30% of the shares. Hitachi has also planned to set up an international purchase centre and one R&D center in China, and Shanghai will be the place for both centers when they are established in 2004. Hitachi is also rectifying its other businesses in China. On April 1, 2003, its two joint ventures in Shanghai –SHHA that dealt mainly in air-conditioners, and the SHEA whose main business was washing machines – were merged to form the new SHEA.

Chapter 11

FOREIGN INVESTMENT SERVICE SECTOR: TRENDS AND SALIENT FEATURES

The most important commitment made by China during negotiations on its accession to WTO was to expand the openness of its service sector. During the year since the nation acceded to WTO there has been a remarkable increase in foreign investment in the Chinese service sector. Some of the service sector which were only marginally opened to the outside world have become more open; and the opening up of some of the service sector formerly closed to the outside world are picking up speed. These opening up efforts are having a positive impact on expanding FDI inflow and raising the efficiency and competitiveness of the Chinese service sector, and such impact will continue in the future.

11-1: GENERAL INTRODUCTION TO FDI INFLOW IN THE CHINESE SERVICE SECTOR

The opening of the Chinese service sector started long before China's accession to WTO. Jianguo Hotel, a joint venture with Chinese and American investment, was one of the first three joint ventures established in China. Since then the service sector continued to open up, and by the eve of the nation's accession to WTO, a considerable number of these industries had already attracted large amounts of FDI.

In 2002, a total of 8,059 new joint ventures were established in the service sector in China, 26.44% up from the corresponding period of the previous year and accounting for 23.59% of the total number of joint ventures newly established during the same period; involving 22.763 billion US dollars in contractual FDI value, up 29.38% from the corresponding period of the previous year and making up 27.51% of national total contractual FDI. The realized FDI amounted to 14.011 billion US dollars, up 27.03% from the previous year and accounting for 26.57% of national total realized FDI.

By the end of 2002, the service sector had attracted a total of 288 billion US dollars in contractual FDI or 34.78% of the national total contractual FDI. See Table 11-1.

Table 11-1: Industrial structure for FDI by 2002

(Unit: billion US dollars)

Sector	Number of Project	Share	Contractual FDI Value	Share
Total	424196	100%	8280.59	100%
Agriculture	12217	2.88%	157.59	1.90%
Manufacturing	310279	73.15%	5242.86	63.32%
Services	101700	23.97%	2880.15	34.78%

Source: MOFTEC database.

The following sections give a general introduction to foreign investment in some important service sector and the latest progress made in this regard after China's accession to WTO.

11-2: The Opening-up of Financial Services Quickened

1. Financial Services

China started attracting foreign investment in banks on a trial basis in 1982. In 1995, with a State Council approval, the number of cities experimenting in attracting foreign investment in banks increased from 13 to 24, and in 1999, the experiments spread to all the central cities across the country. Today, foreign financial organizations can open commercial financial organizations in all the cities in China, and the forms of investment run the gamut from foreign bank affiliates, wholly foreign-owned or joint banks, wholly foreign-owned or joint financial companies, and joint investment banks. Prior to China's accession to WTO, foreign financial organizations could only engage in foreign currency businesses.

Since 2001, Chinese financial services have made many important breakthroughs in the process of opening up to the outside world.

The Renminbi business was opened to foreign-invested enterprises (FIEs) in Shanghai, Shenzhen, Tianjin and Dalian on December 11, 2001, the day China acceded to WTO, and five more cities – Guangzhou, Zhuhai, Qingdao, Nanjing and Wuhan – were added to the list on December 1, 2002. Since the *Regulations of the People's Republic of China on the Administration of Foreign-funded Financial Institutions* and *Detailed Rules for the Implementation of the Regulations of the People's Republic of China on the Administration of Foreign-funded Financial Institutions* were promulgated on February 1, 2002, the People's Bank of China has granted 23 foreign-invested enterprises with the right to deal in Renminbi business. As a result the number of such banks engaged in Renminbi business reached 53, including 30 in Shanghai, 14 in Shenzhen, 5 in Tianjin and 4 in Dalian. By the end of October 2002, foreign banks had opened 181 business organizations in China, including 147 foreign bank affiliates (with 8 branches under them) and 19 corporate entities (with 7 branches under them) registered with Chinese authorities, totaling 37.965 billion US dollars in total assets and 33.797 billion US dollars in gross liabilities, including 49.597 billion RMB in total assets in Renminbi and 42.346 billion RMB in gross liabilities in Renminbi. In January-July, 2002, foreign-invested banks netted a total profit of 184 billion RMB in Renminbi business and 119 million US dollars in foreign exchange business.

A noteworthy phenomenon is that in most cases foreign investment has entered the Chinese banking market by buying shares. Toward the end of 2001, the Bank of Shanghai announced that HSBC and Shanghai Business Bank had invested to become its shareholders and the World Bank's IFC (International Commercial Corporation) had expanded its shares so that foreign investment amounted to 18% of the Bank of Shanghai's total shares, and the total number of Bank of Shanghai shares had increased by 600 million shares from 2 billion to 2.6 billion, with HSBC holding 8% of the shares, Shanghai Commercial Bank of Hong Kong holding 3%, and IFC holding 7% as against 5% when it became a shareholder two years ago. The joint Bank of Shanghai thus became the first to attract foreign banks as shareholders, the first to have several foreign banks as shareholders and by far the domestic commercial bank with the highest percentage of foreign investment. According to incomplete statistics, similar cases have emerged since then. See Table 2.

Table 11-2: Available and forthcoming cases of foreign investment holding shares of domestic banks

Domestic Banks	Foreign Shareholders	Price for acquisition US$ 10000	Shares being held %
	IFC 1999.9	2200	3%
Bank of Shanghai	HSBC 2001.12	3500	8%
	Shanghai Business Bank 2001.12	3000	7%
China Everbright Bank	Asian Development Bank		3%
Nanjing City Commercial Bank	IFC	2700	15%
Shenzhen Development Bank Co., Ltd.	New Bridge Capital Ltd. 2002.10	20000	15%
Shanghai Pudong Development Bank	Citibank 2003.1	6700	-

Foreign investment is also entering the Chinese banking industry by establishing new joint ventures with Chinese and foreign investment. For instance, after four years of preparation, the Sino-German Housing Savings Bank, a joint venture between the China Construction Bank and the Bausparkasse Sparasse Schwabischal, gained the approval of the People's Bank of China and was to be opened in Tianjin sometime in 2003. According to sources, the Sino-German Housing Savings Bank is a company with limited liability with a registered capital of 150 million RMB, with the China Construction Bank holding 75.1% of the shares and the Bausparkasse Sparasse Schwabischalholding 24.9% of the shares. The combination of the successful experience and advanced technology of Bausparkasse Sparasse Schwabischal in managing housing savings banks with the superiority of the China Construction Bank as a state-owned bank enables the joint venture to provide new financial products by combining housing savings and housing loan grants. There is enough reason to believe that this new innovation in the domestic housing financial market will promote the reform of the Chinese housing system, expand the domestic demand and boost the housing consumption. It goes without saying that the housing savings bank also helps attract foreign investment and diversify the risks and pressures on the otherwise wholly owned business of the China Construction Bank.

2. Insurance Services

In 1992 China conditionally opened its insurance market by allowing foreign insurance companies to run affiliates and joint ventures on a trial basis in Shanghai. The experimentation was expanded to Guangzhou in 1995. By the end of 2001, a total of 44 business organizations had been established in China by 29 foreign insurance companies.

After China's accession to WTO, the insurance market has been steadily opened up to the outside world. In 2002 the opening up effort took on a more positive and systematic note, the insurance market was opened in both breadth and depth, and the number of participants in this market continued to increase. The CIGNA Worldwide Insurance Company of the United States, MUNICH RE GROUP of Germany, Swiss Re, Property Insurance of Japan, Liberty Mutual Insurance of the United States, and Standard Life Insurance of Britain gained the green light to prepare for the establishment of insurance companies in the Chinese market, and 15 foreign-invested insurance companies went into operation. By November 2002, a total of 34 foreign insurance companies had been approved to operate in China; these included 19 joint ventures with Chinese and foreign investment, 13 foreign insurance company affiliates, and 2 foreign-invested intermediary organizations. In addition, 112 foreign-owned insurance companies from 19 countries and regions had opened 199 representative offices in 14 cities in China. The opening up effort had expanded gradually from Shanghai to Guangzhou and other places. The business of foreign-invested insurance companies were expanding steadily, with the insurance revenue of foreign-invested and joint venture insurance companies growing from 295,000 RMB in 1992 to 3.329 billion RMB in 2001 or 1.58% of the Chinese market; in 2001, foreign-invested insurance companies garnered a total revenue of 3.2 billion RMB. In Shanghai and Guangzhou, foreign-invested companies accounted for 14.4% and 11.8% respectively of the local life insurance markets and 6.7% and 1.5% respectively of the local property insurance markets. The foreign-invested insurance business has gradually expanded from Shanghai and Guangzhou to Shenzhen, Dalian and Foshan.

In the meantime, for foreign investment to directly hold the shares of domestic insurance companies and indirectly enter the Chinese insurance services have become a convenient way for foreign investment to be involved in China's insurance business. Previously, some foreign financial organizations had already held shares of Chinese insurance companies. Winterthur Swiss Insurance, for instance, was a shareholder of the Taikang Life Insurance Co., Ltd., and the Zurich Insurance Company of Switzerland was a shareholder of the New China Life Insurance Co., Ltd., but their shares were low. In 2002, FDI inflow gained new momentum. In May 2002, for instance, the three insurance companies under the American AEC Group spent 150 million US dollars and gained 22.13% of the shares of the Huatai Insurance Company of China. Limited; in October, HSBC bought 10% of the shares of the Ping An Insurance Company of China for 600 million US dollars to become the third international investor after Morgan Stanley Dean Witter & Co and Goldman Sachs. As a result, both Chinese insurance companies were able to make a big step in replenishing their capital funds, improving their corporate structures and raising their technological and managerial levels.

Moreover, Holland International Group and the Beijing Capital Group announced the establishment of the Capital Safe Life Insurance Company in Dalian, and AIA from United States established an affiliate in Beijing.

The plans of the People's Insurance Company of China and the China Life Insurance Company to introduce joint-stock systems to their life and endowment insurance businesses were officially approved by the State Council on December 23, 2002. Not long ago, the two companies revealed that their introduction of the joint-stock system will enter an essential stage in 2003 and they will strive to issue stocks and become listed companies at an early date. According to sources, the People's Insurance Company of China will raise 5 million US dollars from overseas while the goal of the China Life Insurance Company is 2 billion US dollars. The steps taken by these two companies have unveiled the efforts of large state-owned insurance companies in China to woo foreign shareholders.

What is noteworthy is that when foreign investment flows abundantly into the Chinese insurance market, some foreign-invested insurance companies that had gained the green light to run business offices are withdrawing from China, such as LUNENG of Germany, Swiss Life and Swiss Endowment of Switzerland, the Lincoln Financial Group of the United States. According to incomplete statistics, 22 foreign insurance companies pulled 30 of their representative offices away from China from 2001 to September 2002. The reasons behind this are manifold, including strategic readjustments of foreign insurance companies. For instance, after the 911 terrorist attacks, Luneng Re under Luneng Insurance Group suffered such heavy losses that it had to cut down its frontline. Swiss Life was conducting a global strategic transition. There are also cases in which foreign investors found it hard to adjust to the Chinese market or lacked confidence in the Chinese market. The other factors are concerned with the drawbacks of the Chinese insurance market, such as the lack of public awareness of insurance, inadequate credentials of staff members, unwieldy financial operation, and poor management.

Remarkable changes have taken place in the reinsurance market. At the beginning of 2002, the China Reinsurance Company, the only one of its kind in China, adopted the strategic goal of going all out to develop commercial reinsurance business. This is because when acceding to WTO China committed to abolishing mandatory reinsurance, which happens to be mainstay of the business line of the Chinese Reinsurance Company. The revised *Insurance Law* promulgated in October 2002 deleted clauses on mandatory reinsurance. A China Insurance Regulatory Commission circular issued thereafter called for gradual reduction of the percentage of mandatory insurance as of January 1, 2003, until its total abolishment. In 2002, two global reinsurance companies, the Munich Reinsurance Company and the Swiss Reinsurance Company, gained permission to establish branch companies in China, putting an end to the monopoly of reinsurance business in China by a single company and opening the last protected part of the Chinese insurance market to the outside world. Reinsurance as a secondary risk-diversifying measure is of major significance for the safety and stability of the entire insurance system. Reinsurance in China went off to a late start, and, having all along been under government protection, was handicapped by a low level of commercialization and limited sustainability. The market changes in 2002 helped strengthen the Chinese Reinsurance Company as a whole, boosted the growth of the Chinese reinsurance business, and raised the level of development of the Chinese reinsurance business as a whole.

3. Securities Services

For its WTO membership China has committed to opening up its securities services in three regards: B-stock trading method and niche, establishment of joint-venture securities companies, and establishment of joint-venture fund management companies.

Before China's accession to WTO two securities companies with joint Chinese and foreign investment had already been doing business in China. One was the China International Capital Corporation Limited established in 1995 with American Morgan Stanley that was entitled to sell the stocks of domestic listed companies. The other was BOCI Securities Ltd. established in 2001 with BOC International Holdings Ltd. from Hong Kong.

On December 19, 2002, China Securities Regulatory Commission approved the establishment of the China Euro Securities as the first joint securities company to be established after China's accession to WTO. A joint venture between Xiangcai Securities Co., Ltd. and CLSA, China Euro Securities is registered in Shanghai with 500 million RMB in capital fund, with Xiangcai holding 67% of the shares and CLSA holding 33% of the shares.

China Euro Securities was the first successful case of cooperation between a Chinese securities company and a European investment bank as well as the first joint securities company with Chinese and foreign investment to be established after the promulgation of the *Rules for the Establishment of Foreign-shared Securities Companies*,[1] which heralded the birth of more securities joint ventures in he days to come. China Euro Securities' state business line will include sales of stocks (ordinary Renminbi stocks and foreign-invested shares included) and treasury bonds (government and corporate bonds included), the commissioning of foreign-invested shares, and other businesses approved by China Securities Regulatory Commission.

According to the requirements of China Securities Regulatory Commission, China Euro Securities will be established on June 18, 2003 at the latest, and after it gets the permit for securities businesses from China Securities Regulatory Commission, will take an official part in the operation and development of the Chinese securities market.

In addition, the International Financial Company, BNP Paribas S.A. and Changjiang Securities Co., Ltd. have submitted an application to China Securities Regulatory Commission for the establishment of Cheung Kong Winsan (China) Investment Group PIHL Holdings, and it is expected that this application will be approved within one year's time.

In 2002 China also carried out the qualified foreign institutional investors system, allowing these investors to remit certain quotas of foreign-exchange funds according to rules. This is a quasi-market opening mode whereby these funds can be converted into the local currency and invested in the local securities market through strictly supervised special accounts, and the profits and interests gained from such funds can be converted into foreign exchange and remitted abroad. This is the transitional system carried out by many countries and regions, emerging market economies in particular, before allowing local currencies to be freely convertible. To allow controlled amounts of foreign investment to enter the securities market at a time when capital projects are not yet opened to the outside world helps increase

[1] As a matter fact, Xiangcai Securities Co., Ltd. was already negotiating with CLSA as early as September 2000, and the two sides officially signed a cooperative agreement on February 8, 2001. On July 1, 2002, the day the *Rules for the Establishment of Foreign-shared Securities Companies* was promulgated, Xiangcai Securities Co., Ltd. and CLSA submitted to China Securities Regulatory Commission an official application for the establishment of a joint securities company.

financial sources for the securities market and accumulate experience for the eventual opening up of capital projects to FDI.

In early October 2002, preparations for the establishment of the Guoan Fund Management Company initiated jointly by the Guotai Junan Securities Company Ltd. and Allianz of Germany came under way with the approval of China Securities Regulatory Commission, which represented a major step taken by China to honor its commitments to WTO. The forthcoming Guoan Fund Management Company will have a registered capital of 100 million RMB, with Guotai Junan Securities Company Ltd. holding 67% and Allianz holding 33% of the shares. It will be registered in Shanghai and its business line will encompass the establishment of funds, the management of funds, and other businesses allowed by China Securities Regulatory Commission.

After approval was given for the establishment of the Guoan Fund Management Company, Huabao Trust Co., Ltd. and Societe Generale Asset Management SA. (SGAM) was granted another approval from China Securities Regulatory Commission on October 24, 2002, for the establishment of a fund management joint venture, the Huabao Industrial Fund Management Co., Ltd. with a registered capital of 100 million RMB. On November 28, 2002, Haitong Securities and Fortis Securities Co., Ltd. of Belgium were approved for preparations to establish the Haitong-Futong Fund Management Company, and China Merchants Securities Co., Ltd. and ING of Holland gained green light for preparing for the Merchant Fund Management Company that was officially opened on December 27 of the same year. By the end of February 2003, approval was given for the establishment of five fund management joint ventures with Chinese and foreign investment, while the applications submitted by Everbright Secutities together with Prudential and Shenyin & Wanguo Securities Co., Ltd., French Asset Management Company and International Financial Company were awaiting examination and approval.

In March 2003, the American investment bank Goldman Sachs and China Huarong Asset Management Corporation reached agreement for the establishment of a joint venture to handle bad loans on the mainland of China. The Chinese government has approved this joint venture and Goldman Sachs has purchased 1.9 billion RMB worth of bad loans. According to sources, another joint venture between Huarong and Morgan Stanley Group of the United States will also be approved soon to handle an estimated 10.8 billion RMB of bad loans.

11-3: Commercial and Transportation Services

1. Retailing Sales

In 1992 the State Council decided to run retailing sales joint ventures with Chinese and foreign investment in Beijing, Tianjin, Shanghai, Dalian, Guangzhou and Qingdao and the five special economic zones. In September of the same year, the State Council approved the establishment of the nation's first retailing sales joint venture – Shanghai No.1 Yaohan Co., Ltd. Shortly afterwards, a decision was made to trial-run a chain store in Beijing and another chain store in Shanghai as well as a few retailing sales with Taiwan investment in the hinterland. On June 25, 1999, with the approval of the State Council, the State Economy and Trade Commission, PRC and the Ministry of Foreign Trade Economic Cooperation jointly issued the *Experimental Measures for Commercial Enterprises with Foreign Investment*, expanding the experiments to the capital cities of all the provinces, municipalities and autonomous regions as well as cities with independent accounting units and in special economic zones, and providing specific stipulations on the credentials of Chinese and foreign partners and the ratio between Chinese and foreign shareholders. In the meantime, the nation officially began experimenting with wholesaling business with foreign investment.

FDI inflow in Chinese circulation services has picked up speed after China's accession to WTO. The end of 2002 had given green light to the establishment of 51 retailing sales joint ventures and one wholesaling enterprise. These 51 retailing sales joint ventures had set up 485 branches and totaled 525 million US dollars in accumulated registered capital. These did not include 277 foreign-invested commercial firms approved by local authorities. In 2002, large foreign-invested retailing sales firms had made up 4.6% of national total retailing sales. In Shanghai and Shenzhen where there are more retailing sales joint ventures than anywhere else, these joint ventures had carved out about 12% of the local retailing sales market.

Table 11-3: Business situations of major joint ventures and cooperative enterprises in retailing businesses in 2002

No.	Name	Sales Revenue (billion RMB)	Number of stores	Business type
1	Carrefour	Approx. 12	36	Large supermarkets
2	Pacific Department Store	Approx. 11	8	Department stores
3	Hoyodo	Approx. 10	52	Large supermarkets
4	RT-MART	Approx. 9	35	Large supermarkets
5	Vanguard	8.6	397	Large supermarkets/ supermarkets
6	Parkson	6.8	28	Department stores
7	China UNM	7.3	902	Western food
8	Wal-mart	Approx. 6	26	Large supermarkets/ members-only stores/ community stores
9	Metro	5.3	16	Members-only warehouse shops
10	Cnlogo	Approx. 5	22	Large supermarkets
11	Lotus	Approx. 3.5	12	Large supermarkets
12	McDonald's	Approx. 3.2	543	Members-only warehouse shops
13	Prices mart	Approx. 3	30	Western fast food
14	Bigata	1.8	19	Large supermarkets/ supermarkets
15	Ito Yokado	Approx. 1.7	3	Large supermarkets
16	Makro	1.6	6	Members-only warehouse shops
17	B&Q	Approx. 1.6	8	House building materials stores
18	Auchan	0.8	2	Large supermarkets
19	OBI	Approx. 0.7	4	House building materials stores
20	IKEA	Approx. 0.7	2	House building materials stores
21	Jusco	0.7	2	Large supermarkets
22	7-11	Approx. 6	132	Convenience stores
Total		101	2,285	

Source: China Chain Business Association. In the "Sales Volume" column, eight of the enterprises provided their own statistics; the figures for the other 14 are estimates [indicated with word "approximately"] because the enterprises declined to reveal the exact statistics.

More than 40 of the global 50 leading retailing sales firms have opened shops in China. The renowned American and European transnational enterprises such as Carrefour, Wal-Mart Stores, Metro, Auchan and IKEA have invested in chain stores in China.

The entry of foreign investment into commerce has not only provided better commercial services but also boosted Chinese exports. Foreign-invested retailing sales firms are making substantial purchases in this country. In 2001, the transnational corporations in retailing sales purchased 30 billion US dollars worth of Chinese goods for export, accounting for 12% of national total exports; and in 2002, the figure reached an estimated 36 billion US dollars. On a yearly basis, Carrefour, Wal-Mart Stores, Kingfisher, Metro, Auchan and HKEA each sell hundreds of millions, billions or several dozen billions of US dollars worth of commodities made in China. In 2001, the volume of purchases of Wal-Mart Stores from China amounted to 10.3 billion US dollars, including nearly 1.2 billon US dollars of shoes and about 800 million US dollars of luggage and bags; the figure was 3.5 billion US dollars for Carrefour that had shifted its Asian center of purchase from India and southeast Asia to China, which accounted for 61% of its 2001 purchases from Asia.

2. Transportation and International Freight Commissioning Services

Long before acceding to WTO, China had marginally opened its land, waterway and air transport services to foreign investment. By the eve of its accession to WTO towards the end of 2001, China had approved the establishment of 700-odd joint ventures in land transportation, 60-odd joint ventures in domestic coastal and inland waterway transportation services, and 64 air services joint ventures.

Railway transportation was a latecomer in this opening up effort. China's first joint venture in this field was not established until January 2002. This was the Lanzhou Logistics Co., Ltd, a joint venture of Maersk Shipping Line Co., Canadian Pacific Railway Corp. and the Container Transportation Company of the Lanzhou Railway Bureau, the Container Transportation Centre of the Lanzhou Railway Sub-bureau, the Container Transportation Centre of the Yinchuan Railway Sub-bureau, and the Container Transportation Centre of the Xining Railway Sub-bureau, with its total investment of 429,000 US dollars equally shared between the Chinese and Canadian partners. The joint venture adopts a modern mode of logistics operation, advanced technology and network management expertise so that it can offer enterprises with comprehensive services ranging from purchases and warehousing to production and distribution of supplies and optimize the options to help clients save transportation costs.

After China's accession to WTO, transportation services and international cargo services have shown more openness to the outside world. Towards the end of 2001, the Ministry of Foreign Trade Economic Cooperation issued the *Provisions on the Administration of Enterprises with Foreign Investment Serving as Agents for International Cargo Transport*, according to which foreign investors may establish joint ventures for international cargo services and gain permission within three years after the accession to WTO to set up wholly owned international cargo shipping enterprises. So far China has approved the establishment of over 300 foreign-invested international cargo enterprises, which operate nearly 200 affiliates in other cities in China. Towards the end of 2002, the nation's first foreign-controlled international cargo shipping joint venture was established. The Logistics (Beijing)

Company of the Schenkal Beijing Center of International Technological Cooperation, which has a registered capital of 5.7 million US dollars with the Schenkal Company of Germany holding 70% of the shares and the Beijing International Technological Cooperation Center holding 30% of the shares, began operation in early 2003. A transnational logistics company with a history of 150 years in international logistics services, an annual sales of 6.4 billion euro, a 33,000-strong workforce and 1,100-odd representative offices, the Schenkal Company provides land, ocean and air transportation and comprehensive logistics services and global chain management services. According to the agreement, the joint venture will have completed the first-phase construction of a multifunctional logistics center one kilometer from Beijing Airport by early 2004. Both partners have announced that their joint venture will rely on their superiorities in logistics transportation and warehousing networks on the home and foreign markets, base their operations on domestic business, actively expand their shares of the international cargo market, and promote the degree of internationalization.

New National Express Co., Ltd. and the Canadian branch of the Northern American Greyhound Company, a road transportation giant in the world, signed a cooperation agreement in October 2002. The former is China's only trans-provincial and trans-regional expressway transport enterprise established in 2001 with the approval of the Ministry of Transportation to manage transportation lines between Beijing and Shanghai; the latter, founded in Toronto in 1928, operates transportation lines across North America and takes a considerable share of the North American road transportation market. The cooperation agreement between the two companies indicates that the two partners will work together in such fields as management expertise, parcel express delivery, and domestic and international tourist transportation. Greyhound Canada will transfer to New National Express Co., Ltd. its mature technology, network ticket sales system and safety and management technology and provide personnel training for New National Express Co., Ltd. The signing of this agreement will not only enhance New National Express Co., Ltd.'s management ability but also further open up the Chinese passenger transportation market to the outside world. It also signified the entry of an international transportation giant into the Chinese passenger transportation market.

3. Pharmaceutical Retailing Sales Business

Stardrug, which gets its brands, management expertise and operational assistance from the American MedicineShoppeInternational, the global leading exclusive pharmaceutical retailing sales company, was opened in Shenzhen in September 2002. Because it was the first international retailing sales pharmacy ever to set foot in China, the establishment of Stardrug unveiled the inroads of foreign-invested pharmaceutical retailing sales firms into the Chinese market. Stardrug is targeted at south and east China, with a goal of setting up more than 100 pharmacies before the end of 2003.

11-4: The Opening-up of the Other Fields of the Service Sector

1. Media

Since US IDG invested in and opened the first newspaper, *Computer World*, in China in the early 1980s, a total of 50 media have acquired overseas background in investment and financing in periodicals such as *Fortune China* and *IT Manager World*, television networks such as China Sports Report and Sun TV, and Internet networks such as Maya.Online.sh.cn.

China has speed up opening its media business to the outside world since its accession to WTO. In February 2002, the first large bookselling joint venture, the Fujian-Taiwan Book City, went into business at Zhongting Street, Fuzhou. It is a joint venture under the South Fujian Book City Company run by 12 Taiwan publishers and the Foreign Languages Bookstore of Fujian, and the first of its kind ever established on the mainland of China, with the Foreign Languages Bookstore of Fujian holding 65% of the shares and the Taiwan investors holding 35% of the shares. The joint venture is managed by a board of three trustees from Taiwan and four trustees from the mainland, with the chairman of the board appointed by the Foreign Languages Bookstore and the VP appointed by Yang Rongchuan, chairman of the Wunan Book Company of Taiwan. On September 9, 2002, the TOM Group which is listed on the Growth Enterprise Market The Stock Exchange of Hong Kong Limited announced that it had signed a letter of intent for setting up a joint venture with SDX Joint Publishing Company of Beijing for a term of no less than 20 years with a total investment of 50 million RMB and a registered capital of 40 million RMB, with TOM holding 49% of the shares. The joint venture handles sales, distribution and advertisement of periodicals, distribution, translation and editing of books, copyright businesses, and development of chain bookstores. TOM Group thus became the first investor from outside of the mainland to be granted with the right to run advertisement, distribution and other related publishing businesses on the mainland after China's accession to WTO.

In early 2002, China also approved the Shanghai New Sony Music Company, the nation's first joint venture in independently making and selling audiovisual products with an investment of 29.90 million US dollars from the Sony Company of Japan, and the government also approved the establishment of the first joint venture between Shanghai and Hong Kong motion picture, the Shanghai Yongle Guangyu Movie City Company.

In early 2003, Star TV, an affiliate of the American News Corp. was given the green light to air an entertainment channel in Putonghua in hotels rated with three or more stars and luxury dwellings. Star TV thus became the first foreign television company to be granted with the right to run television programs in China. A short while ago, the Phoenix Satellite Television Holdings Limited had just been approved to run news programs 24 hours a day in luxury hotels and dwellings, whereas Star TV owns 37.6% of Phoenix's shares. Ordinary families in Guangdong were able to receive Star TV and the Chinese and Movie channels of Phoenix Satellite Television beginning from the early 2002.

2. Telecommunications

Prior to China's accession to WTO, the Chinese government prohibited foreign investment in telecommunications services. According to China's commitment to WTO, this field has been opened to foreign investors in a gradual and controlled fashion after the nation acceded to WTO. Towards the end of 2001, the State Council announced the *Provisions on the Administration of Telecommunications Enterprises with Foreign Investment*, which went into effect as of January 1, 2002. According the regulations, foreign-invested telecommunications enterprises may deal in basic telecommunications businesses, value-added telecommunications services and other businesses China promised to open up to the outside world during negotiations on its WTO membership. In 2002, foreign investors were allowed to invest in value-added telecommunications services in Beijing, Shanghai and Guangzhou.

In 2001, Shanghai Symphony Telecom Co., Ltd. was established in Shanghai as the first telecommunications joint venture with Chinese and foreign investment on the mainland. Established by China Telecom Shanghai Branch, the AT&T of the United States and the Shanghai Information Investment Inc., the joint venture introduced a new seamless global connection concept to Pudong Area as the first step to promote telecommunications internationalization under the background of economic globalization. Xintian had basically built up an IP value-added business network by the end of 2001, and when it went into operation in March 2002 it was the first to offer such services as high-grade analogue special-purpose networks, broadband Internet interface and mainframe deposit and its first list of overseas clients to be solicited was targeted at the affiliates of 20 of the global 500 leading transnational corporations running business in Pudong. By the end of 2002, Shanghai Xintian remained the only one large joint venture in China to deal in value-added telecommunications businesses – domestic investors did not arrive in droves as people had expected.

3. Exhibitions

In 2002, a number of giant exhibition companies of Germany finished the first-phase construction of the Shanghai New International Expo Center, the first foreign-invested project of its kind in China with a first-phase floor space of 55,000 square meters. Fifty percent of the shares are hold collectively by Hanover Fairs, Munich Exhibition Company and Messe Duesseldorf GmbH by investing in cash while Pudong Land Holding Development Company takes possession of the other 50% by investing in the use of land. The total investment for this project will eventually exceed 1 billion RMB.

The goal of the project, in which foreign investors were allowed for the first time in China, is to become Asia's largest exhibition center. This was also the first time for Hanover Fairs and its partners to invest in the construction of an exhibition center overseas. Beginning from the latter half of 2002, some giant international exhibition companies moved to China where they had been running successfully for years, and all of them chose the Shanghai New International Exhibition Centre as the venue. The exhibition is a sellout throughout 2003.

4. Travel Services

Joint ventures in the travel services were allowed only in the nation's 12 national tourist resorts before 1998. The first such joint venture was the Yunnan Litian Tourist Company, established with government approval. After 1999, the government lifted this limitation and further opened travel services to the outside world. After China's accession to WTO, China further lowered its standard for the registered capital of a travel service joint venture, and revoked the requirement that a foreign investor could only establish one travel service organization in the country. By the end of 2002, the government approval a total of 12 foreign-invested travel services.

The majority shares of 11 of these 12 foreign-invested travel services were controlled by Chinese partners. In November 2002, China Travel Service Head Office and the European Travel Giant TUI set up a joint venture in Beijing with TUI in control; this was the first Chinese travel service in which a foreign investor held the majority shares.

5. Other Fields

Apart from the aforementioned fields, accounting, law service, asset appraisal, publishing, printing, construction, real estate and realtor management, audiovisual products, catering service and entertainment, maintenance, consultancy, advertisement, medical service, education, leasing, commodities inspection and engineering designing have also been opened to varying degrees to foreign investors, while regulations have been formulated in fields where access for foreign investors is limited. In accounting, for instance, 11 international accounting companies had established 26 member offices in China by the end of 2002. More than 10,000 overseas candidates from 20 countries and regions have sit in accountant credential exams in China, and 405 of them have passed.

11-5: The Role of the Opening-Up Effort in Promoting the Development of Chinese Service Sector

The gap of Chinese enterprises from the advanced world level of products, technology, management and quality in service sector is no less glaring than in the manufacturing industry. Transnational flow of the service sector is more exemplary than that of the manufacturing industry because all its businesses should be carried out through the services provided for clients and it is difficult to keep technological secret. The technological level of a parent company is about the same as that of its overseas affiliates, and while for the manufacturing industry it is possible to retain businesses of higher technological level at the parent company and shift the businesses of middle and lower levels to overseas affiliates, it is impossible for the service sector because counterparts in a host country may find it easy to observe, learn and imitate what these affiliates are doing.

Taking banking as an example, the Bank of Shanghai, the first Chinese bank to have foreign shares, has benefited in many important fields from its introduction of foreign investment. The foreign shareholders have not only further improved the bank's shareholding structure; more importantly, under the guidance of IFC, the bank is able to promote its technological progress, renovate its financial operations and upgrade its management level and economic returns by actively drawing on the advanced managerial experiences of the global modern commercial banks, adopting its foreign partners' global technology and management expertise, and incorporating foreign banks' sophisticated management experience in financial products, marketing methodology and services. Moreover, the global network resources and brands of the HSBC and the International Financial Company have enabled the Bank of Shanghai expand its business space and paved the way for its smooth transition to the overseas financial market.

Take the entry of IFC for instance. After IFC became a shareholder, it brains its influence to bear on the management of the Bank of Shanghai mainly through the following four channels[2]:

(1) Clauses in the legally binding *Purchase Agreement*. As an official document, the *Purchase Agreement* is legally binding on the signatory parties; it also provides IFC with something to go by when offering suggestions and setting requirements for the Bank of Shanghai. In order to strengthen its binding force, the agreement provides a withdrawal clause which stipulates that the Bank of Shanghai shall submit an application for listing on the capital market no later than the end of 2001, become a listed company before 2007, submit to IFC a financial report which has been audited and compiled strictly according to international accounting rules within 120 years after each fiscal accounting year, make sure the dividends to be distributed shall not exceed the net revenue of the previous accounting year, and keep its rate of abundance of capital at no less than 7% towards the end of 1999 and 8% towards the end of 2000 (otherwise it shall not distribute its dividends), and that the loans granted by the Bank of Shanghai to associated parties or parties with a government background shall not exceed 10% of its net capital or 4 billion RMB. If the Bank of Shanghai fails to abide by any one of these stipulations, IFC may exercise its right of transfer, according to which the Bank of Shanghai shall buy its capital from IFC within a specific period of time.

(2) Entering the decision-making body of the Bank of Shanghai by dispatching a trustee to the bank's board of trustees. As a condition for its investment in shares, IFC dispatches an experienced financial expert to the board of trustees of the Bank of Shanghai. The task of this expert is, on the one hand, to improve the functions of the board of trustees, revamp its loose organizational structure and remedy the lack of substance in board meetings and discussions, and on the other, to represent the interests of IFC as an investor, fully exercise his power on the board of trustees, supervise the Bank of Shanghai in honoring its obligations as provided

[2] Established in 1956, IFC is a World Bank affiliate whose capital stock funds come from 156 member states, China included. Its goal is to spur on development of private enterprises in member states, underdeveloped member states in particular, by joining private investment and providing management and technological resources. IFC's financial support includes loan grants and investment in shares. However, when investing in shares, IFC never seeks to become the leading shareholder or control the majority shares, and under normal circumstances, it makes its presence felt on the board of trustees but refrains from taking part in the day-to-day management of an enterprise. IFC has always been concerned with the progress of financial reform in China, hoping to choose an urban commercial bank with good performance and help, by providing technological aids and investing in a small number of shares, turn it into a modern joint-stock commercial bank according to established international norms as a fine example to promote the financial reform in China. After much investigation and consideration, in 1995 IFC chose the Bank of Shanghai for its investment, which thereby became the first project in the Chinese financial industry to be invested by the World Bank Group. After nearly four years of consultations and arduous negotiations, the two partners eventually signed an acquisition agreement in September 1999.

by the *Purchase Agreement*, and, as an international financial expert, offer construction proposals on the management policies and principles of the Bank of Shanghai.

(3) Introducing advanced experience of foreign countries through technological aids. A salient feature of IFC is its ability to provide recipients of its investment with technological aids by taking advantage of its special position as a multilateral international financial organization. IFC has, beginning from the early stage of negotiations, provided technological assistance to the Bank of Shanghai on a number of projects: 1) entrusting, during the early stage of negotiations, the Bank of the Netherlands and the Bank of Ireland to conduct comprehensive appraisals of the business and management of the Bank of Shanghai and, on the basis of these appraisals, present a comprehensive advisory report and proposals for the Bank of Shanghai; 2) dispatch experts from the Office of the Comptroller of the Currency (OCC) of the US Department of Treasury to work with the staff of the credit department of the Bank of Shanghai, help the bank classify its loan grants into five categories, and present the management of the Bank of Shanghai with the *Proposals on Improving the Credit Risk Management of the Bank of Shanghai*; 3) invite financial experts from IFC and well-known transnational banks to give lectures to the trustees, presidents and senior managers of the Bank of Shanghai on credit management, marketing, human resource management, etc, with emphasis on risk prevention.

(4) High-ranking IFC officials making suggestions through writing to the Bank of Shanghai at regular intervals. After hearing reports from its trustee and other financial experts, IFC shall have its East Asia Bureau director and other senior officials make suggestions, in the form of official letters at regular intervals, to the Bank of Shanghai on how to prevent risks and improve its management, and dispatch its trustee to inspect the implementation of such proposals. Attaching due importance to these IFC requirements, the management of the Bank of Shanghai has established a working group to carry out the proposals of the International Financial Company and make it a point to report to IFC on progress in carrying out these proposals. Though the IFC letters of proposals are not legally binding, they have a highly constraining and guiding effect on the behavior of the management of the Bank of Shanghai.

In March 2002, Ericsson (China) Co., Ltd. Nanjing Rep Office repaid its loans from Chinese banks and began borrowing loans from Citibank. Shocked by this event, the Chinese banks started learning and imitating the quality client strategy of foreign-invested banks and renovating their management philosophy and methods. Shortly after the Ericsson incident, Shanghai Pudong Development Bank Hangzhou Branch announced a corporate financial VIP service mode, and brought its first batch of important clients under this special mode of service. The China Minsheng Banking Corp., Ltd followed suit by offering such new services as buyer's interest payment bill discounts, the buying out of foreign exchange bills and insurance and compensation. Some state-owned commercial banks also opened financial management centers one after another to provide considerable financial services for quality clients.

The opening up of the retailing sales has expedited the entry into China of a series of new corporate forms and new management methods and speeded up the renovation of commerce in this country. Warehouse stores, large malls, large supermarkets, chain stores and many other nascent modes of commerce did not mushroom among domestic retail sales firms and became new phenomena in the Chinese commerce until they were brought into China by foreign-invested commercial enterprises. Transnational retailing sales groups have not only introduced new business methods but also played a positive role in solving some of the long-standing problems in circulation fields. For instance, foreign-invested commercial firms use their financial resources to shorten the cycles of payment to suppliers, forcing domestic enterprises to quickly enhance their management and technical level. The revolutionary C&C system introduced to Shanghai by Metro, the world's renowned leading C&C chain store company, had a tremendous impact on both the upper and lower ends of commerce in the city. The company's Putuo Emporium in Shanghai has conducted several hundreds thought deals involving whopping sums of money with 1,500 suppliers since it was opened in 1996. Thanks to its ability to quicken commodity turnover by absorbing and storing large quantities of commodities and selling them on a large scale, Metro is highly appealing to suppliers. Also because Metro's commitment to settling accounts on schedule, making large purchases and quickening its commodity turnover, suppliers are willing to sell commodities to it at low prices.

Baihong Company, China's first wholesale joint venture with Chinese and foreign investment, showed super competitiveness shortly after it went into business in 2001. In order to increase the technological content of its business operations and raise its level of modernization, the company was the first in Chinese commerce to introduce the ERP management software developed by a world-famous software developer and use it to build up an information network to be shared by suppliers, retailers, importers, transportation companies, banks, and the customs. It has also constructed the a 10,000-square-meter high-platform and vertical warehouse that covers an area of 20,000 square meters near Zhenru Railway Station, which serves as the largest logistics center in Shanghai to offer home delivery services for clients at home and abroad. Creative measures like these will set good examples for counterparts and revolutionize the wholesale business in China.

As a result of the entry of foreign-invested wholesaling firms, it has become an irreversible trend for the Chinese wholesaling business to go from center stage to backstage. That is to say, specialized logistics firms, socialized logistics centers, and mixtures of these two forms of logistics services will become major forms of wholesaling business. Information technology will be used as a means to response promptly to demands and provide highly efficient logistics, delivery and other services for producers at the upper end of commerce and retailers at the lower end, thus enabling commodities to increase their value and yield profits in the course of circulation. By forming alliance with information technology, transportation and mechanical automation, wholesaling business will emerge as a high-tech industry and acquire a variety of functions such as the collection and distribution of commodities, the processing of commodities for distribution, as well as information and other services, thereby phasing out traditional wholesaling firms that can only engage in "reselling" commodities. These important changes will have an important and long-term impact on the development of the Chinese service sector and the sharpening of their competitiveness on the market.

Chapter 12

PROMOTING REFORM BY OPENING UP: INVOLVING FOREIGN INVESTMENT IN RESTRUCTURING STATE-OWNED ENTERPRISES

To involve foreign investors in the reform and regroup state-owned enterprises, large ones in particular have been a major breakthrough in China's policy on utilization of foreign investment since the nation acceded to WTO. This move is having an important and profound impact on reform and opening up to the outside world.

12-1: PROGRESS OF REFORM OF STATE-OWNED ENTERPRISES AND CONSTRAINTS ON IT

1.The Stage of Reform without Involving Property Rights

China began transforming its state-owned enterprises after adopting the policy of reform and opening up to the outside world in 1979. The early stage of reform did not involve the property right system of these enterprises; rather, the policy was to increase incentives for enterprises and their workers and staff on the basis of upholding state ownership.

During the period 1979-1983, state-owned enterprises introduced a responsibility system for their profits, and after state's share for profits were fulfilled the surplus profit was divided up between the state and the enterprise. This responsibility system fired the enterprises with enthusiasm, and considerably increased the incomes of both enterprises and workers. In the meantime, however, as state-owned enterprises and individuals did everything they could to curtail the profit to be delivered to the government, this resulted in a rather quick decrease in the portion of state financial revenue in the national income, that is, from 37% in 1979 to 26% in 1983.

To change this situation, during that period 1983-1987 the reform policy was adopted whereby state-owned enterprises were asked to pay income tax instead of turning part of their profits over to the state. The new relationship in distribution brought about by this policy of substituting tax payment for profit delivery stabilized increases in government revenue, but the high tax rate of this policy aggravated the financial burden on enterprises. While the percentage of these enterprises in the total output value was dropping, the portion of their tax payment in the total taxes and profits rose from 79% in 1984 to 83% in 1987, thereby resulting in an increase in the number of state-owned enterprises in deficits and dampening their enthusiasm to work hard.

Drawing on the lessons from these two reforms, the state introduced a contractual management responsibility system to state-owned enterprises during the period 1987-1993. Accordingly, negotiations were held between government administrative departments and enterprises on various quotas for enterprises, such as the portion of profits to be delivered to the state by the enterprises and the rate of increase of such delivery, the speed at which equipment was upgraded, and the margin of increase in wages and salaries. An enterprise that had fulfilled these quotas was allowed to retain a prescribed portion of the surplus profit and its managers were entitled to bonuses according to a prescribed portion. This responsibility system mobilized the ardor of the managers and workers of the state-owned enterprises, but it also spawned problems. Firstly, the enterprises were responsible for profits but not responsible for financial losses so that they were entitled to a portion of surplus profit while leaving the government alone to handle financial losses. Secondly, by allowing enterprises to negotiate with the government once in three years, this egged on their shortsighted behavior, to the neglect of issues of intermediary and long-term strategic importance. Thirdly, because enterprises negotiated their contracts individually with the government, the base numbers varied from one enterprise to another, and there were cases in which an enterprise that performed well during the term of the previous contract was asked to shoulder a heavier financial burden, thus setting competition between the enterprises on an unequal footing.

The 3rd Plenary Session of the 14th Party Central Committee convened in 1993 marked a turning point in reform in China by calling for the establishment of a socialist market economy. In 1994, reform of state-owned enterprises entered a new stage of transforming their management mechanisms and creating new systems. An embodiment of this new stage was to introduce the corporate system to state-owned enterprises so as to transform these enterprises with unlimited liability for the state into limited liability companies each with a number of investors. In the years that followed a total of 2,082 enterprises were transformed into companies. However, reform during this stage was regarded as the "same old stuff with a different label" or "old wine in a new bottle" for the main reason that the administrative department remained in control of the regrouped limited-liability companies, and there was little difference between the decision-making process of the board of trustees and the original government intervention.

2. The Stage of Reform that Touches upon Property Rights Since 1997

The 15th National Congress of the Communist Party of China convened in 1997 was a milestone in the reform of state-owned enterprises in this country. The congress pointed out that the state sector should do something in some fields and resort to non-action in other fields. In other words, state-owned enterprises should be allowed to withdraw from certain fields and the reform of state-owned enterprises can involve changes in the form of property rights. The major breakthroughs in both theory and policy in the *Decisions of the Party Central Committee on Issues concerning Reform and Development of State-owned Enterprises* endorsed at the 4th Plenary Session of the 15th Party Central Committee in

September 1999 will have a major impact on the guidelines and methodology of reform of state-owned enterprises.

The major reform discussed in this chapter involves permission for large state-owned enterprises to revamp their property right structures by selling and transferring part of the state-owned assets. For so long in the past large and medium-sized state-owned enterprises in this country used the method of "keeping the stock intact and adjusting the increment" to form a diversity of property right structures through introduction of the joint-stock system or other forms. That is to say, the available state-owned assets retained their state ownership, while non-state funds are raised by issuing additional shares to the public to establish enterprises of mixed forms of ownership and multiple investors. The new guideline set by the 15th Party Congress and the 4th Plenary Session of the 15th Party Central Committee for the flow and readjustment of the stock of assets of large and medium-sized state-owned enterprises calls for reducing the state stocks of a selected number of state-controlled listed companies that have a good reputation and vast potentials for development so long as state control is not affected; while unlisted state-owned enterprises may liquidate their right to use state-allotted land and part of their assets and may use the funds thus gained to increase their assets and reduce their debts, restructure themselves and replenish their social security funds. This major step will, theoretically and practically speaking, provide a major impetus for the reform of the state-owned enterprises. In actual operation, there are a variety of ways to transform the ownership structure of the enterprises, such as the thoroughgoing method of selling their shares to inside or outside buyers.

3. Main Constraints on Reform of State-owned Enterprises

After the 15th Party Congress and the 4th Plenary Session of the 15th Party Central Committee, the state sector has been required to make step up in some fields and step back in some others. It is thus widely accepted for state-owned enterprises to withdraw from industries of an ordinary competitive nature or let their state assets change hands. This line of thought for reforming and regrouping state-owned enterprises has met little or no obvious obstacle in state policies. Some major constraints, however, do exist in practice, making it rather difficult to promote the reform and regrouping of large state-owned enterprises. A major reason for this lies in the fact that the non-state investors in China are generally lacking the ability to participate in the reform of the property rights of large state-owned enterprises as strategic investors.

The experiences of reform in China and other former socialist countries indicate that it is no easy task to concentrate property right diversification reform on large state-owned enterprises with their large asset and employment scales remaining intact. A few years ago, when government control was relaxed to rejuvenate small enterprises, the lack of investors capable of effective management was already a problem, the problem that there were very few buyers. Some people believe that the problem is rather simple: just liberalize the prices on the property rights, let the prices of the assets of state-owned enterprises drop to an affordable level, and then enough investors will emerge to fulfill the reform to diversify the property-right structure. This way of thinking is problematic in two regards. Firstly, when there is a glaring difference in strength between seller and buyer, to force a deal within a short period of time will inevitably reduce the price of assets to an unreasonably low level and result in excessive inequality in the distribution of assets in the course of reform. Secondly, to sell the shares of state-owned enterprises at a low price cannot improve the efficiency of these enterprises because the formation of an effective governance structure in an enterprise calls for both property right restructuring and the emergence of investors who are highly motivated and capable of supervising the enterprises.

Generally speaking, non-state investors who can bring an effective governance structure to large enterprises are a kind of rare resource in a country where state-owned enterprises hold sway. First of all, non-state investors lack the investing ability. Of all the calculation methods and results available, the most conservative estimate puts the net assets of state-owned enterprises in competitive industries at upwards of 4.5 trillion RMB (though some will argue that according to market value, the net value of the assets of state-owned enterprises is much lower). Although non-state investors have been growing robustly since the adoption of the policy of reform and opening up to the outside world, their investing capacities are falling far short of the task to diversify the property right structure of this colossal amount of state assets. Secondly, for large enterprises the main purpose of diversifying the property right structure is to bring about an effective corporate governance structure and solve the key problem that the behavior of investors is not strong enough to bring any major changes. In other words, investors, such as those on the capital market, are too thinly scattered to render effective supervision over the behaviors of managers in their capacity as investors. The supervisory mechanism of "voting with one's foot", where investors decide if they should invest in an enterprise according to its performance, can hardly play an effective role in China today. Non-state investors who are capable of large-scale investment and earning considerable shares in the total assets of large state-owned enterprises and who are truly concerned with the improvement of corporate efficiency from the perspective of maintaining returns from their assets, are even more a rarity in China.

A main idea to solve this problem is to involve foreign investment in the transformation and regrouping of state-owned enterprises, especially to involve large transnational companies in the transformation and regrouping of large state-owned enterprises. This will become a major aspect of China's policy of reform and opening up to the outside world. Large transnational companies can not only provide huge sums of investment for the transformation of state-owned enterprises, but their business philosophy, technology, global marketing networks and management expertise will come together with their money into the enterprises they acquire. For this reason, we should actively attract investment from transnational corporations, including investment in the form of M&As and turn them into major strategic investors in the reform of state-owned enterprises, large ones in particular.

4. Other Considerations on Encouraging Foreign Investors to Merger or Acquire State-owned Enterprises

Apart from the knotty problems confronting the reform of large state-owned enterprises, the government allows foreign investors to participate in the regrouping of these enterprises in the form of M&As out of the following considerations.

1) The Need to Avoid Increasing New Production Capacities

Excessive production capacities have been a headache for most industries in China since the middle and late 1990s, prompting the government to control the number of new construction projects in these fields. However, during this stage, green field investment has been a major form of utilizing FDI in this country, prompting some to believe that this is a major cause for further expansions of production capacities in some industries and for the failure to remedy the problem of overproduction. Because of this the government began to attach importance to the form of utilizing FDI in merging and acquiring of domestic enterprises, because mergers and acquisitions involve merely the shift of the ownership of enterprises and make it possible to avoid the formation of new production capacities.

2) The Need to Utilize FDI to Dispose of Bad Assets of State-owned Enterprises

A major step taken in the transformation of state-owned enterprises in 1999 and 2000 was to strip bad loans owed to banks from state-owned enterprises. Four ad hoc asset management companies were established to handle these bad loans, and 1.6 trillion RMB of such loans were stripped as a result. However, in the course of disposing of these bad assets domestic enterprises were not enthusiastic enough whereas some foreign banks were willing. To allow foreign investors to participate in dealing with these bad assets is tantamount to giving them the green light to buy domestic enterprise. In 2002, China Huarong Asset Management Corporation, one of the four asset management companies, sold four packages of bad assets worth a total of 10.8 billion RMB to a group of bidders headed by Morgan Stanley, which signified a breakthrough in attracting foreign capital in the reform and regrouping of state-owned enterprises.

3) The Need to Involve Foreign Investment in Resolving Acute Contradictions in Employment

In a general sense, there is not an obvious impact on the aggregates of employment whether foreign investors choose green field investment or M&As. The meanings, however, are different for the government. Green field investment calls for the formation of new enterprises and recruitment of new workers, thereby offering jobs for new workers. Investment in the form of M&As does not necessarily result in the formation of new enterprises and the creation of new jobs, but, on the other hand, a considerable number of the enterprises up for M&As are ill-managed ones that cannot survive without absorbing foreign investment and if they are allowed to go bankrupt they will cause unemployment. If they turn for the better after being merged or acquired they will retain their job opportunities. Because the workers of state-owned enterprises are in a better position to negotiate with the government, if they lose their jobs they will have brought a higher pressure to bear on the government than the widely scattered potential new employees will. For this reason the government is inclined to encourage mergers and acquisitions so as to preserve the jobs.

12-2: The International Experience: Attracting FDI Is a Major Experience for Transforming and Restructuring State-owned Enterprises of Developing Countries

The international experience shows that domestic investors' lack of ability to participate in the transformation and regrouping of large state-owned enterprises is a major problem confronting developing countries and economies in transition when it comes to transforming their state-owned enterprises. In the global upsurge of reforming state-owned enterprises in the past two decades, most developed countries depend on domestic investors while in developing countries, more foreign enterprises are involved than domestic ones. During the period 1987-1999 more than half of the global 50 largest cases of regrouping state-owned enterprises involving foreign acquirers happened in developing countries. See Table 12-1.

Table 12-1: Cases of regrouping state-owned enterprises involving foreign enterprises in developing countries during the period 1987-1999

Rank	Privatized firm	Year	Value of Acquisition (billion dollars)	Country	Acquiring foreign firm	Acquiring Country
1	YPF SA	1999	13.2	Argentina	Repsol SA	Spain
2	Argentina-Airports (33)	1998	5.1	Argentina	Aeropuertos Argentina 2000	United States
3	TELESP (Telebras)	1998	5.0	Brazil	Investor Group	Spain
4	Telesp Celular Participacoes	1998	3.1	Belgium	Investor Group	Portugal
5	Coca-Cola Bottlers Philippines	1997	2.7	Philippines	Coca-Cola Amatil Ltd	Australia
6	Embratel (Telebras)	1998	2.3	Brazil	MCI Communications Corp	United States
7	YPF SA	1999	2.0	Argentina	Repsol SA	Spain
8	Entel Peru SA, Cia Peruana	1994	2.0	Peru	Investor Group	Spain
9	CA Nacional Telefonos de VE	1991	1.9	Venezuela	VenWorld Telecom CA	United States
10	Svyazinvest	1997	1.9	Russian Federation	Mustcom Ltd	Cyprus
11	Sidor	1998	1.8	Venezuela	Consorico Siderurgia Amazonia	Argentina
12	Telecentro Sul (Telebras)	1998	1.8	Brazil	Investor Group	Italy
13	Light SE	1996	1.7	Brazil	Investor Group	United States
14	Telmex	1990	1.7	Mexico	Investor Group	United States
15	Cia de Electricidade do Estado	1997	1.6	Brazil	Investor Group	United States
16	SPT Telecom	1995	1.5	Czech Republic	Telesource consortium	Netherlands and Switzerland

Rank	Privatized firm	Year	Value of Acquisition (billion dollars)	Country	Acquiring foreign firm	Acquiring Country
17	Ferrocarril del Noreste	1997	1.4	Mexico	Transportation Ferroviaria	Mexico
18	Cie Centro Oeste	1997	1.4	Brazil	AES Corp	United States
19	Kaztelekom	1997	1.4	Kazakhstan	Daewoo Corp	Republic of Korea
20	Codensa	1997	1.2	United Kingdom	Saga Petroleum AS	Norway
21	Telesudeste Celular (Telebras)	1998	1.2	Brazil	Investor Group	Spain
22	FSM	1992	1.1	Poland	Fiat Auto SpA (Fiat SpA)	Italy
23	Ceskosiovenska Obchodni Banka	1999	1.1	Czech Republic	KBC Bancassurance Holding NV	Belgium
24	Tengizchevroil	1996	1.1	Kazakhstan	Mobil Corp	United States
25	Bank Polska Kasa Opieki SA	1999	1.1	Poland	Investor Group	Italy
26	Cemig (Minas Gerais)	1997	1.1	Brazil	Southern Electric Brazil	United States
27	Cia Riograndense de Telecomun	1998	1.0	Brazil	Investor Group	Spain

Source: UNCTAD (2000), *World Investment Report 2000: Cross-border Mergers and Acquisitions and Development* (Geneva and New York: United Nations), United Nations publication Table 8, P134.

12-3: Latest Progress in Attracting FDI to Restructure Large State-owned Enterprises of China

1.The Beginning of Foreign Capital's Involvement in Regrouping Large State-owned Enterprises

The involvement of foreign investment in regrouping state-owned enterprises in China did not begin after the nation's accession to WTO. Among the joint ventures with Chinese and foreign investment in China, a considerable number of the Chinese partners are state-owned enterprises. However, prior to China's accession to WTO, the utilization of foreign investment by state-owned enterprises had two characteristics. Firstly, the projects were small in scale – the joint ventures were mostly established in cooperation with medium-sized or small state-owned enterprises. secondly, some joint ventures were in cooperation with large state-owned enterprises, but in this case, these enterprises only contributed a subsidiary or part of its assets —— joint ventures with the entirety of a large state-owned enterprises were few. In either case the need to transform and regroup large state-owned enterprises could not be met.

The Chinese government began to take a positive attitude towards foreign investment in the form of M&As in 2001[1]. In 2001 and 2002, foreign-invested M&As of state-owned

[1] Among the major indications of this positive attitude, at an investment symposium held in Xiamen on September 12, 2001, Xu Ming, a deputy bureau director of the State Economy and Trade Commission indicated that

enterprises, large ones in particular, picked up speed, the scales of projects involved increased, and the forms of such M&As diversified. Among the large cases: on the side of handling bad assets, the China Huarong Asset Management Corporation sold four packages of such assets worth a total of 10.8 billion RMB to a group of bidders headed by Morgan Stanley, HSBC took possession of 8% of the shares of the Bank of Shanghai for 518 million RMB and turned it into China's first commercial bank with several foreign financial organizations as shareholders; New Bridge Capital of the United States spent 1.5 billion RMB and, holding 15% of the shares of Shenzhen Development Bank Co., ltd., became its largest shareholder; HSBC Insurance Group, a wholly owned affiliate of HSBC, bought 10% of the shares of Ping An Insurance Company of China for 600 million US dollars; through its affiliate, Salim (Shanghai) Investment Company, Salim Group of Indonesia took hold of 45% of COSCO Development Co., Ltd.'s shares; Royal Philips Electronics N.V.of Holland signed a share transfer agreement with Suzhou Peacock Electronic Group Co., Ltd. in a deal worth 430 million RMB to increase its share in a joint venture from 51% to 80% while Peacock Electronic's share was reduced from 49% to 20%; and Qingtao Brewery Company Co., Ltd. signed an agreement to issue, in three batches, 182 million US dollars worth of oriental convertible bonds to Anheuser-Busch Inc. from the United States so as to increase the American company's share from 4.5% to 27% and turn it into the company's second largest shareholder.

In 2002, major breakthroughs have been made in the overall joint ventures and cooperation between large state-owned enterprises in China and the world's giant transnational corporations. There are three major cases in point in this regard: first, full-fledged cooperation between FAW and Toyota; second, full-fledged cooperation between the DongFeng Automobile Co., Ltd. and Nissan; and third, the Municipal Government of Shenzhen put the shares of five state-owned groups for international bidding and transfer. All these three cases of corporate regrouping each involved upwards of 10 billion RMB and were therefore landmark events in China's effort to reform its state-owned enterprises.

On August 29, 2002, FAW of China and Toyota of Japan held a ceremony in Beijing to sign a cooperative agreement. FAW is a mainstay enterprise in the Chinese auto industry, and its products cover six series – medium-, heavy- and light-loaded trucks, cars, buses and minibuses – and it had led the Chinese auto industry in both output and sales for ten years running. In 2001, it was cited as the most influential industrial enterprise group in China. Toyota is a world-renowned automaker as well as a globalized enterprise that holds advantages in both technology and management. Although what was signed was merely a framework agreement, both partners announced that they had reached agreement and signed contracts on three lines of production -- medium- and high-grade buses, minibuses, and medium- and high-grade SUVs. It is estimated that the joint venture's annual sales will reach

China wanted to encourage foreign investors to engage in M&As in China and efforts were being redoubled to formulate relevant policies. On February 4, 2001, during his visit to Belgium, the Minister of the Ministry of Foreign Trade and Economic Cooperation Shi Guangsheng said that his country wanted to involve foreign investment in the transformation of state-owned enterprises. At the High Echelon Symposium on Development of China in March 2002, Jiang Qiangui said that China welcomed transnational corporations to participate in the transformation of large and medium-sized state-owned enterprises in the form of M&As. In November 2002, the Ministry of Foreign Trade and Economic Cooperation issued *Circular of the China Securities Regulatory Commission (CSRC), the Ministry of Finance (MOF) and the State Economy and Trade Commission (SETC) on Issues Related to Transferring State-owned Shares and Institutional Shares of Listed Corporations to Foreign Investors.*

300,000-400,000 by 2010. All these three lines of products are FAW's weak points or blanks, whereas Toyota has adequate resources for each line of production. The joint venture between FAW and Toyota will become a major landmark event in the Chinese history of large state-owned enterprises utilizing foreign capital.

On September 19, DongFeng Automobile Co., Ltd. and Nissan announced a plan to fully cooperate with each other to build the largest joint venture in China for the production of full lines of cars, light-loaded commercial vehicles and passenger automobiles. According to the agreement, Nissan will directly invest 1.03 billion US dollars (equivalent to 8.55 billion RMB) in DongFeng Automobile Co., Ltd. so as to earn control of 50% of the joint venture while its Chinese partner will own the other half of the shares by investment in kind and assets. Both partners believe that the DongFeng-Nissan joint venture is totally different from previous joint ventures in the auto industry -- rather, it represents a new mode of regrouping state-owned enterprises in China, for it is no longer cooperation on the basis of a single automobile model but involves the merger of two companies. According to the agreement, Nissan will provide the new company with its managerial expertise in such fields as product planning, purchases, factory productivity, logistics, quality control, brand management, marketing, sales network and financial service. In addition, the new company will, apart from strengthening DongFeng's old commercial vehicle R&D center, establish a new center for the R&D of passenger automobiles. The new DongFeng will include not only projects in cooperation with French PSA and Japanese Nissan but also other central businesses.

In August 2002, the Shenzhen Municipal Government announced to put up 25% to 70% of the shares of the city's energy, water supply, gas, metro service, and foodstuff groups for public international bidding. The bidding involved more than 20 billion RMB worth of the finest state-owned assets. Many global buyers were impressed by the future economic returns of these assets. This was the first time ever in China for the government to directly put large amounts of state-owned shares for international bidding.

Apart from these three cases in point, many local governments have formulated policies to attract foreign investors in M&As. Shanghai, for instance, announced in November 2002 that the city was formulating, in the light of its situations, policies to facilitate foreign investment in mergers and acquisitions of state-owned enterprises. Seven fields were slated for this purpose: first, M&As that involve the introduction of new products, technology and technological processes and the promotion of industrial restructuring and the readjustment of the product mix; second, M&As concerning new agricultural technology, comprehensive agricultural development, as well as such fields as energy, transportation and major materials; third, M&As concerning the use of high technology and the expansion of new industry fields; fourth, M&As for multipurpose utilization of resources and renewable resources as well as the prevention of environmental pollution; fifth, M&As conducive for upgrading products and technology and opening up the world market; sixth, M&As that help raise enterprises' management level and use available assets to improve enterprises' economic returns; and seventh, M&As favorable for the regrouping of state-owned enterprises. To promote this work, Shanghai established ad hoc departments in the Shanghai Property Rights Trading Center and other organizations to offer information for buyers and sellers, handle applications for M&As and provide valuation and trading services.

2. In What Industries Are the State-owned Enterprises the Apple in Foreign Investors' Eyes?

Judging from what has happened in foreign-invested M&As since 2001 and from foreign investors' intentions in contacts and negotiations with Chinese authorities, foreign investors' interest in merging and acquiring Chinese state-owned enterprises relatively concentrated in the following industries:

1) Monopolistic Industries

The monopolistic industries in China are under either natural or administrative monopoly. As things stand today, the monopoly in China is mostly administrative, especially in areas where state-owned enterprises are concentrated. For instance, in finance, telecommunications, power supply, civil aviation, mass media, harbors and urban public utilities industries, barriers abound against the entry of foreign investors and domestic non-state investors. Competition is lethargic at best and the margin of profit is large in these fields due to their relevant seclusion and monopoly, and because of this they have become the most sought-after fields among foreign investors. Moreover, foreign investors, giant transnational corporations in particular, hold much superiority in these monopolistic fields -- their competitive edge being clearly related to their business scales, the number of their networks and global clients and their technical and management levels. Our 2002 survey of the work of involving foreign investment in the transformation and regrouping of large state-owned enterprises in Jiangsu, Shandong and Shaanxi provinces and the city of Shenzhen indicates that urban public services, finance and civil aviation are the three most attractive fields for foreign investors seeking to merge or acquire state-owned enterprises. Those state-owned enterprises that are in a good financial situation and not too large in the monopolistic fields are clearly the apple of foreign investors' eye. These include a number of city banks that have already cultivated a sound network and service system as well as well-defined property rights, scattered shares and a high profitability. Some local air companies are also favorites of foreign investors.

2) Industries with Tremendous Market Potentials

China is in the process of a new round of upgrading the consumer structure, and some of the products and services have commanded the attention of foreign investors because of their vast potentials for market increases. Transnational corporations are only too willing to speed up their entry into China and seize large shares of the Chinese market by fully exploring the state-owned enterprises' large sizes, influential brands, widespread sales channels and thick clusters of sales and service outlets. Because these are the characteristics of such services as finance, insurance, logistics and tourism, foreign investors have shown a strong desire to invest in merging and acquiring the leading state-owned enterprises in these fields.

3) Industries in which Foreign Investors are Allowed to Take Controlling Shares By the Government

The percentage of wholly owned enterprises has been rising quickly among projects invested in China by transnational corporations since the mid-1990s. The share of wholly owned projects in the total realized FDI skyrocketed from 39% in 2000 to 60% in 2002. The fact that foreign investors are in favor of wholly owned projects indicates that firstly, the construction of the market economic system in China has developed to such a point where foreign investors can seek independent business and development on the Chinese market without relying on local partners, and secondly, where the Chinese policy permits, foreign investors hope to keep enterprises under their control, which is a universal phenomenon in global transnational investment. With control in their hands, foreign investors can decide the position and business lines of the enterprises they have invested in China according to their global strategies, and this also enables them to reduce complications and frictions in decision-making and business operations. This desire for control also manifests itself in the behaviors of foreign investors in M&As. According to our survey, in areas where the law does not ban foreign investors from taking majority shares, most transnational corporations have raised the demand to take control of investment projects during negotiations with the Chinese side, and the attitudes of local Chinese governments and state-owned enterprises have become one of the decisive factors that can make or break the negotiations.

12-4: Policies and Legal Framework Involving the Transfer of State-owned Shares

1. China Has Formulated Special Purpose Laws Concerning Foreign-invested Enterprises (FIEs)' Mergers and Acquisitions of State-owned Enterprises

Prior to 2002, there were no legislation governing the merging and acquiring state-owned enterprises in this country. Having combed through the Chinese law, we have found that the related regulations were scattered mainly in the following laws: *Regulations of the Ministry of Foreign Economic Relations and Trade, the State Administration for Industry and Commerce Concerning the Investments Made by the Various Parties to Chinese-foreign Equity Joint Ventures; Supplementary Provisions to Several Provisions Concerning the Investment Made by the Various Parties to Chinese-foreign Equity Joint Ventures; Interim Provisions on Mergers and Acquisitions of Domestic Enterprises by Foreign Investors; and Provisions on the Merger and Division of Enterprises with Foreign Investment.*

Circular of the China Securities Regulatory Commission (CSRC), the Ministry of Finance (MOF) and the State Economy and Trade Commission (SETC) on Issues Related to Transferring State-owned Shares and Institutional Shares of Listed Corporations to Foreign Investors was promulgated on November 4, 2002 as the first piece of legislation in China to cover all the central issues associated with foreign-invested enterprises' mergers and acquisitions of listed state-owned enterprises. The gist of this circular is as follows:

1) Defining the purpose of the transfer of shares. To transfer the state and legal person shares of listed companies to foreign investors is for the purpose of incorporating advanced management expertise, technology and capital from foreign countries, expediting economic restructuring, improving the corporate governance structure of listed companies, enhancing international competitiveness, protecting the lawful rights of investors, and promoting the healthy development of the securities market.

2) Emphasizing the credentials of foreign investors dealing in M&As. The circular demands that foreign investors seeking to possess the state and legal person shares of listed companies have strong management abilities and financial strengths, sound financial

performances and reputations, and the ability to improve the governance structures and promote sustained development of listed companies.

3) Clarifying that for the time being only non-negotiable shares can be transferred to foreign investors. The supervisory authorities have realized that it takes a considerably long period of time to open up the market for non-negotiable A-shares to foreign investors. The involvement of foreign investment in merging and acquiring of listed Chinese companies is, in essence, the transfer of state and legal person shares to foreign investors. The circular has laid down well-defined provisions in this regard but makes no mention whatsoever of the issue of opening negotiable A-shares to foreign investors. In this way foreign investment can be utilized to promote the healthy development of the securities market without causing undue repercussions.[2]

4) Clarifying the duty of management department. The circular stipulates that during the process of transferring the state and legal person shares of listed companies to foreign investors, cases concerning industry policies and enterprise transformation should be checked by State Economic & Trade Commission, while cases concerning the management of state shares be checked by Ministry of Finance, the ones concerning information disclosure and specific acquisitions be charged by China Securities Regulatory Commission, very important cases should be turned in to the State Council.

5) Providing pricing and payment methods. Non-negotiable shares on the Chinese securities market are usually transferred contractually, which has a lot of drawbacks in pricing. The adoption of the open bidding method helps extend the margin of prices and protect the interests of investors. As to ways of payment, the circular proceeds from the actual conditions of China to ban foreign investors from using the internationally established non-cash payment method but allow those foreign investors who have already invested in China to pay with the profits gained from their investment provided that they have been examined by the foreign exchange administrative authorities.

6) Emphasizing the disclosure of related information. The circular stipulates that transfer of state and legal person shares to foreign investors should accord with the stipulations of the China Securities Regulatory Commission's stipulations on the acquisition of listed companies and the disclosure of related information

7) Guaranteeing the justified interests of recipients of shares. The circular stipulates that after acquiring state and legal person shares from listed companies, foreign investors may buy foreign exchange and remit it out of China according to law after their net profits from the listed companies, their incomes from re-transfer of shares and their gains from liquidating the assets of the listed companies have been examined by the foreign exchange administrative authorities. This stipulation serves to allay foreign investors' misgivings.

8) Preventing speculation on government policies and fraudulent practices. The circular stipulates that after transferring its state and legal person shares to foreign investors, a listed company shall carry out original policies and is not entitled to treatments accorded to foreign-invested enterprises. The circular also stipulates that 12 months after foreign investors have

[2] The shares of China's state-owned enterprises listed on the securities market fall into two categories, negotiable shares and non-negotiable shares. The new shares issued to the public by a newly listed enterprise are negotiable shares while their original state-owned shares are non-negotiable shares. The ratio between negotiable and non-negotiable shares of a listed company was approximately 0.35:0.65 towards the end of 2002.

paid up all the money for the transfer of shares, they are allowed to re-transfer the shares they have bought

In January 2003, China issued the *Issues Related to Improving the Administration of Enterprises with Foreign Investment in Terms of Examination and Approval, Registration, Foreign Exchange and Taxation*, which has laid down specific provisions concerning the formalities for the examination and approval of foreign-invested enterprises' mergers and acquisitions of domestic enterprises, as well as time limits for payment.

When a foreign investor acquires the shares of a domestic enterprise, the agreement signed by the two partners on the transfer of shares should define the time limit for the foreign investor to pay up the money for acquiring the shares. The examining and approving authorities shall not grant permission to agreements that provide no clauses on such time limits. Accordingly, a foreign buyer of shares of a domestic enterprise shall pay up within three months after a business permit is granted to the foreign-invested enterprise in question. When a buyer wants to extend the term of payment, he or she may, with the approval of the authorities, pay over 60% of the sum within six months after the business permit is issued, pay up the remainder within one year, and get his or her share of economic returns according to the percentage of paid capital. Before paying up all the money for the purchase of his shares, a shareholding investor shall not have the decision-making power in the enterprise, nor is he allowed to list his rights and assets in his financial reports. The foreign investment and foreign exchange certificates issued by the foreign exchange administrative department of where the seller of shares is located are effective documents proving the payment by a foreign investor.

2. Stipulations in Consideration

Because large state-owned enterprises in China are often leaders in their respective fields and tend to have large teams of workers and staff and complicated debt structures, in M&As they are likely to give rise to such problems as monopoly, unemployment and the regrouping of debt relationships. It is thus the consensus of government and scholars that more detailed and specific stipulations are needed to regulate the behavior of foreign investors arriving in China for merging and acquiring state-owned enterprises. The following are some of the much talked-of points that may be embodied in Chinese legislation in the future:

1) The Probability of Monopoly Arising from M&As

Large-scale M&As should be submitted for examination to see if they may give rise to monopoly. The points of departure to be considered: if a single deal of foreign investment in the Chinese enterprise's shares or single purchase of assets exceeds a boundary, say 30 million US dollars, if the accumulated sums on M&As within a year surpasses a boundary, say 100 million US dollars, if the deals concluded within a year involved more large projects in the same field than is allowed, say ten projects in total, or if through buying shares or assets a foreign investor or a company associated with him has obtained a considerable share of the Chinese market, say one third of it – under these circumstances the Chinese examination and approval authorities should bring the departments, organizations, and interested parties together for a hearing, and pass a decision within a certain period of time – say 60 workdays -- beginning from the day the investigation commences. Moreover, at the request of a domestic enterprise or industrial association involved in a competitive relationship, or in the presence of other major factors that may affect market competition, the examination and approval authorities should also set in motion the aforementioned hearing proceedings.

2) M&As and the Resettlement of Workers and Staff Members

Specific explanation is needed if a foreign-invested enterprise's merger or acquisition of a state-owned enterprise in China is likely to necessitate the resettlement of a considerable number of workers and staff members. It is certainly pointless to ask a foreign investor to totally refrain from laying off workers and staff members or commit himself to resettling them, but explanations are needed about the impact of the merger or acquisition on employment and specifics should be clarified, such as the percentage of old employees to be retained or resettled, and how layoffs should be compensated for.

Both issues are important and merit serious attention. How to prevent the behavior of M&As from giving rise to monopoly is an issue of common concern for various countries. The issue of resettling the workers and staff members is of particular concern for China as the most populous country in the world and as a nation in economic transition. Requirements in both fields, therefore, are likely to be embodied in relevant laws to be promulgated by the Chinese government.

JUDGMENT AND SUMMARY

Permitting foreign investors to participate in the transformation and regrouping of large and medium-sized state-owned enterprises by way of M&As is a major progress achieved in China's reform and opening up to the outside world. It is also an important and concrete embodiment of the effort to promote reform by opening the country wider to the outside world. This process is fraught with uncertainty and instability and has to be tested by time. Only by readjusting government policies and legal framework from time to time can the process of utilizing foreign investment to promote transformation of state-owned enterprises end up in a win-win situation.

Chapter 13

PROSPECTS OF FOREIGN INVESTMENT AND THE SUSTAINED GROWTH OF THE CHINESE ECONOMY

13-1: TO MAINTAIN SUSTAINED FAST GROWTH, THE CHINESE ECONOMY NEEDS TO MAKE MORE USE OF THE OPPORTUNITIES PROVIDED BY ECONOMIC GLOBALIZATION

As a large developing country, China has to make good use of the opportunities provided by economic globalization if it is to maintain the sustained fast growth of its national economy.

1. Employment Is a Long-term Challenge, and it is Vital to Make Good Use of the Global Resources and Market

China is a nation with a lopsided composition of factor endowment. The country accounts for 23% of the global total labor force, but a meager 6-7% of the global capital formation, 7% of the world's total cultivated land acreage, and 4% of the global total verified oil reserve and gas deposits. This lopsided mix of factor endowment determines that China has to integrate itself to a large extent with the global economy and, by massive exports of labor-intensive products and massive imports of resource-intensive products to make up for domestic shortages, provide more jobs for the labor force, alleviate the pressure of employment and sustain its fast economic growth.

Employment will remain the foremost challenge for China in the next few decades of development. In the early 21st century, more than half of the Chinese labor force is still engaged in agriculture. This is not to say that Chinese agriculture today is capable of providing ample employment opportunities, but that the capacity of the manufacturing and service industries to create new jobs has been diminishing, resulting in the stagnation of labor numbers of laborers in farming. Both Table 13-1 and Figure 13-1 attest to a drop in the elasticity of employment of the manufacturing and service industries from 0.41 and 0.36 respectively during the 1979-1985 Period to –0.07 and 0.26 during the 1999-2001 Period.

Table 13-1: Elasticity of employment of the manufacturing and service industries in China

Year	The Elasticity of Employment Growth of the Manufacturing Industry	The Elasticity of Employment Growth of the Service Industry
1979 1985	0.41	0.36
1986 1990	0.34	0.34
1991 1995	0.05	0.20
1996 1998	0.17	0.29
1999 2001	-0.07	0.26

Sources: Table 5-2 (Year-end Numbers of Employees in Three Industrial Categories) and Table 3-1 (Gross Domestic Product) in National Bureau of Statistics of China (2003). *China Statistical Yearbook 2002* (Beijing: China Statistics Press).

Figure 13-1: Elasticity of employment of China's manufacturing and service industries since the adoption of the policy of reform and opening up to the outside world

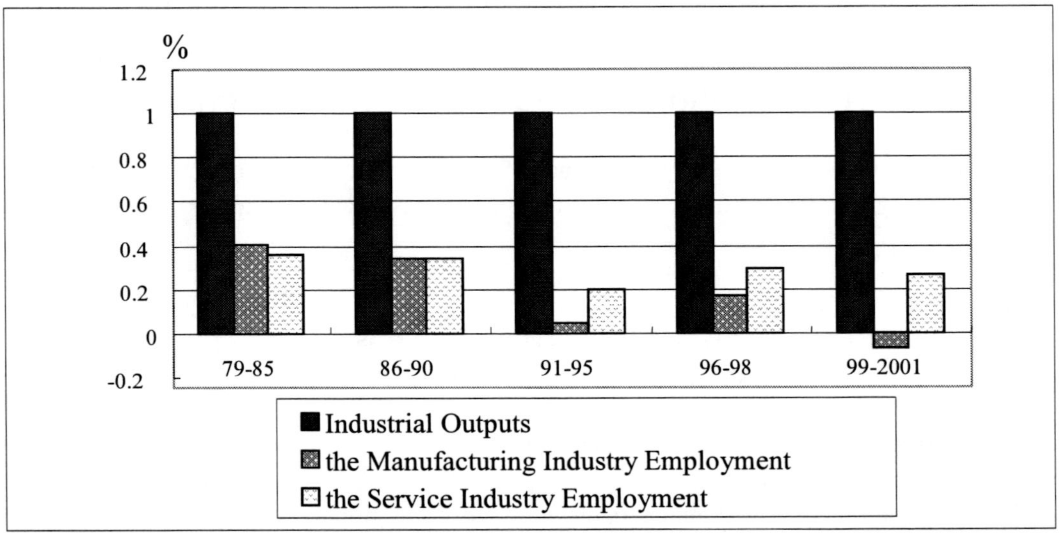

Sources: *Ibid.*

At present agriculture still accounts for half of the national working population. According to a conservative estimation, at least 200 million laborers will have to be shifted from rural areas to somewhere else, averaging 10 million a year. Apart from the shift of the rural labor force, jobs have to be provided for the annual addition of 8 million new laborers. Reform of state-owned enterprises will result in factory layoffs. When these needs are added up, China has to offer 20 million new jobs annually, which account for 5.6% of the 370 million-strong labor force currently working in the manufacturing and service industries. In other words, only when employment grows by 5.6% a year can the need for jobs be basically satisfied. If the economy grows by 7% and employment by 5.6% a year, then the elasticity of employment will increase by approximately 0.8%.

To solve the employment problem it calls for coordinated efforts from various quarters and a package of government policies. An important way to tackle the problem is to open the country still wider to the outside world and take advantage of large-scale international trade and flow of production elements. Thus, on the one hand, more jobs can be provided by incorporating more funds, energy sources, raw materials and other inputs. On the other, it is necessary to boost the development of labor-intensive industries and export as more intensive-intensive products as possible – so that the world market can be utilized to open up the space for the development of China's labor-intensive industries.

2. Upgrading the Chinese Economic Structure Calls for More Foreign Capital and Technology

Increases in China's economic strength and per-capita GDP will inevitably raise the consumption level of some of the Chinese residents and steadily boost the demand of some consumers, urban dwellers in particular, for consumer goods with high incremental value and high technological contents. And they are also becoming more demanding for the high-tech intensity and environmental friendliness of such traditional manufactured goods as textiles, steel products and building materials. For this reason, upgrading the nation's industrial structure is an inherent demand in the effort to maintain sustained economic growth in China. However, the domestic capacities, technological conditions in particular, are falling way short of the needs of the domestic industrial structure. The analysis of Chapter Three indicates that since the mid-1990s, the technology coming alongside foreign investment has been the most important technological source for upgrading the Chinese industrial structure. In the fastest growing fields, such as the electronic and telecommunications and cars industries, foreign-invested enterprises (FIEs) have contributed more than half of the investment and more than two thirds of the outputs.

The international experiences also fully justify the importance of utilizing foreign capital and technology. It shows that it is no difficult task to maintain a relatively high growth rate in the first one or two decades after an economy enters a period of accelerated growth, but it will become relatively difficult to do so after an economy has experienced two or three decades of high-speed development. In the 40 years since the 1960s, only three economies – South Korea, Singapore and Thailand – have kept their average annual growth rates above 7%, only two economies – Hong Kong of China and Malaysia – have maintained an average annual growth rate of 6-7%, and only five economies – including Japan, Indonesia and Turkey -- and two others – have kept their average annual growth rate at 5-6%. See Table 13-2. Many countries have found it hard to maintain a high economic growth rate after two decades of robust development. The reasons differ, but an important one is that when the initial stage of industrialization has come to an end and has to be followed up with domestic industrial upgrading, it is difficult to maintain fast economic growth if a country does not possess the essential conditions for industrial upgrading, such as technological capacities and an ample domestic market. If China is to break this pattern and maintain its high growth on the basis of more than two decades of robust development, it has to be more open to the outside world so as to acquire the needed elements, technology in particular.

Table 13-2: Countries and regions that have sustained high economic growth rate for 40 years

	1960-1970	1970-1980	1980-1990	1990-1999	2000
Economies with growth rate higher than 7%					
R.O.K.	8.6	9.5	9.7	5.7	8.4
Hong Kong	10	9.3	7.1	3.9	7.6
Singapore	8.8	8.5	6.4	8	7.9
Economies with growth rate higher than 6%					
Malaysia	6.5	7.8	5.2	6.3	6.5
Thailand	8.4	7.2	7.6	4.7	7.0
Economies with growth rate higher than 5%					
Lesotho	5.2	7.9	3.1	4.4	5.2
Turkey	6	5.9	5.1	4.1	5.3
Indonesia	3.9	7.6	5.5	4.7	5.4
Pakistan	6.7	4.7	6.3	4	5.4
Japan	10.9	5.0	4.0	1.4	5.3

Sources: World Bank (1982, 1992 and 2000/2001). *World Development Report* (Oxford: Oxford University Press).

3. The Reform of Economic System Has to Be Promoted by Opening Up to the Outside World

Many important issues are yet to be redressed in the economic restructuring of China. The reform of large state-owned enterprises, financial firms and monopolistic industries calls for continued efforts to open up to the outside world.

A main obstacle confronting the reform of large state-owned enterprises is lack of powerful non-state investors in China. The same is true with the monopolistic industries, such as telecommunications, railways, civil aviation, petrochemical industry and urban public utilities. The enterprises in these fields are also large state-owned ones.

Take listed companies for instance. State-owned enterprises and state-controlled companies comprise a major part of the nation's capital market. However, though these enterprises have acquired large amounts of investment from non-state sectors by listing on the capital market, state-owned shares remain in absolute control of the shares of listed companies. In many enterprises the shares are often monopolized by the state and state-owned legal persons. By the end of 2001, companies in which the largest shareholder controls more than 50% of the shares make up 78% of the total number of listed companies, while state shares and state-owned legal person shares account for 91% of the total number of the largest shareholders. This situation had something to do with limitations imposed by the government on the transfer of state-owned shares prior to 1999, and it has been associated with the pounding of the reduction of state-owned holdings on the stock market since 1999. However, the lack of powerful strategic investors at home has all along been a major obstacle for the transfer of state-owned shares and the reform of state-owned enterprises.

By strategic investors we mean those who not only are capable of providing funds but also have technological and management capabilities and who set their eyes on the long-term development of enterprises. The lack of strategic investors who are capable of entering the above-mentioned fields will remain for a period of time. For this reason, to open the doors wider to let in foreign investors while incorporating domestic investors will determine whether the reform of the state sector and monopolistic industries will expedite.

In all, to deepen and broaden the opening-up efforts and further integrate with the global economy is the inherent demand of maintaining the sustained fast growth of the Chinese economy.

13-2: The Steady Progress of Economic Globalization Makes It Possible to Continue Incorporating Foreign Investment and Advanced Technology On a Large Scale

The sustained fast growth of the Chinese economy calls for more utilization of foreign investment, but can this wish come true? Is international capital willing to continue entering China on a large scale? Judging from the international environment and reality, it is still possible for China to introduce foreign investment on a large scale for a certain period of time to come. This possibility is based mainly on two aspects: first, with the process of economic globalization keep accelerating, transnational investment will still arrive in considerable amounts, and the technological transfer by transnational corporations, in particular, will grow in scale; second, with its unique strengths China is likely to remain attractive to foreign investors for a long period of time to come and will land a considerable portion of transnational investment.

1. A New Hallmark of Economic Globalization: Transnational Transfer of Technology Is Continuously on the Rise

Economic globalization has taken on some new features in the course of steady acceleration in recent years. One of these lies in changes in the methods and speed of technology transfer.

In the past, it was an established practice for transnational corporations in developed countries to limit the use of the most sophisticated products and technology they had developed to their own countries before shifting them to other developed countries, and only after a technology had become mature or even outdated did they shift it to developing countries. A developing country will forever trail behind if it depends solely on foreign technology, which is one of the central parts of traditional theory on technology transfer. Great changes have taken place in this situation since the mid-1990s. Firstly, because the speed of technological development has been vastly increased and because investment in R&D and manufacturing is depreciated very fast, an enterprise can recoup its heavy investment in the technology it has developed and make a profit only by putting it to maximum use within the shortest period of time. Secondly, in some important industries, the industrial organization is in transition from vertical integration to horizontal division of work. "Vertical integration" refers to a system in which all the major links on a product's incremental chain are accomplished in a single enterprise, as is the case with IBM prior to the mid-1980s; "horizontal labor division" refers to the practice in which an enterprise is specialized in one or several links on a product's incremental chain, as is the case with Microsoft and Intel. In comparison with vertical integration, enterprises in a horizontal labor division often need the global market to apportion the costs of R&D and maintain their scales. Thirdly, with the number of enterprises at the same technological level on the increase, and with the intensification of competition, an enterprise can become a winner only if it can occupy the market at the fastest speed the in largest possible scale. For these reasons, an enterprise that has just come up with a new technology will invariably seek to put it into global use and manufacturing, enabling the recipient countries to quickly grasp an advanced technology and product. Such a change makes it possible for China to introduce large amounts of advanced technology by utilizing foreign investment.

2. China Will Maintain Its Appeals to Foreign Investors in a Considerably Long Period of Time

China will maintain its appeals as a host country for transnational investment. Such appeals stem from two fields. Firstly, a tremendous market. In the first half of the 21st century, both the Chinese economy and market will continue to expand at relatively high speeds, and the nation's industrial structure will continue to be upgraded. The steady increase in the income level of some of the residents is turning China into a major market for the technology and products of transnational corporations. Given its huge population, China will become an impressive market for transnational corporations even if only a part of the population is earning enough money to become consumers of these corporations' commodities with high incremental value and technological content. For some transnational corporations, China is already the largest overseas market, second only to their home markets, and will become such a market for more transnational corporations in the days to come. Secondly, low costs and a sound industrial foundation. The labor cost in China is around or below one twentieth that of some developed countries and one eighth that of some major emerging industrialized economies. Thus transferring a company's manufacturing capacity to China will obviously enhance its cost-associated competitiveness. China's sound industrial foundations enable make it convenient for transnational corporations to find qualified accessory suppliers. With the increase in the competitiveness of China's domestic enterprises and the steady rise in the number of accessory-supplying enterprises in China, transnational corporations will be able to steadily increase their supply of accessories from domestic companies, thereby reduce costs, speed up production and be more prompt in adjusting their products.

13-3: Prevention of Possible Problems and Risks of An Open Economy

The effort to open the country still wider to the outside world and continue to expand foreign trade and the use of foreign investment will, while bringing about many opportunities, also give rise to new uncertainties and risks. To take the risks into full account and be well prepared against them is the first step for effectively avoiding such risks and keep them under control.

1. Changes In the Global Economy is Likely to Cause Fluctuations In the Domestic Economy

With the doors of the nation thrown wider to the outside world, the changes in the global economy and the economies of some of the major countries in the world will inevitably found their way into China, and the foreign factors are likely to affect the exports and imports and the FDI inflows in this country, causing considerable changes and obvious fluctuations in the annual economic growth rate. The occurrence of unfavorable deficits in both international trade and international investment can aggravate the balance of international revenue and expenditure and cause chain reactions, thereby slow down economic growth.

Figure 13-2, which features a comparison of the growth rate of Chinese exports with that of global exports, indicates that since the beginning of the 1990s, increases in Chinese exports have become highly relevant to increases in global exports. For this reason, fluctuations in the global economy and the global export market unavoidably have a marked impact on Chinese exports.

Figure 13-2: A comparison of the growth rate of China's exports with that of global exports

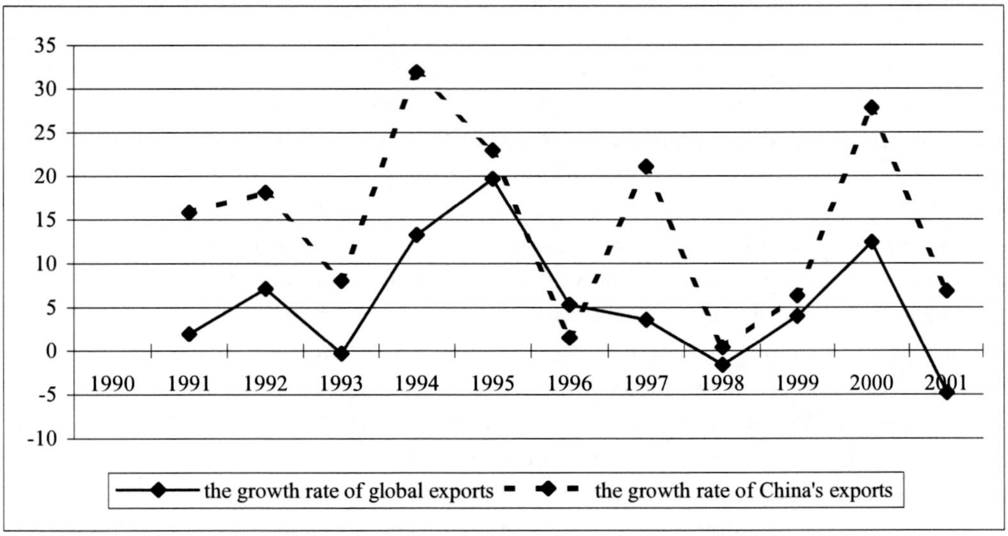

From a long- and intermediary-term point of view, changes in certain inherent conditions in China will spawn destabilizing factors in the course of further opening up to the outside world. Firstly, increases in domestic labor costs and appreciation of the domestic currency. Judging from the international experience, the pressure of appreciation of the domestic currency will be high during this period. For instance, the exchange rate of the Japanese yen to the US dollar was 358:1 in 1970, but it rose by 76% to 203:1 in 1980, and it increased to 135:1 in 1990, which was a 50% rise as compared with what it had been ten years previously and a 165% increase against what it had been 20 years previously. The appreciation of the domestic currency may also destabilize the foreign capital inflows. Secondly, with foreign capital flowing into China on a large scale, and particularly with the gradual increase in the openness of the Chinese capital market, foreign capital's share in the Chinese capital market will grow steadily; any unexpected unfavorable change in the international or domestic economic situation can trigger off a large-scale drain of foreign capital, thereby gravely affect the balance of international revenue and expenditure, and the stability of the domestic economy.

2. The Possibility of Transnational Corporations Abusing their Impact on the Market

With their colossal influence on the global market, transnational corporations are likely to abuse such an influence. This merits serious attention for a host country in transition to an open economy. It is also something that China has to guard against in the days to come.

It goes without saying that all commercial companies – domestic ones and global ones alike -- seek to maximize their profits. In the same token, in the absence of strong market supervision and control, all companies – domestic ones and global ones alike – are likely to resort to unfair or even illegal profit-seeking steps to the detriment of consumer interests and in violation of the principle of fair competition. In this regard, however, a major difference between transnational corporations and domestic enterprises is that the former are commercial giants in the possession of sophisticated technology, powerful research and development capacities, and global financing, production and sales abilities. Because of this, transnational corporations are far more capable of affecting the market than domestic enterprises. When a market is handicapped by inadequate competition and a feeble control framework, the transnational corporations are unlikely not to take advantage of the situation to gain monopoly.

The analyses of Chapter Seven show that as things stand today in the Chinese manufacturing industry, market monopoly is not yet a common and serious problem. Past experiences, however, do not rule out the possibility of market monopoly by transnational corporations in the future. Expanding the Chinese service industry to foreign investors and allowing them to invest in the form of mergers and acquisitions can create chances for new types of market monopoly. But we are still unclear whether or not the use of market forces to adjust foreign-invested enterprises' competitive behaviors in the Chinese manufacturing industry applies to other fields.

After its WTO accession China has vastly increased the openness of its service industry to foreign investment, so much so that most of the service departments have been opened to foreign investors. Services in sales, banking, insurance, securities, telecommunications, transportation and specialties and travel services have all begun to open to the outside world or enhance their openness. Due to lack of competition on the domestic market, the domestic enterprises in some fields of the Chinese service industry are relatively weak in their competitiveness, which differs from the Chinese manufacturing industry where the domestic market was already under adequate competition prior to the adoption of the open policy. If this situation cannot be changed quickly, it is probable to some extent that transnational giants will seize an advantageous position on the Chinese services market and gain high returns from it.

Attracting foreign investment in mergers and acquisitions is also likely to give rise to monopoly. However, given the complexity of the influence of investment in mergers and acquisitions on a market structure, monopoly will not rise, and competition will be intensified, at least under the following two circumstances. Firstly, if the subject of a foreign-invested merger or acquisition is an enterprise in financial difficulties and will be squeezed out of the market without being merged or sold, such a merger or acquisition serves to retain a market competitor and therefore has a positive impact on competition. Secondly, if the subject of a foreign-invested merger or acquisition is second-echelon enterprise in China, such a merger or acquisition can cause this enterprise to be reborn and acquire enough competitiveness to challenge the monopoly of the leading counterparts on the domestic market, thereby intensifying market competition.

Under most circumstances, however, involving foreign investment in mergers and acquisitions can reduce the number of enterprises in competition and set the stage for monopoly. On the negotiation table, there are times when the government permits or acquiesces in a transnational corporation's monopolistic position on the home market in exchange for that corporation's commitments to certain conditions. Monopoly is not the only criterion with which to judge whether a foreign-invested merger or acquisition is in our interests – for example, we may be forced to grant monopoly for a certain period of time or within a certain scope to a transnational corporation because this is the only option available that can exact more commitments to employment and debts. However, such a transaction can be made only when we have taken into full account the serious aftermaths of monopoly. In the Chinese manufacturing and service industries there are large numbers of enterprises that are large and have influential product brands and numerous consumers but are in poor financial situations, and because of this they are major targets for transnational mergers and acquisitions. With their strong positions in negotiations, large transnational corporations are likely to seek monopoly when investing in such mergers and acquisitions.

China is beginning to open some of its naturally monopolistic industries to foreign investors, such as telecommunications, railways, development of natural resources, and power generating. Foreign-investment in merging or acquiring these enterprises will inevitably bring an impact to bear on market competition. Judging from international experience, especially the experiences of developing countries and countries in economic transition, such an opening-up effort is always accompanied by changes in the framework and rules for supervision and control when a foreign-invested merger or acquisition involves a field under natural monopoly, and the conflict of interests, and the lack of experience may cause major controversy and tendencies towards monopoly.

3. Impact on the Security of the National Economy

Countries around the world have been speeding up their opening-up efforts in recent years, and integration of the global economy is going strong. Against this background, however, the global competition in technology and industry is not yet completely marketized. Industries and fields that have an important bearing on the security of national economy and defense, in particular, have never been, and will not be, technological fields for full competition. We cannot possibly obtain from the outside world the key technology for the defense industry or the major technology monopolized by large foreign companies. A foreign company hoping to transfer to China the key technology it has developed for commercial purposes may be intervened or banned by its government if such a technology can be used for both civilian and military purposes.

China has had its feel of obstructions in this regard in the last few years. In the fist half of 2001, SMIC, the well-known American semi-conductor manufacturer, was prepared to establish a chip manufacturing plant in Shanghai for a total investment of 1.5 billion US dollars. To meet its investment need, SMIC applied, through the American Applied Materials Company, for the transfer of two electronic light beam system technologies to China. A technology export examination committee formed by the US Department of Defense, the Department of State, and the Department of Commerce spent the next six months examining the project and finally turned the SMIC proposal down. This is just one of numerous similar examples. In 2001 alone, the US Department of Commerce received 1,294 applications for exporting technology to China. The US Department of Commerce endorsed 72% of them; it rejected 3% of them and declined to deal with 25% of them, citing, in most cases, reasons of "military purposes" and "state security". It is thus clear that research in this category of technology cannot depend on opening up the field and direct technological transfers.

13-4: Seeking a Balance among Expanding Opening-up, Monopoly Prevention and Economic Stability

1. Tightening Up Supervision and Control of the Tendency of Foreign Investment Towards Monopoly

To insist on introducing competition and intensifying it in industries where maybe competitive is the most effective way of supervision and control.

1) Cultivating Domestic Competitors

To cultivate domestic enterprises capable of competing with firms invested by transnational corporations is a major aspect of maintaining market competitiveness. In the last dozen years, a considerable number of Chinese enterprises have, as a result of intense market competition, rapidly increased their level of technology and improved the quality of their products by incorporating foreign technology, and quickly expanded them and acquired high reputations on the domestic and world markets. In the process they have also raised their asset quality and technological level to new heights. However, in their competition with foreign-invested firms, they are treated unfairly in market access, financing and market status, and, being state-owned, they are weighed down by such burdens as over-staffing and debts. As a result, the competitiveness of the domestic enterprises is enfeebled, causing failures in competing with foreign-invested firms. It is therefore imperative to cultivate an effective environment for market competition and place domestic enterprises on a par with foreign-invested firms on the market. To achieve this purpose, firstly, it is necessary to formulate policies to treat domestic and foreign investor equally and eliminate policies that discriminate against domestic investors, and secondly, it is imperative to create an environment with equal systems, remove system-related obstacles from the development of domestic enterprises, speed up transformation of state-owned enterprises, and establish mechanisms to turn enterprises into major market competitors and corporate entities that can make their own management decisions and bear sole responsibilities for their own gains and losses. Only thus can enterprises be as motivated as their foreign-invested counterparts in seeking long-term development. Only by further breaking up rigid administrative divisions, removing the unjustified limitations on the regrouping of enterprise property rights and promoting the reasonable flow of resources according to market rules, can we cultivate a number of large enterprises and large enterprise groups that are fully capable of seeking survival and growth in competition and cooperation with transnational corporations.

2) Promoting the Competition among Foreign-Invested Enterprises

In some fields, domestic enterprises cannot acquire due competitiveness because of high technical and financial barriers. Under these circumstances, investment has to be incorporated from at least two transnational corporations in the manufacturing of a single product so as to bring about competition between foreign-invested firms. A major experience of China in attracting large transnational corporations is that whether an industry is monopolized by a single foreign-invested enterprise or subjected to competition among several such enterprises makes a great difference in enterprises' behaviors in technology transfers and pricing.

3) Promulgating the Competition Law As Soon As Possible

The international experience indicates that the Competition Law is being adopted by more and more countries for the main purpose of restraining and standardizing the behaviors of large transnational companies in competition with the domestic market in an environment where economic globalization is making steady progress. While become increasingly more open to transnational investment, many countries are examining transnational mergers and acquisition as part of their policies on competition. For so many years many developed countries have been using the Competition Law extensively to examine foreign investors' behaviors in mergers and acquisitions. The last 15 years or so have seen some developing countries and countries in economic transition adopt or beef up this system. By the end of 2001, about 93 countries had endorsed a competition law or had been drafting it. We should draw on the experiences of some developing countries in using the Competition Law to constrain behaviors in transnational mergers and acquisitions, lose no time to draft an anti-monopoly law and an anti-unfair transaction law, tighten up the information disclosure system and the auditing of linked transactions that may lead to monopolistic management, and forestall the possible monopolistic and other unfair behaviors of transnational corporations.

2. Be Prepared against Onslaught from the Outside World

From a long-term point of view, stability of the growth of the Chinese economy and health of the financial system, and keeping the risks in the domestic economy under control are the basic conditions for us to cope with the onslaught from the outside world. In the meantime, we should be fully prepared against the risks that may arise from the short-term or sudden fluctuations of a foreign economy.

Firstly, we should formulate anti-fluctuation policies that enable us to promptly readjust domestic policies to prevent fluctuations from spreading and avoid being caught in a vicious cycle whenever reductions in exports or foreign investment inflow have given rise to such fluctuations.

Secondly, we should promote opening up the capital market to the outside world in a gradual manner. Development of the capital market, which can help raise the portion of direct financing, is what is inherently needed in our effort to reduce financial risks, raise the efficiency of the financial market and offer investors with more options; it is a general trend as well. Opening up the capital market to the outside world enables us to use global capital in more ways and better allocate the resources on two markets; as an extension and deepening of the open policy, an open capital market is also a general trend. Another major significance for opening up the capital market is that it enables transnational corporations to domesticate their financing for their businesses and property rights in China and allows domestic investors to share the investment returns of foreign-invested enterprises. Foreign investors can share the benefits of a developing Chinese economy only when foreign-invested enterprises can gain considerable profits and remit such profits out of China. Domestic investors are able to share the economic returns of foreign-invested enterprises only if the latter are allowed to raise funds on the Chinese capital market. However, the opening up of the capital market is a risky undertaking that should be promoted step by step. Firstly, the services of the capital market, such as fund management companies, securities companies, consulting and appraisal companies, should be opened up to the outside world so as to learn from the mature operational and management experiences of foreign countries and promote the sound growth of the Chinese capital market. Secondly, this opening-up effort should take place in a progressive manner and in sync with the growth of effective supervisory and monitoring and management capacities.

Thirdly, it is imperative to strengthen our country's self-reliant R&D capabilities in important fields. In a big developing nation like China, the development of industries and technology that has an important bearing on national economic and military security cannot do without government support. To gain a position in key technological fields and cultivate self-reliant technological abilities is vital to national economic and defense security and to the cultivation of potentials for long-term development. Therefore, while expanding the opening-up efforts, the government has to work together with the nation's industrialists, scientists and technicians to formulate well-defined and effective strategies for the state's technological and industrial development. What merits attention is that because many high technologies associated with state security are developed for the sake of commercial interests, it is wrong to believe no major technologies having to do with state security can be developed without government investment, which can lead to infinite expansion of government intervention. Technologies such as micro-electronic circuits, integrated semiconductors, computer software, robots, optical fibres, super-conductivity technology, and bioengineering technology are for dual purposes with a commercial orientation. It is beyond the government's investment capacity to bring all these fields into the realm of state investment and develop them by solely relying on home resources. A more unfavorable aftermath is that government protection and support can rob the enterprises in these fields of their competitiveness on the market, to the jeopardy of the development of these fields and these enterprises. Therefore, government behaviors aimed at state security should be concentrated on those fields where commercial interests are too inadequate to stimulate domestic investment and where commerce-oriented transnational investment and technological transactions are banned or restricted, or likely so, by parent countries.

RELATED STATISTICS

Total Imports and Exports by FIEs 1986-2002

Unit: US$ 100 Million

Year	Imports and Exports			Imports			Exports		
	National	FIEs	Share %	National	FIEs	Share %	National	FIEs	Share %
1986	738.46	29.85	4.04	429.04	24.03	5.60	309.42	5.82	1.88
1987	826.53	45.84	5.55	432.16	33.74	7.81	394.37	12.10	3.07
1988	1027.84	83.43	8.12	552.68	58.82	10.64	475.16	24.61	5.18
1989	1116.78	137.10	12.28	591.40	87.96	14.87	525.38	49.14	9.35
1990	1154.36	201.15	17.43	533.45	123.02	23.06	620.91	78.13	12.58
1991	1357.01	289.55	21.34	637.91	169.08	26.51	719.10	120.47	16.75
1992	1655.25	437.47	26.43	805.85	263.87	32.74	849.40	173.60	20.44
1993	1957.03	670.70	34.27	1039.59	418.33	40.24	917.44	252.37	27.51
1994	2366.21	876.47	337.04	1156.15	529.34	45.78	1210.06	347.13	28.69
1995	2808.48	1098.19	39.10	1320.78	629.43	47.66	1487.70	468.76	31.51
1996	2899.04	1371.10	47.29	1388.38	756.04	54.45	1510.66	615.06	40.71
1997	3250.60	1526.20	46.95	1423.60	777.20	54.59	1827..00	749.00	41.00
1998	3239.23	1576.79	48.68	1401.66	767.17	54.73	1837.57	809.62	44.06
1999	3606.49	1831.33	50.78	1657.18	858.84	51.83	1949.31	886.28	45.47
2000	4743.08	2367.14	49.91	2250.97	1172.73	52.10	2492.12	1194.41	47.93
2001	5097.68	2590.98	50.83	2436.13	1258.63	51.67	2661.55	1332.35	50.06
2002	6207.85	3302.23	53.19	2952.16	1602.86	54.29	3255.69	1699.37	52.20

Source: MOFTEC FDI Statistics.

Statistics of FDI from United States 1986-2002

Unit: US$ 10000

Year	Number of Project			Contractual FDI Value			Realized FDI Value		
	U.S.A.	National Total	Share %	U.S.A.	National Total	Share %	U.S.A.	National Total	Share %
1986	102	1498	6.81	54148	333037	16.26	32617	224373	14.54
1987	104	2233	4.66	34219	370884	9.23	26280	231353	11.36
1988	269	5945	4.52	37040	529706	6.99	23596	319368	7.39
1989	276	5779	4.78	64052	559976	11.44	28427	339257	8.38
1990	357	7273	4.91	35782	659611	5.42	45599	348711	13.08
1991	694	12978	5.35	54808	1197682	4.58	32320	436634	7.40
1992	3265	48764	6.70	312125	5812351	5.37	51105	1100751	4.64
1993	6750	83437	8.09	681275	11143566	6.11	206312	2751495	7.50
1994	4223	47549	8.88	601018	8267977	7.27	249080	3376650	7.38
1995	3474	37011	9.39	747113	9128153	8.18	308301	3752053	8.22
1996	2517	24556	10.25	691576	7327642	9.44	344333	4172552	8.25
1997	2188	21001	10.42	493655	5100353	9.68	323915	4525704	7.16
1998	2238	19799	11.30	648373	5210205	12.44	389844	4546275	8.58
1999	2028	16918	11.99	601611	4122302	14.59	421586	4031871	10.46
2000	2609	22347	11.67	800089	6237952	12.83	438389	4071481	10.77
2001	2606	26140	9.97	751487	6919455	10.86	443322	4687759	9.46
2002	3363	34171	9.84	815647	8276833	9.85	542392	5274286	10.28

Source: MOFTEC FDI Statistics.

Statistics of FDI from European Union 1986-2002

Unit: US$ 10000

Year	Number of Project			Contractual FDI Value			Realized FDI Value		
	E.U.	National Total	Share %	E.U.	National Total	Share %	E.U.	National Total	Share %
1986	32	1498	2.14	35194	333037	10.57	17853	224373	7.96
1987	40	2233	1.79	42293	370884	11.40	5271	231353	2.28
1988	87	5945	1.46	28531	529706	5.39	15757	319368	4.92
1989	78	5779	1.35	33289	529976	5.94	18761	339257	5.53
1990	82	7273	1.13	22422	659611	3.40	14735	248711	4.23
1991	163	12978	1.26	75939	1197682	6.34	24562	436634	5.63
1992	763	48764	1.56	96360	5812351	1.66	24297	1100751	2.21
1993	1726	83437	2.07	318176	11143566	2.86	67124	2751495	2.44
1994	1464	47549	3.08	562958	8267977	6.81	153769	3376650	4.55
1995	1582	37011	4.27	741977	9128153	8.13	213131	3752053	5.68
1996	1167	24556	4.75	675922	7327642	9.22	273706	4172552	6.56
1997	1040	21001	4.95	422882	5100353	8.29	417115	4525704	9.22
1998	1002	19799	5.06	593938	5210205	11.40	397873	4546275	8.75
1999	894	16918	5.28	409566	4122302	9.94	447906	4031871	11.11
2000	1130	22347	5.06	885516	6237952	14.20	447946	4071481	11.00
2001	1214	26140	4.64	515284	6919455	7.45	418270	4687759	8.92
2002	1486	34171	4.35	450693	8276833	5.45	370982	5274286	7.03

Source: MOFTEC FDI Statistics.

Statistics of FDI from Japan 1986-2002

Unit: US$ 10000

Year	Number of Project			Contractual FDI Value			Realized FDI Value		
	Japan	National Total	Share %	Japan	National Total	Share %	Japan	National Total	Share %
1986	94	1498	6.28	28282	333037	8.49	26335	224373	11.74
1987	113	2233	5.06	30136	370884	8.13	21970	231353	9.50
1988	237	5945	3.99	27579	529706	5.21	51453	319368	16.11
1989	294	5779	5.09	43861	529976	7.83	35634	339257	10.50
1990	341	7273	4.69	45700	659611	6.93	50338	248711	14.44
1991	599	12978	4.62	81220	1197682	6.78	53250	436634	12.20
1992	1805	48764	3.70	217253	5812351	3.74	70983	1100751	6.45
1993	3488	83437	4.18	296047	11143566	2.66	132410	2751495	4.81
1994	3018	47549	6.35	444029	8267977	5.37	207529	3376650	6.15
1995	2946	37011	7.96	759236	9128153	8.32	310846	3752053	8.28
1996	1742	24556	7.09	513068	7327642	7.00	367935	4172552	8.82
1997	1402	21001	6.68	340124	5100353	6.67	432647	4525704	9.56
1998	1198	19799	6.05	274899	5210205	5.28	340036	4546275	7.48
1999	1167	16918	6.90	259128	4122302	6.29	297308	4031871	7.37
2000	1614	22347	7.22	368051	6237952	5.90	291585	4071481	7.16
2001	2019	26140	7.72	541973	6919455	7.83	434842	4687759	9.28
2002	2745	34171	8.03	529804	8276833	6.40	419009	5274286	7.94

Source: MOFTEC FDI Statistics.

Statistics of FDI from Hong Kong 1986-2002

Unit: US$ 10000

Year	Number of Project			Contractual FDI Value			Realized FDI Value		
	Hong Kong	National Total	Share %	Hong Kong	National Total	Share %	Hong Kong	National Total	Share %
1986	1155	1498	77.10	177343	333037	53.25	132871	224373	59.22
1987	1721	2233	77.07	194661	370884	52.49	158794	231353	68.64
1988	4562	5945	76.74	346658	529706	65.04	206760	319368	64.74
1989	4072	5779	70.46	315966	559976	56.42	203690	339257	60.04
1990	4751	7273	65.32	383334	659611	58.12	187600	348711	53.91
1991	8502	12978	65.51	721510	1197682	60.24	240525	436634	55.09
1992	30781	48764	63.12	4004379	5812351	68.89	750707	1100751	68.20
1993	49134	83437	58.89	7393852	11143566	66.35	1727475	2751495	62.78
1994	24622	47549	51.78	4697141	8267977	56.81	1966544	3376650	58.24
1995	17186	37011	46.43	4099555	9128153	44.91	2006037	3752053	53.47
1996	10397	24556	42.34	2760172	7327642	38.21	2067732	4172552	49.56
1997	8405	21001	40.02	1822229	5100353	35.73	2063200	4525704	45.59
1998	7805	19799	39.42	1761328	5210205	33.81	1850836	4546275	40.71
1999	5902	16918	34.89	1332892	4122302	32.33	1636305	4031871	40.58
2000	7199	22347	32.21	1696105	6237952	27.19	1549998	4071481	38.07
2001	8008	26140	30.64	2068586	6919455	29.90	1671730	4687759	35.66
2002	10845	34171	31.74	2520183	8276833	30.45	1786093	5274286	33.86

Source: MOFTEC FDI Statistics.

Statistics of FDI from Taiwan 1986-2002

Unit: US$ 10000

Year	Number of Project			Contractual FDI Value			Realized FDI Value		
	Taiwan	National Total	Share %	Taiwan	National Total	Share %	Taiwan	National Total	Share %
1989	539	5779	9.33	43169	559976	7.71	15479	339257	4.56
1990	1103	7273	15.17	88997	659611	13.49	22240	348711	6.38
1991	1735	12978	13.37	138852	1197682	11.59	46641	436634	10.68
1992	6430	48764	13.19	554335	5812351	9.54	105050	1100751	9.54
1993	10948	83437	13.12	996487	11143566	8.94	313859	2751495	11.41
1994	6247	47549	13.14	539488	8267977	6.53	339104	3376650	10.04
1995	4847	37011	13.10	584907	9128153	6.41	316155	3752053	8.43
1996	3184	24556	12.97	514098	7327642	7.02	347484	4172552	8.33
1997	3014	21001	14.35	281449	5100353	5.52	328939	4525704	7.27
1998	2970	19799	15.00	298168	5210205	5.72	291521	4546275	6.41
1999	2499	16918	14.77	337444	4122302	8.19	259870	4031871	6.45
2000	3108	22347	13.91	404189	6237952	6.48	229628	4071481	5.64
2001	4214	26140	16.12	691419	6919455	9.99	297994	4687759	6.36
2002	4853	34171	14.2	674084	8276833	8.14	397064	5274286	7.53

Source: MOFTEC FDI Statistics.

Statistics of FIE Exports by Country / Region 1991-2002

Unit: US$ 100 Million

Year	Country / Region					Total	Share in that year %
	Hong Kong	Taiwan Province	Japan	European Union	U.S.A.		
1991	53.23		12.18	4.57	9.28		
1992	77.53		19.49	7.13	16.48		
1993	66.14	5.62	54.00	28.94	67.35	222.05	88.01
1994	91.15	8.58	78.59	37.14	88.29	303.75	87.51
1995	119.6	11.5	109.8	48.21	111.89	401.00	85.45
1996	148.91	12.57	148.82	70.30	134.99	515.59	83.83
1997	183.37	15.97	160.09	91.36	168.74	619.53	82.71
1998	174.76	20.39	159.16	115.23	203.32	572.86	83.11
1999	180.44	19.86	176.82	126.60	225.50	729.22	82.28
2000	247.76	25.01	233.40	173.00	287.98	967.15	80.97
2001	285.07	25.61	264.04	192.77	298.76	1066.25	80.03
2002	369.71	37.6	299.86	239.46	405.00	1351.63	79.54

Source: MOFTEC FDI Statistics.

Statistics of FIE Imports by Country / Region 1991-2002

Unit: US$ 100 Million

Year	Country / Region					Total	Share in that year %
	Hong Kong	Taiwan Province	Japan	European Union	U.S.A.		
1991	45.91		25.78	23.47	10.84		
1992	59.43		41.58	32.29	17.39		
1993	51.26	90.67	105.18	63.99	34.20	345.30	82.57
1994	51.56	100.94	141.84	78.75	41.78	414.87	78.37
1995	49.70	104.48	170.30	149.13	53.47	527.08	83.74
1996	49.78	115.35	194.97	113.81	70.92	544.83	72.06
1997	44.04	113.23	195.09	106.15	75.82	534.33	68.75
1998	41.37	114.49	187.74	112.20	77.14	532.94	69.47
1999	41.48	127.60	214.36	124.96	83.10	591.50	68.87
2000	56.85	165.18	284.15	166.23	99.60	772.01	65.83
2001	56.86	178.89	288.97	185.77	115.69	826.18	65.64
2002	68.04	256.27	359.45	189.43	131.07	1004.26	62.66

Source: MOFTEC FDI Statistics.

Realized FDI as a Percentage of Total Investment in Fixed Assets for 1992-2002

Unit: US$ 100 Million

Year	Total Investment in Fixed Assets		Realized FDI	Share in Fixed Asset Investment
	RMB 100 Million	USD Equivalent in $100 million	In $100 Million	(%)
1992	8080.10	1465.22	110.08	7.51
1993	13072.30	2268.71	275.15	12.13
1994	17042.30	1977.34	337.67	17.08
1995	20019.30	2397.23	375.21	15.65
1996	22974.00	2763.22	417.26	15.10
1997	25300.00	3059.97	452.57	14.79
1998	28457.00	3437.29	454.62	13.23
1999	29876.00	3608.00	403.18	11.17
2000	32619.00	3944.26	407.15	10.32
2001	36898.0	4458.11	468.46	10.51
2002	43202	5223.94	527.43	10.10

Note: USD Equivalents are based on the average exchange rate of the year concerned.
Source: MOFTEC FDI Statistics.

Foreign-related Tax Revenues for 1992-2002
(Excluding Customs Duties and Land Fees)

Unit: RMB 100 Million

Year	National Tax Revenues from Industry and Commerce	Growth Rate %	Of which, Total Foreign-related Tax Revenues	Growth Rate %	Share %
1992	2876.1	-	122.26	-	4.25
1993	3970.52	38.05	226.56	85.31	5.71
1994	4728.74	19.10	402.64	77.72	8.51
1995	5515.51	16.64	604.46	50.12	10.96
1996	6436.02	16.69	764.06	26.40	11.87
1997	7548.00	17.31	993.00	29.97	13.16
1998	8551.74	13.3	1230.00	25.94	14.38
1999	10311.89	13.4	1648.86	33.78	15.99
2000	12665.00	12.66	2217.00	35.45	17.50
2001	15165.00	19.74	2883.00	30.04	19.01
2002	17004.00	12.13	3487.00	20.95	20.52

Source: MOFTEC FDI Statistics.

List of Commodities Exported by FIEs in 2002
(Each Item with Exported Value over US$ 100 Million)

Main Commodities Exported	Export Value (US$ 100 Million)	Change (%)
Total	1699.36	27.55
Machinery and electrical products	1050.11	37.00
Hi-tech products	556.57	46.98
Automatic data processing equipment and components	179.03	56.11
Garments and attire assesories	150.97	7.99
Parts for automatic data processing equipment	117.71	70.29
Yarns, fabrics & their products	69.82	25.47
Footwear	55.22	0.72
Mobile phones	52.44	28.86
TV sets, radio receivers & equipment package	37.33	42.33
Integrated circuit & microelectronic	36.83	60.69
Furniture and its parts	34.20	38.17
Bearings	28.44	16.19
Parts and accessories for tape recorder	25.73	34.45
Toys	25.38	11.22
Game players	23.27	212.43
Videocorder & Videoplayers	21.46	59.57
Tape-recorder & radio / tape-recorder / player sets	21.29	18.57
Containers	21.14	0.56
Printed circuits	16.30	18.07
Travel products, suitcase & bag	16.26	10.18
Static converters	15.60	27.16

Main Commodities Exported	Export Value (US$ 100 Million)	Change (%)
On-off system & protective circuit devices and parts	14.93	18.27
TV sets (including SKD/CKD kits)	14.15	15.50
Wire & cable	14.01	31.57
Lamps & lighting products	12.52	26.28
Motors & power generators	12.51	10.36
Aquatic products	11.56	11.14
Diode & similar semiconductor devices	11.23	37.40
Auto parts	10.17	42.97
Wire telephones (including cordless phones)	9.31	0.57
Storage batteries	9.25	38.45
Vegetables	8.44	5.52
Bicycles	7.58	47.31
Condensers	6.98	29.47
Copying machines	6.79	1.07
Electric condensers	6.79	4.66
Pharmaceuticals	6.61	24.35
Amplifiers	6.56	14.49
Cameras	6.54	-23.60
Crude oil	6.31	-2.00
Oil products	6.09	6.74
Pearls, gems & semi-gems	5.99	25.32
Electricity	5.98	-6.18
Laser disk players	5.80	24.52
Electronic calculators	5.78	55.91
Precious metals & jewelry covered with precious metals	5.50	18.42
Non-forged aluminum & products	5.34	34.11
Stainless cooking, dining sets and other household wares	4.96	29.25
Steel products	4.76	30.77
Medical apparatus & instruments	4.74	18.82
Non-forged copper & products	4.18	22.00
Parts for motorcycles and bicycles	4.11	13.12
Paper & paperboard (uncutted)	4.07	9.97
Electric fan	3.94	39.34
Mattresses, bedding & related products	3.86	28.36
Ship & boat	3.84	40.52
Hand or machine tools	3.78	29.68
Christmas products	3.59	28.89
Household or decorative woodwork	2.84	12.69
Primary batteries	2.81	28.70
Glassware	2.77	40.01
Household ceramic products	2.75	32.21
Standard fasteners made of iron, steel or copper	2.59	16.80
Ornamental ceramic products	2.34	11.31
Granite and products	2.33	3.42

Main Commodities Exported	Export Value (US$ 100 Million)	Change (%)
watches	2.27	-9.63
Axles	1.97	8.59
Umbrella	1.96	-5.07
Artificial flowers	1.90	9.58
Cosmetics and skin-care products	1.89	33.94
Synthetic organic dyestuff	1.86	22.46
Casings	1.56	13.22
Textile machineries and parts	1.50	34.19
Clocks for daily use	1.39	13.09
cement	1.30	-18.00
Ordinary sewing machines	1.18	15.46
Lock	1.14	27.61
Stuff feather; down	1.05	-7.76
Frozen chicken	1.02	-44.04
Industrial sewing machines	1.01	26.81

Source: MOFTEC FDI Statistics.

Statistics on Imports by FIEs from Selected Countries and Regions in 2002

Unit: US$ 100 Million

Country / Region	Imports Value	Share in Total Imports by FIEs
Ten Asian Countries and Regions	1042.42	65.04
Hong Kong	68.04	4.25
Macao	0.84	0.05
Taiwan Province	256.27	15.99
Japan	359.45	22.43
The Philippines	22.61	1.41
THAILAND	30.79	1.92
Malaysia	60.45	3.77
Singapore	43.11	2.69
Indonesia	20.01	1.25
R.O.K	180.85	11.28
European Union (15 countries)	189.43	11.82
U.S.A.	131.07	8.18

Source: MOFTEC FDI Statistics.

Statistics on Exports by FIEs to Selected Countries and Regions in 2002

Unit: US$ 100 Million

Country / Region	Exports Value	Share in Total Exports Value by FIEs
Ten Asian Countries and Regions	897.18	52.8
Hong Kong	369.71	21.76
Macao	4.37	0.26
Taiwan Province	37.6	2.21
Japan	299.86	17.65
The Philippines	7.94	0.47
THAILAND	15.93	0.94
Malaysia	30.15	1.77
Singapore	45.03	2.65
Indonesia	11.15	0.66
R.O.K.	75.43	4.44
European Union (15 countries)	239.46	14.09
U.S.A.	405	23.83

Source: MOFTEC FDI Statistics.

Statistics of FDI by Form in 2002

Unit: US$ 100 Million

Form	Contractual FDI Value	Realized FDI Value
Total	691.95	468.78
Equity Joint Venture	175.50	157.54
Contractual Joint Venture	83.00	62.12
Wholly Foreign-owned Enterprise	429.99	238.73
FDI Share-holding System	3.27	5.28
Joint Exploration	0.19	5.11

Source: MOFTEC FDI Statistics.

Cumulative FDI from Certain Countries and Regions as of 2002

Unit: US$ 100 Million

Country / Region	Number of Project	Share %	Contractual Value	Share %	Realized Value	Share %
Total	424196	100	8280.6	100	4479.66	100
Sub-total for 10 Asian investors	340779	80.34	5802.7	70.08	3235.24	72.22
Hong Kong	210876	49.71	3738.06	45.14	2048.75	45.73
Macao	7827	1.85	107.92	1.3	47.73	1.07
Taiwan Province	55691	13.13	614.71	7.42	331.1	7.39
Japan	25147	5.93	495.32	5.98	363.4	8.11
The Philippines	1648	0.39	31.86	0.38	14.25	0.32
THAILAND	3181	0.75	57.1	0.69	23.75	0.53
Malaysia	2538	0.6	62.01	0.75	28.35	0.63
Singapore	10727	2.53	401.5	4.85	214.73	4.79
Indonesia	936	0.22	19.46	0.24	11.19	0.25
R.O.K.	22208	5.24	274.76	3.32	151.99	3.39

Country / Region	Number of Project	Share %	Contractual Value	Share %	Realized Value	Share %
Sub-total for E.U.	14084	3.32	600.88	7.26	339.43	7.58
Germany	3053	0.72	143.22	1.73	79.94	1.78
France	2033	0.48	71.92	0.87	55.43	1.24
Italy	1840	0.43	31.93	0.39	22.29	0.5
Netherlands	1065	0.25	89.74	1.08	43.38	0.97
Belgium	403	0.1	9.07	0.11	5.61	0.13
Luxembourg	80	0.02	5.57	0.07	1.07	0.02
U.K.	3418	0.81	196.33	2.37	106.96	2.39
Ireland	52	0.01	1.1	0.01	0.35	0.01
Denmark	225	0.05	13.31	0.16	4.77	0.11
Finland	155	0.04	5.44	0.07	3.53	0.08
Sweden	517	0.12	11.56	0.14	8.1	0.18
Austria	509	0.12	9.08	0.11	3.48	0.08
Greece	41	0.01	1.07	0.01	0.29	0.01
Spain	626	0.15	10.41	0.13	3.54	0.08
Portugal	67	0.02	1.13	0.01	0.69	0.02
Sub-total for North America	43320	10.21	866.59	10.47	432.47	9.65
Canada	6040	1.42	103.77	1.25	33.58	0.75
U.S.A.	37280	8.79	762.82	9.21	398.89	8.9
Sub-total for Some Free Ports	8552	2.02	641.09	7.74	305.09	6.81
Virgin Islands	6659	1.57	493.48	5.96	243.88	5.44
Cayman Islands	706	0.17	94.81	1.14	38.03	0.85
West Samoa	1187	0.28	52.8	0.64	23.18	0.52

Source: MOFTEC FDI Statistics.

FDI Utilized by East, Central and West Parts of China as of 2002

Unit: US$ 100 Million

Region	Number of Project	Share %	Contractual Value	Share %	Realized Value	Share %
Total	424196	100	8280.59	100	4479.66	100
East	345054	81.34	7171.01	86.60	3854.55	86.05
Central	49443	11.66	625.14	7.55	397.02	8.86
West	29699	7.00	484.44	5.85	228.09	5.09

Eastern region: Beijing, Tianjin, Hebei, Liaoning, Shanghai, Jiangsu, Zhejiang, Fujian, Shandong, Guangdong, Hainan

Central region: Shanxi, Jilin, Heilongjiang, Anhui, Jiangxi, Henan, Hubei, Hainan

West region: Inner Mogolia, Guangxi, Sichuan, Chongqing, Guizhou, Yunnan, Shaanxi, Gansu, Qinghai, Ningxia, Xinjiang, Tibet

Source: MOFTEC FDI Statistics.

Top 15 Foreign Investors in China as of 2002

Unit: US$ 100 Million

Country/Region	Number of Project	Share %	Contractual FDI Value	Share %	Realized FDI Value	Share %
Total	424196	100	82805981	100	44796597	100
Hong Kong	210876	49.71	37380600	45.14	20487523	45.73
U.S.A.	37280	8.79	7628190	9.21	3988943	8.9
Japan	25147	5.93	4953212	5.98	3633986	8.11
Taiwan Province	55691	13.13	6147086	7.42	3311028	7.39
Virgin Irelands	6659	1.57	4934803	5.96	2438765	5.44
Singapore	10727	2.53	4014955	4.85	2147270	4.79
R.O.K.	22208	5.24	2747593	3.32	1519896	3.39
U.K.	3418	0.81	1963261	2.37	1069550	2.39
Germany	3053	0.72	1432209	1.73	799367	1.78
France	2033	0.48	719215	0.87	554335	1.24
Macao	7827	1.85	1079181	1.3	477322	1.07
Netherlands	1065	0.25	897448	1.08	433815	0.97
Cayman Irelands	706	0.17	948071	1.14	380333	0.85
Canada	6040	1.42	1037740	1.25	335789	0.75
Malaysia	2538	0.60	620053	0.75	283544	0.63

Note: Listing in order of realized value
Source: MOFTEC FDI Statistics.

Statistics of Cumulative FDI by Form as of 2002

Unit: US$ 100 Million

Form	Number of Projects	Share %	Contractual FDI Value	Share %	Realized Value	Share %
Total	424,196	100.00	8280.59	100.00	4479.66	100.00
Equity Joint Venture	225,883	53.25	3275.48	39.56	1922.04	42.91
Contractual Joint Venture	52,965	12.49	1633.19	19.72	827.86	18.48
Wholly Foreign-owned Enterprise	145,165	34.22	3325.38	40.16	1656.16	36.97
Joint Exploration	183	0.04	46.54	0.56	73.64	1.64

Source: MOFTEC FDI Statistics.

FDI Stock as of Year-end 2002

Unit: US$ 100 Million

Year	Number of Project	Contractual Value	Realized Value
Total	390,025	7452.91	3952.23
1979-1982	920	49.58	17.69
1983	638	19.17	9.16
1984	2,166	28.75	14.19
1985	3,073	63.33	19.56
1986	1,498	33.30	22.44
1987	2,233	37.09	23.14
1988	5,945	52.97	31.94
1989	5,779	56.00	33.93

Year	Number of Project	Contractual Value	Realized Value
1990	7,273	65.96	34.87
1991	12,978	119.77	43.66
1992	48,764	581.24	110.08
1993	83,437	1114.36	275.15
1994	47,549	826.80	337.67
1995	37,011	912.82	375.21
1996	24,556	732.76	417.26
1997	21,001	510.03	452.57
1998	19,799	521.02	454.63
1999	16,918	412.23	403.19
2000	22,347	623.80	407.15
2001	26,140	691.95	438.78
2002	34171	827.68	527.43

Source: MOFTEC FDI Statistics.

Sectoral Distribution of Cumulative FDI as of 2002

Unit: US$ 100 Million

Sector	Number of Project	Share %	Contractual FDI Value	Share %
Total	390,025	100.00	7452.91	100.00
Agriculture, Forestry, Animal Husbandry & Fishery	11,242	2.88	140.71	1.89
Industry	285,000	73.07	4631.60	62.14
Construction	9,315	2.39	215.14	2.89
Transport, Warehousing, Post & Telecommunications	4,324	1.11	172.70	2.32
Wholesale, Retailing, Catering	19,642	5.04	247.94	3.33
Property and Utilities	40,756	10.45	1688.76	22.66
Health Care, Sports & Social Welfare	1,069	0.27	49.06	0.66
Education, Culture, Arts, Broadcasting, Film Industries	1,364	0.35	21.95	0.29
Scientific Research & Technical Services	2,706	0.69	27.79	0.37
Other Sectors	14,607	3.75	257.26	3.45

Source: MOFTEC FDI Statistics.

FDI Distribution by Province and Municipality as of 2002

Unit: US$ 10000

Locality	Number of project	Share %	Contractual value	Share %	Realized value	Share %
Total	424196	100	82805981	100	44796597	100
Beijing	18386	4.33	3625080	4.38	1789125	3.99
Tianjin	15119	3.56	3183070	3.84	1699004	3.79
Hebei	10597	2.50	1607418	1.94	825008	1.84
Shanxi	2254	0.53	415195	0.50	197142	0.44
Inner Mogolia	1674	0.39	216154	0.26	92493	0.21
Liaoning	25025	5.90	4706395	5.68	2077230	4.64

Locality	Number of project	Share %	Contractual value	Share %	Realized value	Share %
Dalian	10601	2.50	2501624	3.02	1163846	2.60
Jilin	6646	1.57	669883	0.81	350401	0.78
Heilongjiang	6637	1.56	661423	0.80	436017	0.97
Shanghai	27502	6.48	8107277	9.79	3690367	8.24
Jiangsu	49971	11.78	12002579	14.49	6083489	13.58
Zhejiang	24059	5.67	3595876	4.34	1647531	3.68
Ningbo	6910	1.63	1259856	1.52	589620	1.32
Anhui	5276	1.24	696975	0.84	375477	0.84
Fujian	31262	7.37	7298224	8.81	4126679	9.21
Xiamen	5518	1.30	1930975	2.33	1224739	2.73
Jiangxi	6136	1.45	670194	0.81	419059	0.94
Shandong	36172	8.53	5551551	6.70	2936407	6.55
Qingdao	10695	2.52	2067100	2.50	1040781	2.32
Henan	6836	1.61	966588	1.17	517935	1.16
Hubei	8990	2.12	1165163	1.41	904481	2.02
Hunan	6472	1.53	920562	1.11	695373	1.55
guangdong	96357	22.72	19829993	23.95	12145813	27.11
Shenzhen	21030	4.96	3390208	4.09	2103683	4.70
Guangxi	7567	1.78	1446687	1.75	774447	1.73
Hainan	9310	2.19	1228868	1.48	720865	1.61
Sichuan	5908	1.39	925836	1.12	395622	0.88
chongqing	3412	0.80	535108	0.65	306118	0.68
Guizhou	1537	0.36	184753	0.22	48888	0.11
Yunnan	2249	0.53	337474	0.41	114604	0.26
Tibet	25	0.01	1465	0.00	3	0.00
Shaanxi	3622	0.85	731845	0.88	375774	0.84
Gansu	1500	0.35	132785	0.16	59176	0.13
Qinghai	321	0.08	67898	0.08	10343	0.02
Ningxia	646	0.15	63174	0.08	16736	0.04
Xinjiang	1120	0.26	133419	0.16	40901	0.09
Central Ministries & Commissions	1608	0.38	1127069	1.36	924089	2.06

Source: MOFTEC FDI Statistics.

Industrial Structure of FDI Stock as of 2002

Unit: US$ 100 Million

Industry	Number of Project	Contractual FDI Value	Share %
Total	424196	8280.59	100.00
Primary Industry	12217	157.59	1.90
Secondary Industry	310279	5242.86	63.32
Tertiary Industry	101700	2880.15	34.78

Source: MOFTEC FDI Statistics.

Industrial Outputs by FIEs as a Percentage of National Industrial Outputs

Unit: RMB 100 Million

Year	National Industrial Outputs	Industrial Outputs by FIEs	Share (%)
1990	19701.04	448.95	2.28
1991	23135.56	1223.32	5.29
1992	29149.25	2065.59	7.09
1993	40513.68	3704.35	9.15
1994	76867.28	8649.39	11.26
1995	91963.28	13154.16	14.31
1996	99595.55	15077.53	15.14
1997	56149.70	10427.00	18.57
1998	58195.23	14162.00	24.00
1999	63775.24	17696.00	27.75
2000	73964.94	23145.59	22.51
2001	94751.78	26515.66	28.05
2002	101198.73	33771.09	33.37

Source: MOFTEC FDI Statistics.

Composition of Commodities Exported by FIEs 1991-2002

Unit: US$ 100 Million

Item	1991		1992		1993		1994		1995		1996	
	Value	%	Value	%	Value	%	Value	%	Value	%	Value	%
Total value	120	100	173.56	100	252.28	100	347.09	100	468.91	100	615.06	100
Primary products	7.89	6.5	10.49	6	18.32	7.2	26.2	7.5	29.99	6.3	116.45	18.93
Foodstuff & live animals for food	5.65	4.6	8.12	4.6	13.62	5.3	15.35	4.4	16.3	3.4	16.7	2.71
Beverage & tobacco	0.23	0.1	0.26	0.1	0.13	0	0.24	0	0.82	0.1	12.91	2.1
Non-edible raw materials (excluding fuel)	1.02	0.8	1.51	0.8	2.91	1.1	3.55	1	3.93	0.8	14.07	2.29
Fossil fuel, lubricants & related materials	0.31	0.2	0.14	0	0.51	0.2	2.83	0.8	5.14	1	8.4	1.37
Animal and vegetable oils, fat & wax	0.67	0.5	0.45	0.2	1.15	0.4	4.24	1.2	3.8	0.8	38.56	6.27
Industrial manufactures	113	93	163.07	94	233.96	93	320.89	92	438.93	94	497.15	80.83
Chemicals and chemical products	2.46	2	3.71	2.1	5.12	2	8.01	2.3	12.14	2.5	24.06	3.91
Manufactures classified by raw materials	17.2	14	22.15	13	30.63	12	40.94	12	56.94	12	150.59	24.48
Machinery and transport equipment	31.3	26	45.44	26	61.99	25	102.32	29	162.31	35	24.19	3.93
Miscellaneous	55.4	46	91.78	53	136.18	54	169.61	49	207.53	44	216.29	35.17
Other unclassified products	6.29	5.2			0.03	0	0.01	0	0.01	0	75.8	12.32

Item	1997		1998		1999		2000		2001		2002	
	Value	%	Value	%	Value	%	Value	%	Value	%	Value	%
Total value	749	100	810	100	886.3	100	1194.41	100	1332.35	100	1699.9	100
Primary products	140.8	18.8	47.1	5.82	52.21	5.89	200.07	16.75	226.53	17	94.8	5.58
Foodstuff & live animals for food	18.19	2.43	30.3	3.74	32.58	3.68	22.14	1.85	25.37	1.9	56.27	3.31
Beverage & tobacco	13.98	1.87	0.84	0.1	0.83	0.09	13.52	1.13	19.64	1.5	4.29	0.25
Non-edible raw materials (excluding fuel)	21.19	2.83	7.22	0.89	7.65	0.86	38.63	3.23	52.17	3.9	12.11	0.71
Fossil fuel, lubricants & related materials	10.8	1.44	6.58	0.81	10.27	1.16	18.01	1.51	56.19	4.2	21.48	1.26
Animal and vegetable oils, fat & wax	44.4	5.93	2.2	0.27	0.88	0.1	62.34	5.22	73.16	5.5	0.65	0.04
Industrial manufactures	606.3	81	762	94.2	834	94.1	991.26	82.99	1105.82	83	1605.1	94.4
Chemicals and chemical products	31.05	4.15	25.2	3.11	26.1	2.94	32.32	2.71	36.42	2.7	48.17	2.83
Manufactures classified by raw materials	164.3	21.9	109	13.4	115.7	13.1	194.13	16.25	211.46	16	198.31	11.7
Machinery and transport equipment	31.9	4.26	328	40.5	383.2	43.2	50.1	4.19	52.61	4	900.08	53
Miscellaneous	279.2	37.3	301	37.1	309.1	34.9	565.46	47.34	661.49	50	457.98	26.9
Other unclassified products	93.04	12.4	0.02	0		0	138.35	11.58	143.84	11	0.56	0.03

Source: MOFTEC FDI Statistics.

BIBLIOGRAPHY

Chen Baosen (1999). *Global Competition among American Transnational Corporations* (Beijing: China Social Sciences Press).

Chen Hongwei (2002). "GE Grows Alongside China", *Foreign Investment in China*, No. 1.

Chen Youjiu (1998). *OPEC and World Economy* (Beijing: Petroleum Publishing House).

Cheng Dongsheng, Wei Houyan et al (1996). *The Road for West of China to Economic Rejuvenation* (Shanghai: Shanghai Far-east Publisher).

Customs General Administration People's Republic of China (1993-2001). *Customs Statistical Almanac of the People's Republic of China* (Beijing: *Customs Statistics* Editorial Department of Customs General Administration People's Republic of China).

Department of Foreign Investment of the Ministry of Foreign Trade and Economic Cooperation (2001). *Statistics on FDI in China 2001*, not for sale.

Department of Foreign Investment of the Ministry of Foreign Trade and Economic Cooperation, 2002, *Statistics on FDI in China 2002*, not for sale.

Department of Trading Materials of the National Bureau of Statistics of China (ed.) (1992). *Complete Statistics concerning China's Foreign Economics 1979-1991,* provided by the China Statistical Information Consulting and Service Center.

Jiang Xiaojuan (1996). *A Research on the Relationship between Industrial Development and Foreign Economy and Trade* (Beijing: Economic Management Press).

Jiang Xiaojuan (1997). "A survey on Foreign Investment in the Detergent Industry of China", *A Collection of the Foreign Investment Journal*, Volume I, Transnational Investment Research Centre of the Chinese Academy of Social Sciences

Jiang Xiaojuan (2000). "A Study on Foreign-invested Enterprises' Behaviours of Research and Development in China", *Science & Technology Review*, No. 9.

Jiang Xiaojuan (2000). "Investment of Large Transnational Corporations: Impact on China's Industrial Structure, Technological Progress and Economic Globalization" in Wang Luolin (ed.) *China Foreign Investment Report 2000* (Beijing: China Financial and Economic Publishing).

Jiang Xiaojuan and Jing Linbo (2001). "Attracting Investment of Transnational Corporations in Forms of Mergers and Acquisitions: Significance, Trends and Strategic Countermeasures", *Management World*, No. 3.

Jiang Xiaojuan, Yang Shengming and Feng Lei (ed.) (2001). *Frontier Theories on China's Foreign Economics and Trade* (Beijing: Social Sciences Documentation Publishing House).

Li Jingwen (1999). "Forecast and analysis on the development of China's Economy (2000-2050)" in Zhang Zhuoyuan (ed.). *Discussion of Experts on the issues about China's Economy in 21st Century* (Zhengzhou: Henan People's Publishing House).

Li Xunlei and Hong Xiaobin. "A New Milestone for Capital Market", *Securities Post*, November 21, 2001.

Lin Ling and Liu Shiqing (2000). "Discussions on the Strategy of Go To West", *Reform*, No. 2.

Ministry of Foreign Trade and Economic Cooperation of the People's Republic of China (2001). *White Paper 2000 on China's Foreign Economy and Trade* (Beijing: China Social Sciences Press).

Ministry of Foreign Trade and Economic Cooperation of the People's Republic of China (2002). *White Paper 2001 on China's Foreign Economics and Trade* (Beijing: China Social Sciences Press).

National Bureau of Statistics of China (1997). *Regional Economies of China in 17 Years of Reform and Opening Up to the Outside World* (Beijing: China Statistics Press).

National Bureau of Statistics of China (1997-2002). *China Statistical Yearbook* (Beijing: China Statistics Press).

National Bureau of Statistics of China (2002). *China Statistical Abstracts 2001* (Beijing: China Statistics Press).

Pan Wenqing, Li Zinai, and Zhang Wei (2001). "Prospect on China's Economic Growth in the first 20 years of 21st Century", *Forecast*, No.3.

Ping An Securities Comprehensive Research Institute (2002). *Impact of Foreign-invested Mergers and Acquisitions on Listed Companies*, No. 005.

Qin Chenglin (1997). *A Study on the Gap among Regional Economies in China* (Beijing: China Economy Publishing House).

Qu Weizhi et al (2001). *Research Report on China's Export of Electronic and IT Products* (Beijing: China Economy Publishing House).

Section of International Enterprises of the Bureau of Industrial Policies of the Ministry of International Trade and Industry of Japan: *Japanese Enterprises' Overseas Undertakings and Activities*

Shi Guangsheng (2001). *Readers on China's WTO Accession* (Beijing: People's Publishing House).

State Administration of Taxation of China (1999-2002). *Tax Year Book of China* (Beijing: China Taxation Press).

Sun Yan (2001). "A Roundup of the World's Oil Refining Capacity in 2000", *International Petroleum Economics*, No. 5.

The Editorial Board of *Almanac of China's Economy* (1997-1999). *Almanac of China's Economy* (Beijing: China's Economy Almanac Press).

The Editorial Board of *Almanac of China's Foreign Economic Relations and Trade* (1999-2001). *Almanac of China's Foreign Economic Relations and Trade* (Beijing: China Foreign Economic Relations and Trade Publishing House).

The Editorial Board of *Almanac of China's Foreign Economic Relations and Trade* (1996-1998). *Almanac of China's Foreign Economic Relations and Trade* (Beijing: China Economy Publishing House)

The Editorial Board of *China Electronic Industry Yearbook* (1997-1999). *China Electronic Industry Yearbook* (Beijing: Electronics Industry Publishing House).

The Editorial Board of *China Light Industry Yearbook* (1997-2001). *China Light Industry Yearbook* (Beijing: China Light Industry Yearbook Press.

The Torch High-tech Industrial Development Center of the Ministry of Science and Technology (2001). *A statistical report on the ten-year development of national high-tech industrial development zones* (Beijing: Scientific and Technical Documents Publishing House).

Wang Cailiang. "*A Century in the World Petroleum Industry*", serialized in the 2000-2001 issues of *International Petroleum Economics*.

Wang Luolin (ed.) (2000). *China Foreign Investment Report 2000* (Beijing: China Financial and Economic Publishing).

Wang Luolin (ed.) (2002). *The Strategy of Go To West in the Next Half-Century* (Beijing: Bejing Publishing House)

Wang Xiaolu (2001). "The Sustainability of China's Economic Growth and the Reform of System" in Wang Xiaolu and Fan Gang. *Sustainability of China's Economic Growth* (Beijing: Economics Sciences Press).

Wang Zhile (1996). *Famous Transnational Corporations' Investment in China* (Beijing: China Economy Publishing House).

Wang Zhile (1998). *Investment of Japanese Enterprises in China* (Beijing: China Economy Publishing House)

Wei Houkai (2000). *Strategy for Industrial Development in Central and Western China in the 21st Century* (Zhengzhou: Henan People's Publishing House).

Wei Houkai (2002). "New Trends in Chinese Development of Regional Economies after China's WTO Accession", *Economic Perspectives*, No. 6.

Wei Houkai. *Regional Changes in Foreign Investment after China's WTO Accession*, a working thesis of the Institute of Industrial Economics of the Chinese Academy of Social Sciences

Xie Sanming (ed.) (2001). *Research on the Potential of China's Economic Growth and Business Cycles* (Beijing: China Plan Press).

Xu Xianchun (2002). "China's Economic Growth in Future and Prospect of its International Economic Position", *Economic Research Journal*, No.3.

Xue Muqiao (ed.) (2000-2001). *Almanac of China's Economy* (Beijing: China Economy Almanac Press).

Yang Yuchuan and Duan Wenbin (ed.) (1994). *Foreign Exchange Market and Business in Foreign Exchange* (Beijing: Economic Management Press.

Yang Zhigang, Ding Lin and Wu Binzhen (2000). "An Empirical Study on the Burdens of Value-Added Tax and Income Tax on Enterprises", *Economic Research Journal*, No. 12.

Yang Zipeng (ed.) (2000-2001). *China Light Industry Yearbook* (Beijing: China Light Industry Yearbook Press).

Zhou Xiaochuan (1994). "Renminbi: March towards Convertibility", a thesis submitted to the International Symposium on China's Strategy for Foreign Economy and Trade in the 1990s held in 1994

UNCTAD (1999). *World Investment Report 1999: Cross-border Mergers and Acquisitions and Development: Foreign Direct Investment and the Challenge for Development* (Geneva and New York: United Nations), United Nations publication.

UNCTAD (2000). *World Investment Report 2000*: *Cross-border Mergers and Acquisitions and Development* (Geneva and New York: United Nations), United Nations publication

UNCTAD (2001). *Word Investment Report 2001: Promoting Linkages* (Geneva and New York: United Nations), United Nations publication.

World Bank (1982, 1992 and 2000/2001). *World Development Report* (Oxford: Oxford University Press).

World Bank (1993). *World Development Report 1993: Investing in Health* (Oxford: Oxford University Press).

World Bank (1999). *World Development Report 1999/2000: Entering the 21st Century* (Oxford: Oxford University Press).

World Bank. World Development Report 2002: Building Institutions for Markets. From World Bank Website: *http://econ.worldbank.org/wdr/WDR2002/text-2394/.*

World Bank. World Development Report 2003: Sustainable Development in a Dynamic World. From World Bank Website: *http://econ.worldbank.org/wdr/wdr2003/text-17926/.*

Richard J. Barnet and John Cavanagh [USA](1999). *Transnational Corporations and New World Economic Order*, Chinese Version (Haikou: Hainan Publishing House).

About the Author

Jiang Xiaojuan has been working in the Chinese Academy of Social Sciences (CASS) since 1989, when she was graduated with a doctor's degree in economics from the Academy's Graduate School. She first worked as assistant researcher and then as senior research fellow of the Academy's Institute of Industrial Economics, holding such posts as deputy director and director of the institute's Department of Industrial Development. At present, she is the director of the Institute of Finance and Trade Economics, CASS and concurrently secretary-general of the International Investment Research Centre of CASS.

Jiang's forte is industrial structures and industrial organization, the industrial policy, transnational investment, and economic systems in transition. She is the author of nine books and numerous essays. Most representative of these are the books *The Industrial Policy during Economic Transition in China, Relationship between Industrial Development and Foreign Economic Relations and Trade*, *China's Industrial Transition: Organizational changes, Efficiency Gains, and Growth Dynamics.* and such essays as "Issues Concerning Public Choice in Pursuing the Industrial Policy in China", "Overcapacity and the Issue of Exit of State-owned Enterprises", and "Development of Transnational Companies and High and New Technology in China".

Jiang is a three-time winner of the Sun Yefang Prize for Economic Science, the top honour in the Chinese economic circles. Among the other awards under her belt are a national top prize awarded to young social scientists for best scientific research results, a national award for distinction in the research of foreign economic relations and trade, and a first-class Chinese Academy of Social Sciences award for fine research results.

She has been cited as a "National-calibre Young Expert Who Have Made Outstanding Contributions" by the State Council, an "Outstanding Female Worker" by the Working Committee of Central Government. She is also one of the Ten Best Young People of the Chinese Academy of Social Sciences. For her distinguished achievements she has been granted with a State Council special monthly allowance.

Jiang is a consultant for top-echelon government policy-makers. She has participated in the drafting of a number of major central government documents concerning China's economic restructuring and development, and she works on the advisory or experts' committees of some central government departments and provinces. She also hold lectures to the Standing Committee of Political Bureau of Community Party of China in year 2002 and 2003 in the fields titled “New Trends of Globalization” and “Challenges We are

Facing". As a distinguished economist she is also a trustee of a number of listed companies and high-tech enterprises.

INDEX

K

L

M

N

O

P

R